SMALL
dolls
of the
40s & 50s

IDENTIFICATION & VALUE GUIDE

- TODDLERS GINNY, GINGER, WENDY, MUFFIE •
- COUNTLESS LOOK-ALIKES •
- BRITISH DOLLS •
- ADVERTISING DOLLS •
- BABY DOLLS •
- AND MORE •

Carol J. Stover

COLLECTOR BOOKS
A Division of Schroeder Publishing Co., Inc.

Cover design by Beth Summers

Book design by Heather Warren

COLLECTOR BOOKS
P.O. Box 3009
Paducah, Kentucky 42002-3009
www.collectorbooks.com

Copyright © 2002 Carol J. Stover

The current values in this book should be used only as a guide. They are not intended to set prices, which vary from one section of the country to another. Auction prices as well as dealer prices vary greatly and are affected by condition as well as demand. Neither the author nor the publisher assumes responsibility for any losses that might be incurred as a result of consulting this guide.

Searching For A Publisher?

We are always looking for people knowledgeable within their fields. If you feel that there is a real need for a book on your collectible subject and have a large comprehensive collection, contact Collector Books.

❦ Contents ❦

❦

❦ About the Author ❦

Carol J. Stover launched her marketing career in Boston, Massachusetts, after graduating from Cornell University's School of Hotel Administration in 1965. Almost 30 years later, Carol's attention turned from marketing to dolls as she decided to replace her long-lost 1950s Ginny dolls. As she searched, Carol became so fascinated with Ginny's story that she began researching the doll's maker, Vogue Dolls, Inc., interviewing Vogue's chief designer and the daughter of Vogue's founder, Virginia Graves Carlson, former Vogue home sewers and employees, other collectors, and anyone else who knew about Vogue.

Carol put her Vogue knowledge to good use in 1998 when she co-authored with Judith Izen, *Collector's Encyclopedia of Vogue Dolls*, now dubbed the Vogue "Bible" by avid collectors. The comprehensive 344-page hardbound book documents all of Vogue's dolls since its 1922 founding (including today's Ginny), values, Vogue history, and more.

As her own Ginny doll collection blossomed, Carol noticed how many other '50s doll makers tried to recreate Ginny's look. In her new book, *Small Dolls of the 40s & 50s*, she now shares her research on dozens of '50s toddler dolls with her readers and opens up the world of all '50s small dolls including toddlers, storybook dolls, display dolls, baby dolls, and related dolls from the '40s and '60s.

She also lectures on Vogue and other modern dolls, and on the art of collecting and writing about Baby Boom era dolls. She has authored over 60 magazine articles on dolls, toys, and collectibles for publications including *Antique Trader, Collector's News, Contemporary Doll Collector, Doll Reader, Dolls Magazine, Doll Magazine (UK), Doll World, Antiques & Collecting Magazine, Big Reel, Toy Shop, UFDC Doll News, Warman's Today's Collector, The Chicago Tribune*, and many others. Carol is a member of United Federation of Doll Clubs' "Yankee Doodle Dollers of Massachusetts" and the UFDC "Windy City Doll Guild" chapters, and she is a member of the Independent Writers of Chicago.

The story of Carol's original quest for a replacement Ginny has a happy ending. Not only did she find a replacement much like her 1953 strung Ginny in a bright green felt cowgirl outfit, but her dad later found her '54 walking Ginny (thought to be long gone) in the attic with her trunk, outfit ensemble, and all!

❧ Acknowledgments ❧

I would like to thank the enthusiastic collectors, writers, and doll fans for sharing their dolls and expertise with me for my research to compile this book. They truly encouraged me to identify and to untangle the web of small and lesser-known dolls from the 1950s. Also, thanks to fellow writers who have generously lent their time, expertise, photographs, and archival materials over the years. Without all this help, neither my doll writing nor this book would have been possible:

Johana Gast Anderton, Vickie Ashelford, Kathy Bailey, Lynn Blumenthal, Kathy Barry-Hippensteel, Heather Browning Maciak, Jan Cahill, Edna Cooper, Karen Corriel, Judy Cullen, June Dove, Gidget Donnelly, Louise Fecher, Laura Fluhr, Maureen Fukushima, Jan Glaser, Vickie Glover, Linda Hawkins, Bunny Henckel, Amy Hirsch, Carolyn Johnson, Pam and Polly Judd, Nancy Kerson, Chree Kysar, Louie Laskowski, Sandi Lynfrey, Ursula Mertz, Peggy Millhouse, Mary Miskowiec, Bev Mitchell, Dyan Murphy, Shari Ogilvie, Deirdre Olson, Karen Payne, Veronica Phillips, Tina Ritari, Lani Spencer-McCloskey, Susan Steelman, Joyce Sziebert, Sydney Ann Sutton, Brenda Thomas, Deedee Townsend, Suzanne Vlach, Sandi Winfrey, and Dian Zillner.

Also, thanks to these super-collectors and doll experts for help with specific chapters: Jo Barckley for sharing her extensive knowledge of Virga, Schiaparelli, and International and British dolls as well as of sewing dolls and kits, for allowing me to photograph her special dolls, and for contributing her own photos; Sandy Johnson-Barts for her expert contribution and for allowing me to photograph her special Betsy McCall, Vogue, Ginny, and Muffie dolls; Shirley Bertrand for her expert knowledge of dolls of all eras and for allowing me to photograph her special ones; Lee Ann Beaumont for her special knowledge and photos of dolls, especially of British, Canadian, and international dolls, and for allowing me to photograph her dolls; Linda Chervenka for her enthusiasm and knowledge of Ginny and small '50s dolls; Sue Fay for generously sharing her Flagg dolls; Toni Ferry, an unsurpassed doll costume designer always willing to create, share and compare, especially Vogue; the Henrietta Doll Lovers Club, Henrietta and Rochester, NY area for information about Ontario Plastics and to the following members for enthusiastically detailing and photographing their Paula Sue dolls: Mary Britton, Sue Ring, Margaret Daggs, Dorothy Dailey, and Carolyn Owen; Judith Izen, co-author, friend, for her encouragement and willingness to explain and share information and photos, especially on Vogue and Ideal; Vicki Johnson for sharing and allowing me to photograph her Ginny and Flagg dolls; Barbara Lamb, Darleen Foote, and Jana Cornell for information about the Jane Miller company; Mary Miskowiec for sharing her rare Virga items, information, and photographs; Patsy Moyer, a fellow writer who generously shared information and photos; Jeanne Niswonger, doll historian and author for her expert knowledge about Vogue and small '50s dolls and for sending her dolls for photography; Mary Lu Paulett especially for comparing and sharing her Mary Lu dolls for photography; Lillian Roth for her extensive Muffie expertise; Patricia Smith, author and researcher, for sharing her photos and extensive expert knowledge about small '50s dolls; Tina Standish and her mother Mayene Miller for their tireless comparisons, information, and photographs of Ginger, Andrea, and the Stashin Doll Co.; Mary Van Buren-Swasey for comparing and sharing information on little-known dolls of the '50s and permitting me to photograph them; Billie Nelson Tyrrell, vintage and celebrity dolls authority who generously shared her photos and her time; Barbara Rosplock-Van Orman for allowing me to photograph rare dolls from her extensive Ginny collection, as well as Betsy McCall and Ginnette, and for sharing information; Marty Abrams, Abrams Gentile Entertainment, for the history of MEGO.

Thanks also to the corporate and institutional doll world professionals who are never too busy to answer questions and to assist with my work: Gigi's Dolls and Sherry's Teddybears, and Gigi Williams and Sherry Baloun; Shirley's Dollhouse, Shirley Bertrand; Yesterdolls, Sue Johnson; Barbara Frasher, Frasher's Doll Auctions; McMaster's Auctions, Shari McMaster; Theriault's Auctions, Debbie Thompson; Wenham Museum, Mary Ellen Smiley.

One very special expression of my gratitude goes to collector and researcher Marge Meisinger for sharing her endless knowledge about modern dolls including all 8" dolls, her in-depth knowledge of all Alexander dolls, her fabulous archival library, and for the wonderful treat of learning about celebrity dolls of all eras from her. Marge and Earl have opened their home and their wonderful world of dolls to me.

And finally thanks so much to my wonderful parents, Louise and Lowell Gibbs, and to my brother John Gibbs who are always so encouraging, and to my wonderful children, Adam Summerfield and Jason Summerfield and his wonderful wife Marie, and to my loving grandmother, Ora Adams, who gave me one of my first dolls, a rag doll named Bessie. Last, but never least, to my wonderful husband Frank Stover who has patiently and even enthusiastically listened to my doll stories, helped me with my doll searches, proofread countless pages of copy, and shared my happiness in the doll community.

🍇 Introduction 🍇

Small dolls are fond favorites with modern doll collectors. The diminutive storybook dolls, display dolls, and baby dolls of the '40s and '50s are all much sought after today. And then there is Ginny, the supreme '50s toddler doll of all time. Ginny hit her stride in the post-WWII era and became the leading toddler doll in the "fabulous fifties." As expected, countless look-alikes soon flooded the '50s doll market. No wonder that collectors remember the cute little toddlers so vividly and enjoy finding them today. Perhaps the, "Ah, those were the days," factor is also at work on collector's recollections. Sweet little '50s dolls represent a time when children led playful, uncomplicated, non-computerized lives. Little girls wore hats, gloves, and Mary Jane pumps and enjoyed playing "tea party" with their dolls. In this high tech era, recollections of playing dolls (for boys and girls!) can be far more appealing than video games.

For those less emotionally connected to '50s small dolls, the numbers prove that their popularity today is not only about nostalgia. The brisk secondary market sales of '50s dolls like Vogue's Ginny or Alexander's Wendy not only confirms their popularity but also that they become more valuable every year. Believe it or not, these innocent little 8" dolls can bring as much as $2,000 to $5,000 each on today's auction blocks. Traditional porcelain doll lovers once dismissed the little cuties as "just modern dolls," but at those prices, this is more than sentimentality to some – it is big business.

As the price of top-quality, well-known toddler dolls escalates today, they are now out of reach for some. Undaunted, collectors have turned their attention to the lesser-known toddlers that can be just as cute...and wonderfully affordable. So now begins our book about the well-known, the not-so-well-known, and even the obscure toddler and other small dolls of the 1950s.

History

As you read through the company sections, you will note that some of the '50s toddler dolls look just alike, yet they have different names and other makers. Why? That is because they probably are the very same dolls bought from a common maker, but re-dressed and renamed for sale. In this book we will explore who owned whom in the '50s doll-dom, and why in-breeding was especially common for the lesser-known, unmarked dolls.

You will also note that '50s toddler doll costumes may all begin to look alike to you. You are not imagining this either. To keep costs down, dollmakers bought from one another, lent costumes from one line to another, and, of course, copied each other. For example, angular cap sleeve dresses were a common Fortune Doll Co. style in

the '50s. Their 9½" Pam's red taffeta dress, their 8" Jeanette's #104 "Red Afternoon Dress" and their 8" Ninette's #13/7 "Red ensemble" are so similar that you will blink twice. The fabrics may vary, but they all had the same unique angular cap sleeve style, and they all closed with a "P" pattern round metal snap. But you'll also find that Fortune's competitor, Duchess Dolls, used the very same dress for their toddler Randi's #102 "Red Ensemble." This can confuse collectors for sure.

How did this look-alike doll mania happen? Would it help to know that Cosmopolitan's Ginger appears to be the common denominator for many of these dolls' bodies and their angular cap sleeve dress styles? Cosmopolitan was likely the original source for many of the early '50s competitors, but there were others too. Who cares? If you aren't "into" '50s dolls, then you may not care. But for those of us who collect them, we like to know what doll we have in order to date her, to dress her appropriately, and, finally, to value her. The same is true for the baby, storybook, display dolls, and others. So we must study up to tell one doll from another.

Book Guidelines

As you read, please note that I have followed these guidelines in writing this book:

1. The term look-alike is used throughout the book. It generally refers to dolls that "looked like" the competitive small doll leaders in the '50s, Vogue's 8" Ginny and her 8" baby sister Ginnette. Others may regard their favorite 8" doll as the '50s toddler leader. However, Vogue earned the notoriety when they brought the chubby dolls into the hard plastic doll world in 1948 and added sleep eyes in 1950. This precedes Alexander's Muffie, Nancy Ann Storybook's Wendy hard plastic toddlers introduced in 1953, and Cosmopolitan's Ginger introduced c.1954. Also, Vogue developed revolutionary promotions for the doll and her fabulous wardrobe, so Vogue is generally known as the pioneer of this genre in the '50s. Happily, the Vogue Doll Company still produces wonderful Ginnys today.

2. The term "small dolls" is also used throughout this book. I generally defined a "small" doll as one measuring up to 9" tall. Most of these dolls are display dolls (i.e., souvenir dolls), storybook dolls, or toddlers. However, if one of these dolls had a taller doll in the line, or if a maker had a small teen doll in the "family," I have included that doll up to 10½" tall. Related 10½" fashion dolls are mentioned in passing, but I have not included details on them because they seem to occupy a category all their own.

3. Chapter One lists individual '50s doll makers alphabetically and covers information on that individual compa-

ny's small '50s dolls. Comparisons among the small dolls by different dollmakers appear in Chapter Five.

4. If my personal research about a particular doll's maker is not completed at this point, I have noted that and have presented what is known to date. I would welcome hearing from any collector, past employees, or doll company family member that may have further information on these dolls and/or doll makers.

5. I have concentrated on small 1950s dolls, but if small dolls from the '40s or '60s are relevant to complete the saga of a maker's toddler doll family, I have also included them.

6. Most of the baby dolls I have included are related to a specific toddler doll family, and most are 8" tall. If a larger baby doll is relevant to a doll family, I have included it up to 9", or, in rare cases, up to 10½" tall.

7. Entire books have been written about advertising dolls. For brevity, I have not included the soft or plush advertising dolls in this book, concentrating instead on the hard plastic and vinyl small advertising dolls, and on toddler dolls in particular.

8. Values indicated throughout the book were estimated informally based on current prices seen at doll shows and on the secondary market. Auction prices realized and regional differences have also been factored in but should still be considered in interpreting the values suggested. Values are for dolls without boxes. The (+) indicates that the value shown may exceed that indicated based on rarity of costume, exceptional condition, boxes, tags, etc. Poor coloring, played-with condition, incomplete outfits, etc. will result in lesser values than the one shown.

9. Some captions have auction prices in parentheses after a specific photograph. These amounts reflect the price realized for the specific doll shown at one particular auction. The amount shown may or may not correspond with secondary market prices, and may not be realized at other auctions. The auction price realized for a doll includes a box only if indicated.

So enjoy the book, enjoy the dolls, and by all means, enjoy collecting!

Carol J. Stover

Values in this book should be used as a guide only. They are not intended to set prices which vary from one section of the country to another. Auction prices as well as dealer prices vary greatly and are affected by condition as well as demand.

Neither the author nor the publisher assumes responsibility for any losses that might be incurred as a result of consulting this guide.

Hard Plastic Dolls & Babies

🍇 A&H Doll Corporation 🍇

A&H Doll Corporation was founded after WWII, specializing in small hard plastic dolls. Their first dolls were display type dolls, but eventually they jumped into the Ginny market of 8" toddler dolls. In 1955 they aggressively advertised their toddler Gigi, but they also sold lesser-known dolls for budget markets named Julie, Judy, and Lisa. The Gigis most often found are unmarked Ginger type dolls, so they are difficult to identify today without boxes. However, they also used hybrid type hard plastic dolls interchangeably for both Gigi and Julie. In other words, this is a very difficult company to pin down for doll type. The descriptions below are the most often found, but probably not the only A&H toddler doll types used. In 1956 A&H also sold an 8" vinyl baby sister named "Gigi's Lil' Sister."

Display Dolls

Marks on Doll: None.
Boxes Marked: Either A&H or Marcie.

Colored Hair Display Dolls, 6" c. 1950s

A&H sold some 6" display dolls with mohair wigs dyed blue (presumably in other colors too), sleep eyes, and moving head and arms. They were dressed in stapled-on tulle gowns edged at the hem with pastel ribbon, and felt hats were stapled on the head. The boxes had round window lids. Note: A&H also sold 8" toddler dolls with pastel colored wigs (see Toddlers & Baby).
Value: Estimated $20.00 – 25.00 MIB (no specific values known).

Marcie Read & Play Creations, 8" c. 1951

A&H filed for a patent for "A Marcie Read & Play Creation" (last letter A not E) in 1951. The first in the series was, Alice and her Books. The Marcie doll wore an outfit matching the heroine, and she was advertised as 8" (actually measured 7½" inches), with jointed head and arms and sleep eyes. Her outfits were not removable. She was packaged with a small Wonder Book in a window box. Advertising read, "Imagine reading this wonderful story while holding an exact replica right in your hands." By 1952 there were 12 doll and book sets in the series including Heidi, Come Visit My Ranch, The Surprise Doll, Peter Pan, and Playtime for Nancy.
Value: MIB $50.00+.

Donna Dolls, 12" c. 1952

Hard plastic 12", fully jointed, sleep eye dolls with "life like" wavy hair in bridal, international, historic, and other nonremovable costumes. They were introduced as "big sister" dolls to Marcie dolls, and there were 18 dolls in the set. These same 12" dolls were also sold as A&H "Dolls of Destiny."
Value: MIB $30.00.

Marcie Dolls 8" c. early 1950s

Marcie dolls were advertised as 8", but they actually measured 7½" inches. They had either painted side-glancing eyes or sleep eyes; molded-on shoes with three incised lines in front. By 1953 Marcie advertised 80 different costumes and dolls with "Moving eyes, lifelike hair and movable heads and arms." Clothes were not removable. Some Marcie dolls were packed in "sparkling bell-shaped containers." Others were packaged in attractive window boxes with a pink and blue window design.
Value: MIB $30.00.

Marcie Undressed Dolls 11", 8" Undressed Dolls c. 1950s

Marcie advertised an 8" (may be the same doll above measuring 7½") hard plastic girl dolls and an 8" boy doll with "mov-

Heidi Child of the Mountains, a Marcie Read and Play Creation, c. 1950s, with storybook and hard plastic doll packaged together. Courtesy Ruth Leif.

Donna Doll advertisement, c. 1950s.

8

A Marcie Doll, #817 Sweetheart 7½" hard plastic sleep eye doll with strung head and arms doll in window box, c. 1950s.

The Surprise Doll, a Marcie Read and Play Creation, c. 1950s, with a storybook and hard plastic doll packaged together. Courtesy Mary Fontaine.

Marcie sleep eye 7½" doll Pilgrim in a plastic dome carrying case with handle on top.

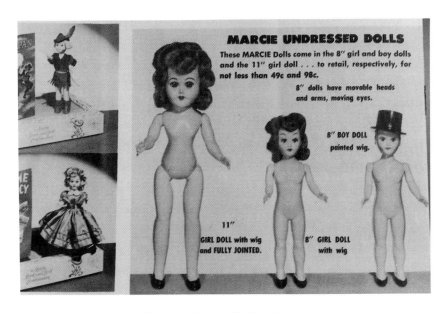

Marcie undressed dolls advertisement.

Marcie Doll #844 7½" hard plastic Ice Skater with sleep eyes, c. 1950s, in bright fuchsia costume with red mohair wig.

able heads, arms, and moving eyes." The girls had synthetic wigs, and the boy had painted-on hair. Their feet had painted shoes with three incised lines. These dolls were popular as inexpensive "dress me" dolls. $15.00 – 30.00

Toddlers & Baby

Gigi Toddler 8" c. 1955
Marks on Doll: None.
Boxes Marked: Gigi/ A&H. Two types of boxes: Gray and red or black and red diagonally striped boxes; pink window boxes; other dolls sold seated in a "Crystal-Clear Dome" with a handle on top.

Doll Characteristics: A & H advertised Gigi in 1955. She was a fully jointed, 7½" – 8" hard plastic toddler doll with sleep eyes and molded eyelashes, and C-shaped arm hooks. Despite these common characteristics, identifying Gigi is difficult because different dolls were used. Two types were shown in a single Gigi brochure!

TYPE #1: Molded lash sleep eyes; flesh tone plastic; the mouth painting has a down-turned look at the corners; mold line behind ear; regular jointed straight leg walker with smooth feet and no toe detail; arms with C-shaped hook; 2nd and 3rd fingers molded together on the right hand and finger tips are separate from knuckles on the left; with or without two lines at the

elbows. Note: It is neither a Ginger head, nor a Pam, nor a Virga Playmate head. Note: Type #1 Gigi is the same doll as A&H's "Lisa" doll (see Lisa, p. 15), Dollyana's "Dorrie," Riegel's "Miss 1962."
Value: $65.00; MIB $95.00.

TYPE #2: Molded lash sleep eyes; peach color tone plastic; the mouth painting has a down-turned look at the corners; mold line behind ear; pin-hip straight leg walker with toe detail; arms with C-shaped arm hook; 2nd and 3rd fingers molded together on the right hand and finger tips are separate on the left; with or without two lines at the elbows. Note: This is the same doll as the pin hipped Mindy (see Active Doll Co.).
Value: $50.00; MIB $85.00.

TYPE #3: Medium eye dolls with Ginger characteristics, (i.e., head mold seams through the center of the ear, regular jointed straight leg walking, toe detail.)
Value: $50.00; MIB $85.00.

TYPE #4: Type #2 or #3 Gigi dolls with bent knees.
Value: $50.00; MIB $85.00.

TYPE #5: Pastel hair Gigi was advertised in the brochure. The only example found MIB has "pastel" hair, the same head as Gigi Type #2 with mold behind the ear, but has molded T-strap shoes (see Gigi Pastel-Colored for specifics) and regular jointed walking legs.
Value: $65.00; MIB $95.00.

Gigi Pastel-Colored Wig 8" c. mid-1950s
Marks on Doll: None.
Boxes Marked: Unknown; one pastel hair doll has been found in a pink window box marked "Gigi/ Walking Doll."
Doll Characteristics: A&H advertised a "Selection of dolls with pastel-colored hair...with dress to match." Each of the five dolls in this series had a different shade of pastel-colored hair with matching outfits. The pastel-colored hair Gigis are a hybrid mix of doll parts: medium or wide eye Mindy #1 and Gigi #2 type heads with mold line behind the ear, C-shaped arm hooks and separate finger tips on left hand, and 2nd and 3rd molded together on the right. However, they have T-strap molded shoes instead of toe detail like Mindy. Note: This is the same as MEGO Julie #1.
Dress Characteristics: Gigi pastel hair dolls wore a ribbed taffeta dress with embroidered nylon ruffle pinafore sleeves and hem trim.
Value: $55.00+; $85.00 in box.

Wig Characteristics, all types
Wig material was not specified in Gigi's brochure. It was a synthetic wig sewn to a thin backing strip, usually one row of stitching, and glued to the head.
Dress Characteristics: Over 30 different removable Gigi outfits were shown in the black and white brochure which read,

Face detail on Types #1 & #2 Gigi: (L to R): Type #1: Large sleep eyes (or can be medium), mouth with down-turned look, mold line behind ear; Type #2: Smaller sleep eyes, mouth with down-turned look, mold line behind ear. Courtesy Marge Meisinger.

Two different Gigis (L to R): Type #1: Straight walking legs, smooth feet with no toe detail; sleep eye, mold line behind ear; Type #2: Pin-hipped, straight walking legs with toe detail, sleep eye, mold line behind ear. Courtesy Marge Meisinger.

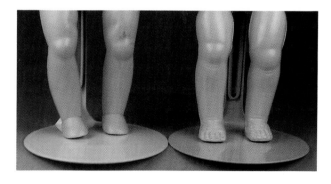

Toe detail on Types #1 & #2 Gigis: (L to R): Type #1: Smooth feet, no toes; Type #2: Detailed toes. Courtesy Marge Meisinger.

Two different Gigis. (L) Type #3: Wide or medium eye Ginger type with straight legs; (R) Type #4: Wide or medium eye Ginger with bent knees. Courtesy Marge Meisinger.

Gigi in jeans outfit #7270 with a red and white checked shirt, straw hat, and sunglasses. The brochure shows uncuffed knee-length jeans. Courtesy Marge Meisinger.

Two Gigis Majorette walking dolls in #7200 majorette costume (L to R): Type #1: Gigi majorette doll with straight legs and smooth toes; Type #2: Gigi majorette on right is a pin-hip walker with toe detail. Both costumes have white satin skirts, felt bodice, gold braid, gold belts, and baton. Courtesy Marge Meisinger.

Type #5: Pastel wig Gigi has some similarities as Gigi Type #2 (with same head and mold line behind ear, arms, body, and peach colored plastic) except Gigi #5 has regular jointed legs, molded T-strap shoes, and a pastel wig.

Gigi outfit snaps: (R) Smooth round metal snap; (L) Donut-shaped snap. Courtesy Marge Meisinger.

Bent knee walking Gigi Type #4 in red print dress outfit #7140 trimmed with yellow rick-rack, lace with matching bonnet. Courtesy Marge Meisinger.

11

"I'm voted best dressed dolly of the year." The outfits had finished waist seams, closed back seam below dress opening. Dresses coordinated with matching hats and pants; outfits included with vinyl slip-on shoes and socks. Early outfits closed with a round, smooth metal snap, but later with metal donut-shaped snaps painted or unpainted. Many dress styles were direct look-alikes to Ginny. Gigi was also dressed in international costumes, but they were not shown in her brochure. A photo of Gigi in a Davy Crockett type outfit with coonskin cap was advertised in '55 and '56. Outfits were also sold in separate boxes. **Value** (all types): $55.00; MIB $75.00+.

Advertisement for "Pastel Dressed Doll Series" in Gigi brochure c. 1955.

A&H Gigi brochure c. 1955.

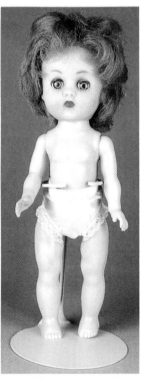

A&H Gigi Type #5 doll with "Pastel" bright yellow wig and special yellow dress. There were six pastel colors in the series with matching dresses advertised in the Gigi brochure. She is Type # 5 Gigi walker with T-strap molded shoes.

Gigi advertisement, c. 1957, for Gigi with "vinyl head with rooted hair" in a revolving carousel with wardrobe and accessories.

Undressed 8" vinyl headed Gigi marked "GIGI" on the neck, with rooted hair, sleep eyes, lashes painted under eyes, hard plastic body, arms, and walking legs with toe detail.

Gigi Vinyl Head Toddler 8" c. 1957

Marks on Doll: GIGI or "U" on neck.

Boxes Marked: Unknown but probably Gigi/A&H, bell, Gigi, A Walking Doll.

Doll Characteristics: 8" sleep eye walker with toes, marked Gigi, advertised with a vinyl head and a hard plastic body c. 1957. She was sold in a "revolving carousel wardrobe." Also sold in bell, marked U on neck, smooth feet.

Wig Characteristics: Advertised as "rooted hair that may be combed, curled." Bell label: Rooted hair, combable, washable, brushable.

Dress Characteristics: Same as for hard plastic Gigi. Outfit characteristics, same as above with donut snaps. New nylon styles were added to the previous lines for the vinyl head dolls

Value: $50.00; $90.00 in carousel. Note: See Uneeda for U-marked dolls.

Gigi's Lil' Sister Baby Doll 8" c. 1957

Marks on Doll and Boxes: On neck: Gigi's Lil' Sister

She was also sold in a "Carousel Wardrobe" that revolved to reveal sections in which garments were hung and shelves for other

Two Gigi boxes with black or gray diagonal stripes. Courtesy Marge Meisinger.

Straight leg walking Gigi dolls (probably Type #1) with original boxes and brochure: Gigi #7210 in beach costume with knit top and matching hat and Gigi #7020 in coral organdy dress and bonnet ($225.00 both dolls MIB); Boxed Gigi outfits (L to R) Top: Black and white taffeta dress in pink box; #710 orange dress with forest green jacket and hat; Bottom: #714 Cotton print dress and hat #714; Nurse costume, cape and cap ($90.00 lot of 4 MIB). Prices realized courtesy Frasher's Doll Auctions.

Advertisement for Gigi c. 1955-56 wearing a special Davy Crockett outfit and six other outfits.

Gigi wears a "Spanish" costume with a red taffeta skirt, black felt bodice, and black lace mantilla. Same as A&H's Julie and Lisa dolls. Note pink box. Courtesy Marge Meisinger.

A&H advertising card for Gigi in "Crystal Clear Dome" along with Lil' Sister and display dolls. Gigi appears to be Type #2 or #3. Vinyl head doll also sold in bell. Courtesy Marge Meisinger.

A&H flier advertising Gigi and other A&H dolls to dealers at Toy Fair c. 1955. Courtesy Marge Meisinger.

Separate Gigi outfit including white taffeta and black lace dress closing with donut snap, straw hat with flower and black tulle veil; slip-on vinyl shoes, and socks. The outfit is undocumented and has no number on box.

Advertisement for Gigi "Lil' Sister" 8" vinyl baby doll in Living for Young Homemakers, November 1956.

Gigi's "Lil' Sister," separate outfit marked "bride" on the box with a white taffeta gown and panties.

items. Included were four outfits, and accessories like a bottle, rattle, and hangers; at some point she was packaged seated holding a bottle in a "Crystal-clear dome" with a handle on top.

Doll Characteristics: Around 1957 A&H advertised "Lil' Sister," an 8" drink and wet baby doll, some "coo" with sleep eyes. Soft vinyl with straight legs and lashes painted under eyes, a Ginnette type. She came in her Carousel Wardrobe that had a section for the doll and one for her clothes. Fingers separate, with dimples.

Wardrobe Characteristics: Lil' Sister's wardrobe had finished waist seams, closed back seam below dress opening, and closure with a donut snap. Interestingly, one outfit box was marked, "Bride." Young bride! No photo example available of the doll.

Value: $45.00; $90.00 in carousel.

Julie 8" c. 1957

Marks on Doll: None.

Box Marks: I am Julie/ A&H; some window boxes were blue with red print.

Doll Characteristics: The inexpensive Julie doll was advertised c. 1956-57 as an 8" hard plastic doll. She was a toddler look-alike. Ginger characteristics: medium or wide eyes, straight leg walking doll with toe detail, C-shaped arm hook with separate fingers, and mold line through center of the ear. Julie was discounted in stores like Davison's Basement in Atlanta for $1.50 dressed or 88 cents on sale. Note: Another 8" toddler doll named "Julie" is found in boxes marked MEGO (see MEGO section).

Wig Characteristics: Glued-on synthetic wig of medium quality.

Dress Characteristics: Julie dresses had closed back seams, waistlines finished with factory overcast stitching, and closure with circle donut snaps. Many of Julie's outfits were identical to A & H's Gigi dolls such as the majorette, a formal gown, and the distinctive dress with a black and white diamond-patterned skirt shown on Gigi's brochure cover. Julie's interna-

1957 Julie, Davison's store advertisement. Note some outfits are A&H's Gigi outfits in Julie boxes. Courtesy Marge Meisinger.

tional costumes were also identical to Gigi's, such as the Spanish dress with red skirts and black felt bodice. However, while some Julie outfits were identical to Gigi's outfits, some were quite different and not well made. For example, Julie's tulle ballerina costume was less attractive and not as well made as Gigi's ballet costume. Separate Gigi outfits were sold in window boxes.

Value: $40.00; MIB $55.00 (in red and blue box); MIB $70.00 (in Easter Egg box).

Julie 8" doll in blue print taffeta dress with separate outfits. (L to R) #254 Plaid skating outfit, blue taffeta dress with gold trim; red fringed cowgirl skirt, plaid top, and red boots ($130.00 MIB Julie and outfits). Realized price courtesy Frasher's Doll Auctions.

Julie 8" toddler in a blue box with red letters wears a Greek costume of white taffeta with black felt jacket edges with gold picot trim and red felt cap trimmed with a feather.

Julie 8" toddler in blue window box wears a "Spanish" costume of red taffeta with black felt bodice and lace mantilla. A&H's Gigi and Lisa dolls had the same costume.

Separate pink taffeta gown in box marked Julie/ A&H. It appears to be the same as A&H's Gigi's gown #7260.

1957 newspaper advertisement for undressed Julie, outfits, and hatbox. Not shown: Julie in formal gown #247; Nun #245. Courtesy Marge Meisinger.

Lisa 8" c. 1950s

Doll Marks: None.

Marks on Box: Lisa.

Doll Characteristics: A&H's 8" hard plastic toddler doll named Lisa was virtually unadvertised. She was sold in boxes marked A&H and printed, "I am Lisa. I walk, I sit, I sleep, Dress Me, Curl My Hair." Lisa is a mixture of different doll parts: her head is the same as Type #2 Gigi (same as Active's Mindy); hands are also like Mindy with C-shaped arm hook; hands have separate fingers on the right hand with 2nd and 3rd fingers molded together on left or they can be slightly separated depending on unmolding; prominent mold lines on arms; her straight walking legs have smooth, flat feet with no toe or shoe detail. Note: The same smooth feet were used by competitors, including A&H's Gigi #1, Linda Doll Co.'s Linda #1, and the vinyl headed Janie by Uneeda. (See Comparisons chapter.) The entire Lisa is the same doll used by Riegel for "Miss Riegel-1962," for Linda Doll Co.'s Linda, and for Dorrie by Dollyana. A&H may have also used their other doll types in Lisa boxes.

Wig Characteristics: Synthetic wig material not known, but a nice quality.

Dress Characteristics: The MIB Lisa examples found to date were undressed dolls with panties, and no shoes.

Only one separate Lisa outfit has been found to date, and it is the identical Spanish outfit for A&H's Julie and Gigi dolls, with the same closures and finishes noted above.

Value: $40.00; MIB $55.00.

Close-up of heads of brunette Lisa on left and Type #1 Gigi on right.

Lisa was an 8" toddler that A&H sold to compete with their own Gigi and Julie dolls. Lisa combined the head of Type #2 Gigi with the smooth feet and no toes of Gigi #1.

Two smooth feet A & H dolls. (L to R) Lisa with brunette wig on left has the same head as Type #2 Gigi; Gigi Type #1 on right with smooth feet.

Separate Lisa Spanish outfit is the same as Gigi's and Julie's Spanish costume.

Marcie Daily Dolly 9" c. 1955

Marks on Doll: None.

Box Marks: Unknown.

Doll Characteristics: Marcie Daily Dolly was advertised for Toy Fair 1955. She was a 9" pin-hipped walker, fully jointed with sleep eyes and molded lashes. Her fingers were separate fingers, she had two dimples on her knees and toe detail, and had prominent mold lines down the sides of legs and arms. Note: This same doll was sold by Virga as their 9" walking Lucy doll.

Dress Characteristics: Marcie Daily Dolly had 16 costumes sold separately that were well made and closed with a regular hand-sewn metal snap. Waist seams are finished with factory overcast stitching.

Wig Characteristics: Saran wig in braided or flip styles sewn with two parallel rows of stitching to backing.

Value: $45.00 undressed; MIB dressed $65.00.

Not Shown: Sluggo Dolls, A&H boxed 8" dolls as Sluggo and Girlfriend. They were apparently Plastic Molded Arts' strung toddler dolls c. 1950s. (See pg. 263.)

Advertisement for Marcie Daily Dolly in McCall's Needlework Magazine, Fall/Winter '54–'55. Courtesy Marge Meisinger.

A little booklet, c. 1956, advertised 16 costumes for 9" Marcie Daily Dolly. She was also sold dressed only in panties, socks, and shoes. Courtesy Jo Barckley.

Flyer for A&H's 9" Marcie Daily Dolly walking doll wears outfit #605 Gardening Costume, a yellow flowered print with lace trim.

❦ Active Doll Company ❦

Active Doll Co. in Brooklyn, New York sold low to mid-market dolls in the 1950s. They are best known for their display dolls and for Mindy, their cute 8" hard plastic toddler look-alike doll, c.1957. Active advertised that, "Your better neighborhood stores all carry Mindy and Minnette [baby sister] fully clothed, as well as separate wardrobes for each." Brochures for the "walking" Mindy and for the "bending knee" Mindy yield details about the line. Active also sold the little-known toddler "Judy."

Toddlers

Mindy 8" c. 1956 – 1957

Marks on Doll: Unmarked.

Boxes Marked: Mindy/ Active Doll Corporation on window lid boxes; cardboard trunks are marked "Mindy."

(L to R) Mindy Type #1 Black pin-hip walker doll with toe detail; Type #1 Pin-hip walker with toe detail; Type #2 Straight leg walker Ginger type doll with toe detail.

Doll Characteristics: Mindy can be difficult to identify since she had more than one head and body type, and brochures show that these were used simultaneously, a common practice in the 1950s. The following are the most often found examples, but there may have been other variations:

TYPE #1: At first glance, Mindy's face appears to be the same as Virga's Playmate or Fortune's Pam, however, there are differences. Mindy's eyes are more round, and the plastic has a more "peach" color tone; mouth painting has a down-turned look at corners; pin-hip straight walking legs with toe detail; C-shaped

arm hooks; 2nd and 3rd fingers molded together on the doll's right hand but separate from knuckles on the left. Note: This is the same doll head and body as the pin-hipped Gigi Type #2 (see A&H section).

TYPE #2: A straight leg walking doll; wide or medium sleep eyes, mold line through center of the ear, C-shaped arm hook; separate fingers; walking doll with straight legs and toe detail. Note: This doll head has Ginger characteristics (see Cosmopolitan section).

Mindy: Type #3 Ginger type bent knee walker doll with toe detail.

TYPE #3: Walking doll with Ginger characteristics (same as Mindy #2) but has bending knees (see Virga and Cosmopolitan sections).

Wig characteristics: Advertising reads, "Curl, Brush, and Comb her hair." The Dynel wig was sewn with one row of stitching to a strip of backing and glued to the head.

Clothing Characteristics: Clothes were relatively well made, mid-market quality, using velvet and flowers for trim. Advertisement read, "All of Mindy's dresses are just the prettiest and tailored in beautiful material...they all have snaps so that you can dress Mindy easily and quickly." The back dress seam was stitched closed below the dress opening, and all seams were left unfinished. Dresses closed with hand-sewn, square metal snaps, and some dresses had a strip of stiff net sewn inside along hem stitching. The box brochure shows Mindy dressed in 24 outfits and accessories. "Mindy's Skate Case," a cardboard "Traveling Trunk," and a counter display of Mindy outfits in acetate cases selling for $1 each. A second brochure advertised "bending knees" Mindy dressed in 36 different outfits but no cases or accessories.

Value: $55.00 for doll; $75.00 in small suitcase box; $90.00 in cardboard trunk.

Mindy dress construction detail showing closed back seam, metal snap, and net hem reinforcement.

Mindy and Her Skate Case
$4.98

A real case to carry your skates in comes with Mindy, the bride, and her complete bridal outfit, even to the bouquet in her hand. You get a lace trimmed negligee or pajamas, two dress outfits, a hat, comb, mirror and two bows for Mindy's hair.

Also available with skater instead of bride.

Brochure advertisement for Mindy and her "Skate Case" with doll in bride gown, two dress outfits, pajamas, negligee, and accessories. Courtesy Marge Meisinger.

All About
Mindy

SHE WALKS

SHE HAS
GO-TO-SLEEP EYES

CURL, BRUSH,
COMB HER HAIR

Completely Dressed, in handsome package, 8″ size, **$1**⁹⁸
Also available in 11″ size.

Meet Mindy, the Doll all America is in love with.

Read about Mindy, her 24 lovely dresses, her keen skating case and her traveling trunk.

Cover of an early straight leg walking Mindy brochure featuring 24 outfits. Courtesy Marge Meisinger.

Mindy's Dresses $1.

Fits all 8 inch Dolls.
Also available in 11″ size

This is just one of Mindy's 24 dresses in her own little see-through handbag. All of Mindy's dresses are just the prettiest, and tailored in beautiful materials just like the "grown-up" dresses that Mommy has.

They all have snaps so that you can dress Mindy easily and quickly. Turn this sheet over and see Mindy all dressed in her 24 best. Now that you have started your collection of Mindy's outfits, I am sure you will want every one of her party, play and fun outfits. You can dress Mindy or any doll of her size in all of these dresses because they're just made to fit.

Be sure you get the genuine Mindy costumes, so lovely and so well made. Look for the Mindy see-through handbag with Mindy's name, in her own attractive display box.

Brochure photo of separate dress in acetate case. Courtesy Marge Meisinger.

Mindy in outfits from brochure, c. 1956 - 1957.

Mindy Type #1 with her cardboard wardrobe trunk in a taffeta "Party Dress" #14 with felt hat, vinyl slip-on shoes. Courtesy Marge Meisinger.

Mindy and Her Trunk   **$2.98**

Some "traveling music" for Mindy with her big wardrobe trunk. Mindy's trunk has a real snap-lock and many labels from far away lands. Mindy's pajamas hang on a plastic hanger and Mindy herself is dressed in one of her nicest dresses. A terrific value for $2.98.

Mindy with her trunk and extra pajamas.

Also available in 11" size.

Brochure advertisement for dressed Mindy and her trunk with extra pajamas. Courtesy Marge Meisinger.

Mindy Type #1 pin-hipped, straight leg walking doll with sleep eyes wears a taffeta Party Dress #14 with velvet and flower trim, net hat, and slip-on shoes. Original elastic still in her hair.

Full-page advertisement for Mindy Type #2 straight leg walking dolls by Sue Marlin Associates in Philadelphia. Courtesy Marge Meisinger.

Back of Mindy dress closes with a circle donut snap.

Walking Mindy Type #1 in a small cardboard case with window front and carry handles.

Mindy Type #1 in Gypsy #22 cotton outfit with yellow cotton scarf, green cotton bodice, ribbon taffeta skirt.

End label of Mindy Clown #100/30 doll box.

Mindy Type #2 straight leg walker in red and white #25 Tennis costume with slip-on vinyl shoes and tennis racket. Courtesy Jo Barckley.

Mindy Type #3 bent knee walker wears her diamond taffeta print Clown #100/30 costume with attached net ruffle collar and clown matching hat in original window box.

Left: Mindy in School Days #23 in her cardboard trunk with large check dungaree outfit not shown in Mindy catalog. ($425.00); right: Mindy in Gypsy #22 or #35 ($150.00). Prices realized courtesy Frasher's Doll Auctions.

Mindy bent knee walker in original box with separate outfits ($275.00 for all). Prices realized courtesy Frasher's Doll Auctions.

Active's Judy 8" walking doll was a wide-eye Ginger type doll mounted on cardboard and displayed in Active's "Sight-Selling" visual package.

Judy 8" c. 1950s

Marks on Doll: None.

Boxes marked: Cardboard with "bubble" window to display doll: "Judy/The 8 inch Walking Doll/Another 'Sight-Selling' Visual Package created by Active Doll Corp."

Doll Characteristics: This is an 8", hard plastic, wide-eye Ginger doll bought by Active. She is a straight leg, head-turning walker; head mold through center of ear, flat feet with toe detail, toes are unpainted, arms have C-shaped hook and separate fingers.

Wig Characteristics: Synthetic wig with single-stitch part on strip backing.

Dress Characteristics: Sold undressed in taffeta panties trimmed in lace.

Value: Doll only $45.00; on original bubble card (rare) $75.00+.

Baby

Minette Baby 8" c. 1958

Marks on Doll: Unknown.

Boxes Marked: Unknown.

Doll Characteristics: Active Doll Company's Minnette was an 8" all-vinyl drink and wet baby doll, fully jointed, with sleep eyes, molded lashes, and curved legs. Minnette was a Ginnette look-alike and was marketed as the baby sister to 8" Mindy.

Wig Characteristics: Curly baby-cuts; ads read, "My rooted curly hair is so real and natural that you can comb it, wash it, and wave it as often as you please."

Clothing Characteristics: Finishes are unknown, but Minnette's brochure showed seven outfits including a christening gown, coat ensemble, play suit rompers, and bunting.

Value: $55.00.

(No actual MIB examples of this doll have been found to photograph.)

"I'm Minnette, and I'm so cuddly. I'm sure you'd love to adopt me. My rooted, curly hair is so real and natural that you can comb it, wash it and wave it as often as you please. I'm eight inches tall, and my vinyl skin is life-like to the touch."

She's a real pet In her coat set.

Minnette's so lovely to caress In her pretty party dress.

Minnette had seven dresses and play outfits and a christening gown. These are two dresses shown in her brochure.

Baby sister 8" Minnette drink and wet sleep eye doll with curly rooted hair, advertised in brochure with sister Mindy.

🍇 Admiration Doll Company 🍇

Admiration produced dolls for the low-end market in the '50s and '60s. Many dolls were the display type dolls, but they also entered the toddler doll market in the '50s and '60s.

Admiration also entered the vinyl doll and high heel doll market in the '60s.

Display Dolls

Admiration boxed a number of display dolls, and these are two of the types found:

Marks on Doll: Unmarked.
Boxes Marked: Square pink boxes with window lids, "BROADWAY DOLL/A NEW CAROL CREATION/ THE ADMIRATION DOLL CO. INC/ NEW YORK CITY."
Also: Square blue boxes with window display lids, "THE STARLET DOLL/ AMERICA'S LOVABLE PERSONALITY."
Also: Admiration featured display dolls in boxes with other names and various designs.
Doll Characteristics: A 7½" hard plastic doll with sleep eyes, jointed at head and arms, fixed legs with molded plastic rectangular bows with one horizontal crease.
Dress Characteristics: Stapled-on dresses or gowns without hems with ribbon for bodice.
Wig Characteristics: Wavy mohair glued to the head.
Value: $25.00 MIB.

Carol-Sue the Little Mother's Darling 8"
Marks on Doll: None.
Boxes Marked: Carol-Sue/ Midwestern Mfg. Co. The folding red and blue window boxes are the same as Admiration's toddler doll boxes with the addition of "The Little Mother's Darling" printed below the window.

Display type doll "Carol-Sue, The Little Mother's Darling" with moveable head and arms and fixed legs, sleep eyes with molded lashes. She wears a stapled-on red cotton dress gathered and stitched to a yellow ribbon, and slip-on white vinyl shoes.

One of Admiration's 7½" hard plastic display type dolls with sleep eyes, The Broadway Doll, A new Carol Creation, in a stapled-on taffeta gown.

Broadway Doll 7½" doll on original box.

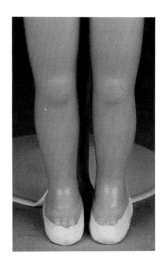

Broadway Doll feet with rectangular bow with one horizontal crease, painted white.

Doll Characteristics: These 8" inexpensive blow molded plastic dolls had sleep eyes, moving arms and head, fixed legs. Two types "Carol-Sue The Little Mother's Darling" dolls were used with slightly different heads. One has larger eyes with molded lashes, and the other also has lashes painted above the molded lashes.

Clothing Characteristics: Stapled-on clothes of inexpensive cotton with unfinished skirt gathered onto a ribbon; a strip of fabric is wrapped around neck and tucked into skirt for bodice; slip-on vinyl shoes.

Wig Characteristics: Glued-on wavy hair, not sewn to a backing.

Value: $35.00 MIB.

Toddler Doll

Carol-Sue

In the early 1960s Admiration Doll Co. advertised in *Playthings* magazine, and one of their dolls was Carol-Sue (per Pam and Polly Judd, *Hard Plastic Dolls II*).

Unfortunately, the Carol-Sue box does not have the name of the maker but is attributed to Admiration.

Marks on Doll: Unmarked.

Boxes Marked: Carol-Sue; boxes were red or blue folding window boxes.

1958 newspaper ad by White's Notions for inexpensive Carol-Sue doll with stapled-on dress and felt hat. Reads, "Fancy dressed, moveable arms, legs, head. Eyes open and close. Gaily dressed." They sold 2 for $1. Courtesy Marge Meisinger.

Display type doll "Carol-Sue, The Little Mother's Darling" with moveable head and arms and fixed legs, sleep eyes with molded lashes, and painted lashes above eye. Wears a stapled-on taffeta dress with blue taffeta print skirt and white ribbon top.

Carol-Sue c. 1958, Type #1, with blonde wavy hair, stapled-on dress with red ribbon top, and white taffeta skirt with red and blue stars gathered on a blue waist ribbon. She is missing her hat.

Doll Characteristics:

   TYPE #1 – This 7½" doll has Ginger characteristics with wide sleep eyes (some wider than others), molded lashes, head mold seams through center of the ear; C-shaped Ginger type arm hooks with separate fingers. Her body was the same as Ginger and had apparently been a walker. However, the walking mechanism was removed, and she was strung through the hole that once held the walking rods, giving her a "no neck" look. Her straight legs have separate toes that are usually painted white. This is a very good clue to her identification. However, occasionally Carol-Sue is found MIB without painted toes. Note: Carol Sue with stapled-on clothes has the same head and body as Midwestern's Mary Jean, but Mary Jean has removeable clothes. Also, A&H's "Judy" dress-me uses this same doll but without painted feet.

   TYPE #2 – Same body and painted feet as Type #1, but some have heads with smaller eyes, lashes painted under the eyes, and head mold line behind ear.

Clothing Characteristics: Admiration's Carol-Sue dolls were affordable dolls with simple dresses. Her clothes were stapled-on at the stomach and back, and the skirt is made of unfinished taffeta, unhemmed and stitched, gathered onto a ribbon; the bodice is formed from a ribbon tucked inside the skirt. Some dolls have stapled-on felt bonnets; no shoes but painted white feet. Interestingly, "Dress Me" is printed on the box even though the clothes were stapled to the doll.

Wig Characteristics: Wavy mohair or wavy synthetic strands are glued to the head with no backing. A large eye Ginger type doll has been found with staple marks and a stapled-on Carol-Sue hat, and she has blue hair. This leads to speculation that Carol Sue dolls also had pastel hair, but this is not documented at this point.

Value: MIB $45.00.

Comparison of two types of Carol-Sue dolls. (L) Type #1 with typical Ginger wide eyes with mold line through center of ear; (R) Type #2 one with smaller eyes, lashes painted below the eyes, and mold line behind the ear. Both have Ginger bodies with white painted feet and stapled-on clothes. Carol-Sue is basically the same as Midwestern's Mary Jean but has stapled-on clothes instead of removeable clothes.

Close-up of Type #1 & #2 Carol-Sue dolls.

Blonde Carol-Sue c. 1958 Type #1 has typical wide eyes with molded lashes but does not have lashes painted under the eyes. Her dress is stapled-on with a dotted black top and blue taffeta flowered skirt, pink ribbon waist band, black felt hat, and painted white toes instead of shoes. Blue and gold design box with acetate window lid.

Brunette Carol-Sue c. 1958 Type #2 has wide sleep eyes with molded lashes that are slightly smaller than some, lashes painted under the eyes, and mold line behind the ear. Her stapled-on magenta and blue flowered dress is lace-trimmed with a stapled-on pink felt hat; she has painted white toes instead of shoes and a red and gold design box with acetate window lid.

Blonde Carol-Sue c. 1958 with stapled-on red and blue striped dress with blue taffeta skirt and red felt hat. Most had painted white toes instead of shoes, but these toes are not painted. Red and gold design box with acetate window lid. Courtesy Marge Meisinger.

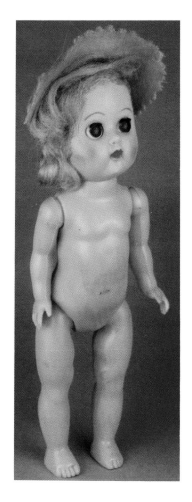

(Right) This played-with doll has stapled-on felt hat and staple marks on her stomach and back, the same as Carol-Sue. However this doll has blue hair, indicating that Carol-Sue may have had pastel hair, no doubt competing with Virga's Lolly Pop dolls (see Virga section). Courtesy Jeanne Niswonger.

(Left) Brunette Carol-Sue dolls c. 1958 Type #1 on left with stapled-on dress and felt hat and painted white toes instead of shoes. Doll on right with painted toes has slightly larger eyes and is either Carol-Sue or Midwestern's Mary Jean with removeable dress. Courtesy Mary Van Buren Swasey.

❧ Madame Alexander Doll Company, Inc. ❧

Madame Alexander founded her famous doll company in 1912, and she quickly became known for quality dolls sold to the high-end market. Some feel that her dolls are the standard by which all others are judged. Her hard plastic dolls of the 1950s included a number of small dolls, but space allows a review of only the most popular.

Toddler Dolls

Wendy (also Wendy-Kins, Wendy-Ann, Alexander-Kins) 8" c. 1953

Marks on Doll:

1953 – 54 – ALEX on back: Strung, straight leg, not a walker, tannish flesh tone and dark red lips, molded lashes with lashes painted under eyes.

1954 – 55 – ALEX on back: Straight leg, now a walker, lighter plastic tones and lips; can look bisque, molded lashes with lashes painted under eyes.

1956 into 1964 – ALEX on back: The same walking doll as '54-'55 but with bent knees.

1965 – 72 – ALEX on back: bent knee, non-walker, and darker lower lashes into '70s.

1973 – 76 – Bent knee non-walker with rounder eyes and whites showing below eyes, pinker flesh tones.

1977 & later – "Alexander" on back: Straight leg non-walkers, eyes more centered paler flesh tones.

Boxes Marked: Early boxes- "Alexander-Kins"; later boxes- "Madame Alexander."

Doll Characteristics: Wendy was a darling 7½"- 8" hard plastic, fully jointed toddler doll with sleep eyes introduced c.1953. She was marketed with the above names, but "Alexander-Kins" was dropped c.'63 in favor of "Wendy-Ann." Over time she was made from different plastics and changed from a strung doll to a straight leg walker, and then to a bent knee walker per above dates. Her arms' "hooks" were metal rings, and she had separate fingers on the right hand, but second and third fingers molded together on the left hand. A brochure c. '56 states, "Alexander-Kins are molded of finest hard plastic, are fully jointed and walk. To bend her knee pull gently on the leg to unlock the walking device and bend knee."

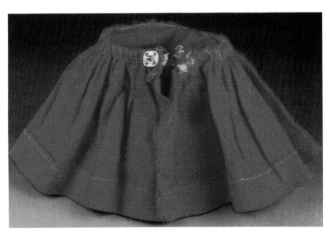

Inside Wendy dress: '53-'56: Finished overcast stitched waist seam; unfinished center back seam below waist opening; straight stitched deep hem.

Alexander Wendy on left wears '54 scoop neck, sleeveless ballerina dress; on right polished cotton pinafore dress c. 1953-56 school dress with rick-rack trim that came in different colors with different floral print pinafores. 1955 outfits with straw hat but some "School Outfit" c. '53 had matching bonnet.

(L)Wendy's face c. '54; (R) Wendy's face c. '55 doll; both faces are the same, and both are straight leg walkers.

Wendy '55 "Lady in Waiting" #487 satin gown is hemmed with machine hem stitch. Courtesy Marge Meisinger.

Dress Characteristics: *Quality & Style* – Outfits were beautifully made, well fitting, and were tagged with an MA tag. *Neckline* – Most dresses had round or scooped necks, some with attached collars, or bibs, or cowl collars. Some styles were wrap-around with no neckline. *Sleeves* – Most were sleeveless with rick-rack or lace trim or had elbow-length sleeves with no shoulder seam. Some elbow-length puffed sleeve styles did have shoulder seams. Pinafore dresses had regular waistlines with separate aprons. Wrist-length sleeves were uncommon except on jackets for dress ensembles or for gowns. *Skirts* – Full with regular or pleated gathers and seamed at the waist. The single back dress seam was stitched together below the dress opening. *Slips* – Usually no attached slip. *Pants* – Usually lace-trimmed cotton organdy gathered at the leg, some with 3 rows of attached ruffles on the back. *Finish* – Deep hems were turned and straight-stitched to finish. Some fine satin gowns were machine stitched with a looped hemming stitch. The single back dress seam was stitched together below the dress and edges left unfinished. The waistline seam was overcast with industrial machine stitching to finish edges. *Closures* – Most outfits were closed with square snaps machine stitched on only two sides; if all 4 snap sides are stitched, it is probably homemade or a competitor's dress. Some small flat two-hole buttons and some round pearl buttons were also used.

Wig Characteristics: The early strung Wendy wigs for straight leg and bent knee dolls were stitched down both sides of a center seam, so there are three rows of parallel stitching. Other wigs had a distinctive zigzag stitching down the center. This type wig is found especially on bent knee walkers introduced in 1956 and sold through '64 and on bend knee non-walkers until '72. A brochure c. '56 stated,

Wendy closures c.'53-'56: Top left: Snap sewn on two sides; Top right: Apron with metal eyelet; Bottom: Two-hole pearl buttons. Not shown: Round brass buttons.

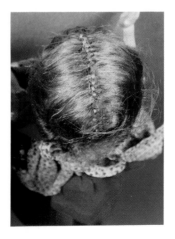

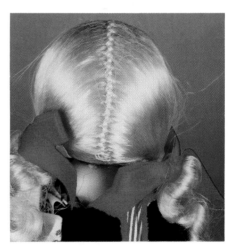

Alexander Wendy (also Alexander-Kins and Wendy-Kins) in early wig c. '53-'55 with three rows of parallel stitching.

The Alexander Wendy braided wig c. 1956 has unique stitching, a center row with zigzag stitches sewn over. Courtesy Marge Meisinger.

"Each wig is woven, washable, and can be combed and curled," but Wendy's synthetic wig material isn't specified.

Value Undressed: '53-$300.00; '54-$275.00; '56-$175.00; '65-$100.00.

In Party Dress: '53-$500.00+; '54-$450.00+; '56-$375.00+; '65-$275.00.

Dressed Dolls

Wendy Ann in gowns, all with pantaloons and straw hats c. 1953 (L to R): "Country Picnic," pink and white cotton gown with waist jacket, lace edging; "Little Victoria," blue organdy dotted Swiss organdy gown with tulle sleeves, Alexander-Kins wrist tag; "Little Edwardian," blue and white star print gown with white tulle sleeves. Realized $550.00, $800.00, $400.00 respectively. Courtesy Frasher's Doll Auctions.

1953 Alexander 8" Wendy strung non-walker, "Little Madeline" from Ludwig Bemelman's stories, dotted pink cotton dress and matching bonnet. Dress tagged "Alexander-Kin," matches larger MA doll.

End box label for Ballerina #554 stamped "cornflower blue" color, with tosca hair color.

1954-56 Wendy straight leg walker ballerina #554 with original box in tutu with blue taffeta top with 3 faux rhinestones and tulle full skirt. The style matched ballerinas in 15" and 18" sizes and also came in yellow, pink, and lavender. Walking dolls were phased in beginning 1954.

1954 straight leg walker in variation of Guardian Angel #480 with pale pink gown edged with gold picot trim and gold braid, with white wings and a gold halo secured with a chin strap. Silver tie slippers and toy harp. Courtesy Marge Meisinger.

Alexander-Kin 1954 straight leg walker Guardian Angel #480 in blue gown edged with silver picot trim and gold braid, with white wings and a gold halo secured with a chin strap. Silver tie slippers and toy harp Tagged: "Guardian Angel/Madame Alexander/ Reg.U.W. Pat. Off/ New York, N.Y." Courtesy Billie Nelson Tyrrell.

Wendy straight leg walker '55 "Wendy Ready for Plane Journey" #425 wears pleated skirt with blue felt jacket, matching cap with red pom pons. Courtesy Marge Meisinger.

"Wendy's Train Journey" #468 1955 wears a red plaid dress and white felt jacket with matching beanie cap with red pom pons. Tagged "Alexander-Kins." Courtesy Marge Meisinger.

Wendy straight leg walker '55 "Lady in Waiting" #487 pink satin gown with tulle side panniers trimmed with flowers and silver edging. Courtesy Marge Meisinger.

"Wendy's Train Journey" #468 1955 variation with white tam and red pom; the catalog showed a beanie. Courtesy McMasters Auction.

Basic Alexander-Kin doll #500 c. '56 and '58 on right with lace-trimmed panties, socks, and shoes; basic doll #600 on left in elastic leg pants. Courtesy Marge Meisinger.

1956 straight leg walker "Wendy Helps Mommy" #428 in a navy taffeta dress with red and white striped cotton tie-on apron and bloomers. Courtesy Marge Meisinger.

1956 "Wendy's First Long Dancing Dress" #606, in a lovely pink tulle gown with green velvet sash. Doll had a special hairstyle for the outfit. Courtesy Marge Meisinger.

Bottom (L to R): Wendy Carries Her Milk Money #553 c.'56, red and white striped pinafore buttoned to a blue body suit ($300.00); Wendy in striped Leotard ($300.00); Blue cotton pinafore with red rick-rack ($500.00). Top (L to R): Wendy Goes Ice Skating # 555 c.'56, white felt skirt over red leotard ($326.00); Wendy in a red polished cotton dress (possibly "Wendy is Fond of Morning Dresses #345 c. '57) ($550.00); Wendy Changes Outfits for Rainy Day #439 c.'55, red and white taffeta coat and hat over red polished cotton dress ($400.00). Realized courtesy of Frasher's Doll Auction.

Wendy in FAO Schwarz exclusive 1956 trunk ensemble, a red patent case with plaid lining and a plastic window door to hold Wendy and clothes. Courtesy Marge Meisinger.

Wendy straight leg walker '55 "Wendy Dressed for Maypole Dance" #458 blue taffeta dress edged with lace and organdy yoke, fabric flowers backed with felt. Courtesy Marge Meisinger.

1957 bent knee walker, "Wendy has Many School Frocks" #368 red taffeta dress with white pinafore laced with red satin ribbon which also came in other colors and plaid. White straw hat trimmed with red velvet flowers. The souvenir pin commemorates the style. Courtesy Marge Meisinger.

1957 bent knee walker, "Princess Ann" #393, in a lace dress trimmed with satin ribbon sash, and straw hat trimmed with flowers. Sold for $450 by McMasters Auction.

1957 bent knee walker, "Prince Charles" #397, in blue suit, short pants, and cap. Realized $410 at McMasters Doll Auction.

1958 bent knee walker "Edith the Lonely Doll" #850 in pink cotton check dress, white cotton apron. Note the brass circle earrings and upswept hairstyle. Character is from book by Dare Wright. Courtesy Marge Meisinger.

1958 "Billie" #567 in blue suit with matching cap. Courtesy Marge Meisinger.

Madame Alexander sold girls' dresses to match 8" Wendy doll dresses c. 1961, like this pink cotton dress with white ruffled top. Courtesy Marge Meisinger.

1965 bent knee, non-walker "Wendy in Organdy Dress" #621, a pink dress edged with rows of lace on the bodice and skirt. Small pink hair bow, original wrist brochure, tagged "Wendy-Kin." Courtesy Marge Meisinger.

1965 "Scarlett" #785 in white organdy gown with green rick-rack trim, straw hat, and original wrist booklet. Courtesy Marge Meisinger.

Wendy "Hawaiian" bending knee doll with dark wig and brown eyes, flower in hair, made from 1966 to 1969 and discontinued.

Wendy Bride c. 1966-68 with nylon gown edged with lace and puffed sleeve and tulle veil. (Same style bridal gown with straight sleeves c.'69-'72.) Groom c. 1956 #577 with felt tuxedo. Courtesy Vicki Johnson.

"Africa" made from '66-'71 with dark hair and brown eyes, bending knees, wearing bright cotton costume, white scarf, and brass loop earrings; marked ALEX on back.

Back of "Africa" with Alexander tag.

Maggie Mix Up 8" c. 1960

Marks on Doll: ALEX on back.

Doll Characteristics: Maggie came in 8" and 16" sizes, both with straight red or blonde hair, with bangs and freckles and green sleep eyes with molded lashes. The hard plastic bent knee 8" size was similar to Vogue's "impish" type Wee Imp also introduced in '60, but with a different knee joint. Maggie was a hard plastic doll using the Alexander-kins body with a different head.

Dress Characteristics: Maggie was sold undressed or dressed in a variety of play outfits. In 1961 Madame introduced 8" "Maggie Mix-Up Angel" #618 in a blue silver-trimmed or in a white gold-trimmed gown like the 1954 "Guardian Angel" except with the solid foil wings. Also, Madame, perhaps tellingly, eliminated her halo and harp!

Wig Characteristics: Glued-on red wig with center part stitching and bangs.

Value: $400.00+.

1961 "Maggie Angel" #618 with red hair and freckles in blue gown with embroidered silver yolk, silver picot trim, lined sleeves, and silver wings sewn on back. Courtesy Marge Meisinger.

Maggie Mixup bent knee walker "Skater" #615 wears a knit body suit with blue pleated skirt, attached red ribbon waist band, knit cap, and brown leather skates. Courtesy Marge Meisinger.

Quiz-Kin 8" c. 1953

Quiz-Kin c. 1953, 8" fully jointed, hard plastic baby with molded and painted hair, or wig over molded hair; straight legs, non-walking; two buttons on back to

1953-'54 Quiz-Kins girl in white organdy dress and Quiz-Kins boy with molded hair in red jersey and yellow and white striped cotton pants. Courtesy Marge Meisinger.

Quiz-Kins 8" c. 1953 with back buttons controlling "yes" or "no" head moves. Courtesy Marge Meisinger.

❦ Madame Alexander Doll Company, Inc.

move doll's head "Yes" and "No." From TV show "Quiz Kids," they were dressed in jersey knit bodysuits to facilitate access to buttons.
Value: $550.00.

Baby Dolls

Little Genius 8" c. 1956 – 1962
Marks on Doll: ALEX on back; dress tags: "Little Genius by Madame Alexander.
Boxes Marked: Madame Alexander.
Doll Characteristics: Alexander's 8" drinking and wetting baby "Little Genius" had a hard plastic head and body, vinyl limbs, fully jointed body, sleep eyes, a nursing open mouth, and a hole in the lower back to wet. She was sold to the high end of the market. Note: The Little Genius should not be confused with Alexander's baby c. 1949 with the same name and a Magic Skin head and cloth body.
Wig Characteristics: She has a curly baby-style caracul wig which appears to be Saran.
Dress characteristics: Beautifully made and tagged dresses, close with buttons; the 1956 brochure showed 11 lace trimmed outfits of organdy or polished cotton including a christening outfit, party dress, bonnet, and sunsuit,
Value: $200.00; $300.00+ for fancy or christening outfit.

Littlest Kitten 8" c. 1963 – 1964
Marks on Doll: ALEX on back.
Boxes Marked: Madame Alexander
Doll Characteristics: Alexander's 8" Littlest Kitten was not a drink and wet doll, but was a darling all-vinyl baby with slightly bent legs. She had sleep eyes with molded lashes and lashes painted under the eye.
Wig Characteristics: Straight rooted hair; material not specified but appears to be Saran type.

Little Genius 1956-64 in pink organdy coat ensemble trimmed with lace and matching bonnet ($295). Price realized and photo courtesy McMasters Doll Auction.

Left: Little Genius c.1956-8" curly top baby doll with hard plastic head and body and vinyl limbs, nursing mouth, and a hole in the lower back to wet like the others; caracul wig. Right: Alexander's 8" Littlest Kitten c.1964 was not a drink and wet doll but was a darling vinyl baby with bent legs and straight rooted hair.

Dress Characteristics: Beautifully made and tagged dresses, close with buttons.
Value: $225.00+.

Fisher Quints (set) 8" c. 1964
Marks on Doll: On tag "Original Quintuplets."
Doll Characteristics: These 7" dolls used the hard plastic Little Genius head with open nursing mouths, but bodies, arms, and legs were vinyl. They came with four pink baby bottles and one blue labeled "Original Quints."
Dress Characteristics: Came in white undershirts and diapers or with jumpsuit tagged "Quints," wrapped in a blanket bunting.
Wig Characteristics: Molded hair.
Value: $450.00 set.

Fisher Quints c. 1964, hard plastic head with vinyl body with sleep eyes, open nursing mouth in replaced vintage Alexander outfits. Courtesy Marge Meisinger

36

❦ American Character ❦

American Character Doll Co. (AC) manufactured fine-quality composition dolls as early as 1919. They entered the lucrative post-WWII doll market with hard plastic and vinyl dolls, introducing Tiny Tears around 1950, and Betsy McCall in 1957. Both Betsy McCall and Tiny Tears are now doll classics.

Small Doll

Betsy McCall 8" c. 1952

Betsy McCall was originally a magazine paper doll character developed around 1951 to help sell McCall's sewing patterns. In 1952 Ideal introduced a 14" Betsy doll, but around 1957 American Character was granted a license for the 8" doll. American Character also sold larger Betsys, but their tiny doll is a favorite today.

Marks on Doll: In a circle on the back: "McCall (c) Corp."

Boxes Marked: "Betsy McCall" on lid and "Betsy McCall/McCall Doll" on end.

The rectangular boxes were white with blue star pattern and gold dots. Dolls that were sold through catalog companies had solid pink boxes.

Doll Characteristics: Betsy was an 8" hard plastic doll with rigid straight vinyl arms, second and third fingers molded together, blue sleep eyes, single stroke eyebrows, and molded lashes. The first-year Betsys had peg-based jointed knees, and the second year knees were metal pin-jointed. Betsy's hard plastic was a lovely bisque color, and she had a high forehead, lovely rosy cheeks, and a closed mouth with red lips. Her advertising reads, "She can sit, stand and walk." The Betsy McCall mold is likely to separate at the crotch, and the knees will split as the doll ages.

Wig Characteristics: The first-year Betsy had a mesh based Saran wig; second year she had rooted Saran hair in a rubber skullcap; metal barrettes were clipped at the temple on each side.

Dress Characteristics: Dresses were well made, *continued on page 41*

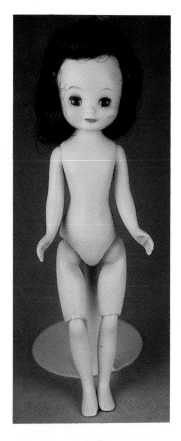

Undressed brunette Betsy McCall. Note the splitting knees, a common problem with aging Betsy McCall dolls today.

An American Character 8" blonde Betsy McCall in nylon chemise, white vinyl side snap shoes, and knit socks. Her plain pink box indicates she was a mail-order doll.

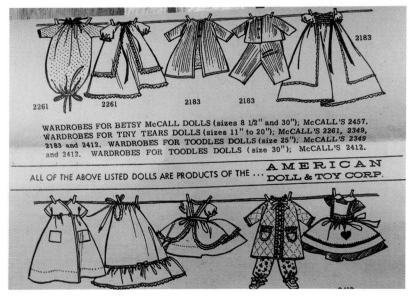

WARDROBES FOR BETSY McCALL DOLLS (sizes 8 1/2" and 30"); McCALL'S 2457. WARDROBES FOR TINY TEARS DOLLS (sizes 11" to 20"); McCALL'S 2261, 2349, 2183 and 2412. WARDROBES FOR TOODLES DOLLS (size 25"); McCALL'S 2349 and 2412. WARDROBES FOR TOODLES DOLLS (size 30"); McCALL'S 2412.

ALL OF THE ABOVE LISTED DOLLS ARE PRODUCTS OF THE ... AMERICAN DOLL & TOY CORP.

Flier from Betsy McCall's mail order box advertises McCall patterns available for American Doll & Toy Corp. (American Character) Betsy McCall, Tiny Tears, and Toodles.

Betsy McCall, hard plastic, blue sleep eyes with molded lashes, single stroke brows, painted lower lashes, brunette Saran wig. She has jointed knees and is dressed in original nylon teddy, socks, and shoes in original box with two booklets. Separate outfits: Ice Outfit and Sunday Best Outfit. Courtesy McMasters sold for $1,050 at auction.

Betsy McCall 8" c. 1957 in brown and red plaid cotton trimmed with white rick-rack, black shoes. Courtesy Barbara Rosplock-Van Orman.

Betsy McCall 8" c. 1957 in original box with brochure and separately boxed "Sweet Dreams" negligee outfit # 840/250. Courtesy Shirley's Doll House.

Betsy McCall 8" c. 1957 in red jumper and blue and white striped shirt, with red vinyl shoes. Courtesy Barbara Rosplock-Van Orman.

Spiegel 1962 catalog advertisement for Betsy McCall and her carrying case. Courtesy Marge Meisinger.

Betsy McCall in 1957 Sun n' Sand costume. Courtesy Sandy Johnson Barts.

Sugar & Spice and Sunday Best on larger Betsy McCall. Courtesy Sandy Johnson Barts.

Page from 1962 catalog showing jointed Betsy McCalls. Courtesy Sandy Johnson Barts.

8" Betsy McCall from store display with white hat stapled to head. Courtesy Sandy Johnson Barts.

Recess and Bar-B-Q; blue grill and hot dogs are original to the 2-piece outfit. Courtesy Sandy Johnson Barts.

Betsy McCall in "At the Zoo" outfit. Courtesy Sandy Johnson Barts.

Standard case offered for Betsy McCalls. Courtesy Sandy Johnson Barts.

Inside Betsy McCall case. Courtesy Sandy Johnson Barts.

Betsy McCall in Farm Girl outfit; brown duck is original. Courtesy Sandy Johnson Barts.

Bottom row (L to R): "On the Ice," brown wig, red jersey, red felt skirt, velveteen vest, felt hat, white ice skates ($190.00); "On the Ice," with white felt skirt ($140.00); "Town & Country," black and white checked cotton coat ensemble ($220.00); "Holiday Fashion," white taffeta body suit and rose pink velveteen skirt ($190.00); "Playtime," Betsy McCall white taffeta printed skirt and gray felt coat ($250.00). Top row (L to R): Betsy in pink flocked nylon party dress ($210.00) Betsy in original box in nylon chemise (2)($350.00 & $500.00); pink taffeta dress with lace overskirt ($200.00); pink nylon formal with velveteen bodice and black flocked accents, nylon stole, attached petticoat ($300.00). Courtesy Frasher's Auctions.

11" Tiny Tears with hard plastic head, vinyl body, sleep eyes with tear ducts, open nursing mouth, drinking and wetting doll, rooted hair, good color in replica ensemble by Toni Ferry.

and many closed with smooth round metal snaps, painted and unpainted. Outfits were sold separately in McCall boxes.
Value: $200.00 doll in chemise; $350.00+ for doll in original box.

Babies

Tiny Tears 11" c. 1950s – 1960s
While Tiny Tears came in many sizes over the years, these are the smallest sizes.
Mark on Doll: American Character on head; Marked "Pat. No. 2675644.
Boxes Marked: Tiny Tears/American Character Rock-A-Bye Eyes/Rock her slowly/to sleep in/your arms. The presentation box included a pink/white cotton dress, diaper, bubble pipe, bottle, sponges, tissues, and wash cloth.
Doll Characteristics: In the 1950s the 11" doll had a five-piece jointed vinyl body, hard plastic head with tear ducts, rooted tosca hair, blue sleep eyes, brush lashes, open pink mouth with bottle hole; she drinks and wets. Beginning in 1963 she was all vinyl.
Dress Characteristics: Well-made dresses closing with buttons, sleep wear, and large assortment of boxed separate clothing.
Wig Characteristics: Rooted hair in curly baby cut.
Value: $100.00 – 150.00 doll only; or $350.00+ in original, complete case.

Teeny Weenie Tiny Tears 8" c. 1964
Marks on Doll: Marked on head "1964/AM Char Doll."
Boxes Marked: Unknown.
Doll Characteristics: The 8½" Teeny Weeny Tiny Tears c. 1964 was a fully jointed vinyl baby with rooted hair, sleep eyes, an open mouth, and she had a curved right hand. She was a nursing doll but without tear ducts like Tiny Tears.
Dress Characteristics: Well-made mid-market baby dresses, hemmed, open down the back, and closing with a single metal snap at the neck. She wore pastel dresses or dresses with a white apron and bib yoke.
Wig Characteristics: Rooted hair in ear-length bob.
Value: $45.00.

8½" Teeny Weeny Tiny Tears c. 1964, vinyl with rooted hair and sleep eyes. Open mouth, nursing doll with no tear ducts. Marked 1964/AM Char Doll on head. Fully jointed with curved right hand, wearing original yellow cotton dress with white apron and bib yoke. Rooted hair. Courtesy Marge Meisinger.

8½" Teeny Weeny Tiny Tears c. 1964, vinyl with rooted hair and sleep eyes wearing original pink cotton dress with white collar edging. Marked 1964/AM Char Doll on head.

❦ Arranbee Doll Co. (R&B) ❦

Arranbee Doll Co. imported bisque dolls as early as the 1920s as well as selling their own composition dolls in many sizes through the '20s, '30s, and '40s. Their small, 7"-9", composition toddler and storybook dolls were very popular in the '40s. R&B sold their 8" composition dolls to other companies such as Vogue Dolls, Inc. who dressed them for sale under their own label.

The R&B Company entered the hard plastic doll market in the late '40s, and they were well known for their 14" or larger dolls such as Nancy, Nancy Lee, and Nanette. R&B's 10½" hard plastic Littlest Angel was also popular. They did not specialize in 8" toddler dolls, but they did offer the 10" hard plastic Coty Girl c.1958, a high heel fashion doll. They also sold 10" vinyl Li'l Cupcake baby and Sweet Pea dolls, but there is little documentation on them. At this point, no R&B hard plastic 8" toddler doll has been documented. In 1958 R&B was sold to Vogue Dolls, Inc. who continued their Littlest Angel and also used the mold for their Li'l Imp c. 1959.

R&B Composition Toddler & Baby, 7½"-8" c. 1940s
Marks on Doll: R&B Doll on back.
Boxes Marked: R&B.
Doll Characteristics: R&B's 7½" -8" composition doll was a strung and fully jointed toddler with painted features and side-glancing eyes. Typically R&B did not paint eyelashes over the doll's almond-shaped eyes, and they did not paint eyebrows on some. Some of the toddlers in the early '30s dolls had curly molded hair and were featured in a Nursery Rhyme Series. Other 8" toddler dolls had a distinctive single curl in the center of the forehead. R&B put bent baby legs on the 8" toddler and sold them as "Ink-U-Bator-Baby" or as "My Dream Baby" to compete with Alexander's Dionne Quints. Vogue Dolls, Inc. bought R&B's 8" composition toddler with straight legs and sold it as "Toddles" and the baby as "Sunshine Baby." (See Vogue section.)
Wig Characteristics: Molded hair was painted, but some had mohair wigs glued to the head.
Dress Characteristics: R&B outfits were colorful but inexpensively made and closed with a button or pin. Vogue Dolls Inc. also sewed for R&B's dolls, and the outfits were well-made fashions of the day or storybook costumes closing with a hook and eye. Note: See Vogue chapter for comparison photos of R&B and Vogue 8" composition dolls.
Value: 7½" Storybook characters with curly molded hair, $200.00+

7½"-8" Toddlers with straight legs, $200.00+ or more in box.

8" Baby with bent legs, $250.00 or more in box.

R&B 8" composition doll c. 1940s marked "R&B" on back and with painted brows, wearing an inexpensively made Scottish costume with felt pants and a glued-on cap over molded hair.

Back of R&B Scottish Girl showing outfit closing with button. Note crack at neck, a common problem with composition dolls.

R&B's 7½"-8" composition toddler doll, strung with painted side-glancing eyes, no eyelashes, and a single molded curly lock in the middle of forehead. Note that there are painted brows but no painted lashes. This R&B costume closes with a button.

R&B's 7½"-8" "My Dream Baby" uses the same mold as their 8" toddler doll but with bent baby legs. Typical of R&B, the baby has no painted lashes or brows and has a single molded curl on the forehead. This doll wears a pale pink organdy gown trimmed with lace, with matching bonnet. R&B also sold these dolls in sets of five as quints. Vogue bought these baby dolls from R&B and sold them as "Sunshine Babies."

Rare R&B box with lid for "Little Angel," marked "Style/ 1010."

R&B's all hard plastic 10½" Little Angel Bridesmaid in pink dotted gown on the left with straight legs and Littlest Angel in red and white striped taffeta dress on the right with bent knees. Both are pin-hipped, head-turning walking dolls; doll on right has bent knees.

R&B's "Littlest Angel" hinged lid box, picturing all of her features on the cover.

Little Angel/ Littlest Angel 10½" - 11" c. 1954

Doll Marked: R&B on head (sometimes very faint).

Boxes Marked: Little Angel or Littlest Angel/ R&B.

Doll Characteristics: First were all hard plastic, with sleep eyes and molded lashes, open closed mouth; jointed at the head, neck, and shoulders; pin-hipped, head-turning walkers with straight legs and later, jointed knees. R&B added vinyl heads c. '57. Vogue bought R&B in '58 and continued the line with vinyl heads c. '59.

Wig Characteristics: Synthetic wigs.

Dress Characteristics: Clothing was well-made and sold in separate boxes.

Value: $200.00+ MIB.

Li'l Cupcake 10" c. 1950s

Doll Marked: VM or VM 1½" back of head.

Boxes Marked: Little Cupcake/ R&B.

Doll Characteristics: All vinyl 10" fully jointed drink and wet doll with sleep eyes and molded hair; arms have separate fingers, and feet have toe detail.

Dress Characteristics: Well-made organdy, taffeta, and cottons with lace trims, closes with bottons.

Wig Characteristics: Molded hair.

Value: This doll is hard to find and values fluctuate; she has fetched as high as $275.00 at auction or as little as $35.00 in an Internet auction; has been seen at doll shows for $75.00 – 150.00 in box.

R&B's 10" vinyl fully jointed drink and wet Li'l Cupcake baby doll with molded hair wears an organdy dress and coat ensemble with matching bonnet. Courtesy Lani Spencer McCloskey.

❦ Carlson Manufacturing ❦

Very little is written about Carlson, but they distributed a series of dolls in the 1950s including 7½" display dolls with well-made and colorful costumes. The sleep eye display dolls had jointed head and arms and wrist tags reading, "Manufactured with the founders of America in mind to keep Americans aware of our heritage, Made in U. S. A." Examples of display doll costumes ranged from bride dolls to internationally costumed dolls. They apparently also sold 8" toddler dolls, as a toddler Santa doll found has the Carlson label glued to the front of the jacket.

Toddler

Santa Doll 8" c. 1950s
Marks on Doll: Unknown; clothing label "Carlson Manufacturing Doll."

Santa Claus 8" doll by Carlson appears to be a strung Plastic Molded Arts doll with sleep eyes, molded lashes, and lashes painted under. Carlson Manufacturing tag is on the velvet Santa costume leg. Courtesy Mary Van Buren-Swasey.

Marks on Box: Unknown.
Doll Characteristics: An 8" strung doll with sleep eyes and molded lashes with lashes painted underneath. Since clothes are glued to the doll, they cannot be removed to examine toe detail, fingers, etc. Note: From the doll's eye, face, and body characteristics, it appears to be a Plastic Molded Arts doll c. 1953.
Dress Characteristics: The two examples found are both dressed in a red velvet Santa costume with faux fur trim, with glued-on leatherette gloves and shoes. The Santa hat is glued to the head.
Wig Characteristics: No wig is visible under Santa's glued-on hood, but a wavy white mohair beard is glued to the chin.
Value: $35.00 – 45.00+ with box.

Santa Claus 8" doll by Carlson has a glued-on red velvet costume with faux fur trim and leatherette gloves and boots.

❦ Commonwealth Plastics ❦

Commonwealth Plastics made dolls for companies such as Vogue Dolls Inc. for their 8" Ginny and 8" Ginnette dolls in the 1950s. However, Commonwealth also labeled and sold their own dolls at the same time, including hard plastic "dress me" dolls, display type dolls, an 8" toddler "look-alike" doll, an 8" vinyl baby, and other vinyl dolls.

It was common for makers of inexpensive dolls to give one name to an entire line, regardless of height or doll type. Thus, it can confuse collectors that Commonwealth Plastics gave the name "Carol" to both their 8" display dolls and to their chubby 8" toddlers. Commonwealth also began to display the "Lingerie Lou" logo on their advertisement c. 1957, so it is assumed there was a merger or tie-in at that point. The following are Commonwealth Plastics' best-known small dolls in the '50s and '60s under their own label.

Display Dolls

DRESS ME DOLLS
Marks on Doll: Unmarked.
Marks on Package or Box: Unknown.
Doll Characteristics: These slim 6", 7", 8", 9", and 11" dolls were advertised as "sturdy plastic dolls" with "moving arms, heads and eyes" in the 1960s, but were undoubtedly sold in the '50s too. They also made an "Adult walking doll with high heel feet" which was fully jointed. They were popular for sewing, crocheting, and souvenir dolls. Note: It is reported Commonwealth also sold a 10" Carole (with an "e") "dress me" type doll shown on pg. 56 of P. Smith's *Modern Collector's Dolls Eighth Series.*
Value: $25.00 – 35.00 doll only; $30.00 – 40.00 in original package.

Toddler

Carol 7½" c. mid-'50s – '60s
Marks on Doll: Unmarked.
Marks on Card stapled to plastic package: CAROL/DRESS-HER/YOURSELF/DOLL/COMMONWEALTH PLASTICS; STYLE D-81P/ COLORFUL TODDLER DOLL WITH MOHAIR WIG AND COLORFUL PANTY.
Doll Characteristics: Commonwealth adapted the large eye Ginger type doll for their "Carol" doll and advertised her as an 8" toddler doll, but she actually measured 7½". She was sold to the low-end market at hardware stores, dime stores, etc. Carol had sleep eyes with molded lashes, high cheek color, straight arms with C-shaped hooks and separate fingers. To lower the doll's cost, the walking mechanism was left out, and she was strung through the neck slit that once held the bar controlling the doll's turning head. The head was strung over a metal bar inside the head, and the legs swing but do not turn the head. These dolls were advertised in *Playthings* magazine in the mid-'50s, but they were probably sold into the '60s as well. Note: This non-walking large eye Ginger doll was also adapted for Admiration's Carol-Sue and for Midwestern's Mary Jean. A&H also used the head-

turning version of the large eye Ginger for their "dress me" toddler "Judy."
Dress Characteristics: The doll came undressed in the plastic package with white panties trimmed with lace at the bottom.
Wig Characteristics: The package tag is printed "8" toddler doll with mohair wig and colorful panty." The wavy wig was glued directly to the head.
Value: $35.00 doll only; in original package $45.00.

Commonwealth Plastics packaged this toddler c. 1957, "Carol Dress-Her Yourself Doll" in a plastic bag. She was an 8" strung doll with wide eye Ginger characteristics. This same doll was used by Admiration's Carol-Sue and by Midwestern for Mary Jean.

❦ Other Composition Doll Companies ❦

Mayfair/Gardel Industries

"Mayfair" and "Birthstone Doll" were patented doll names filed by Gardel Industries, New York, NY, in 1945. A 7½" composition bride doll with painted side-glancing eyes and jointed arms has been found in a box marked "Mayfair/Dolls of Distinction/New York, N.Y. Pat. Pend., and it is assumed this is the same company using the "Mayfair" name patented in '45. What other doll they may have sold is not known for sure.

Mayfair Birthstone Dolls, Composition 5" c. 1945
Marks on Doll: None.
Boxes Marked: Boxes stamped with the doll's month and #; brochure in box: "Mayfair Dolls/Present/ Birthstone/ Dolls/Of the Month." Boxes had red stars in the same pattern as Hollywood Doll's boxes with blue stars. Some sources indicate a tie-in with that company, but no documentation has been found.

Mayfair's 5" Birthstone Doll "Opal" in original box with brochure and poem card for month of October.

Characteristics of Doll: All composition 5" one-piece body and head with strung arms; painted features with side-glancing eyes, lashes painted above eye; black painted shoes. Cheeks and chin are less prominent than Eugenia's 5" doll.
Dress Characteristics: Good quality gowns sewn onto doll. There were 12 gowns in this series, each named for monthly birthstone. Most dresses were crisp taffeta with felt accents and ribbons or felt bonnet stapled in hair. Faux monthly "birthstones" trimmed the gown's bodice; sewn-on pantaloons. Note: There is no documentation to tie this company into Mayfair Products Ltd. in Canada.
Wig Characteristics: Wavy mohair glued to head.
Value: $45.00 in box.

Eugenia Doll Co., Inc.

Eugenia Doll Company advertised small composition dolls in the '30s and '40s. Among these were some cute 5"-6" storybook type dolls sold through Ward's and mail order houses. Series included Touch of Paris and Bridal Party. According to Pam and Polly Judd in *Compo Dolls 1928 – 1955*, Eugenia may have bought their dolls from Ideal. Later Eugenia dolls were hard plastic, including one of the first permanent dolls c. 1949, a 14" doll named "Pam The Perm-O-Wave Doll" with human hair. However, no small hard plastic toddlers have been attributed to Eugenia.

Touch of Paris Series 5" c. 1945
Marks on Doll: None.
Boxes Marked: On a gold label, "Touch of Paris/Copyright 1945"; doll's series name; wrist tags glued-on, "Touch of Paris/Eugenia Doll Co.;" boxes are navy and white or red and white diagonal stripe.
Doll Characteristics: All composition 5" one-piece body and head with strung arms c. 1945; painted features with side-glancing eyes, lashes painted above eye, prominent cheeks and chin; black painted shoes.
Dress Characteristics: Good quality, sewn onto doll, felt hat stapled to head.
Wig Characteristics: Wavy mohair glued to head.
Value: MIB $45.00.

Unknown Maker

Fairy-Land With Illustrated Story Book
This doll is typical of the scores of unmarked composition dolls sold with no mark on doll or maker shown on the box.
Marks on Doll: None.
Boxes Marked: Fairy-Land, Made In USA.
Doll Characteristics: Inexpensive 7" Red Riding Hood composition doll with fixed head and legs with painted side-glancing eyes, socks, and shoes; jointed at arm.
Wig Characteristics: Wavy mohair glued on.
Value: $50.00.

Mayfair's 5" composition "Birthstone Doll" for October was named Opal. She had painted features, mohair wig, jointed arms, and three faux "opals" on her gown's bodice.

Eugenia 6" composition doll c.1948 "Flower Girl" #41 with jointed arms and painted features (missing eye paint) in yellow and blue taffeta dress with felt hat from Bridal Party Series #40; original box and wrist tag.

Fairy-Land 7" unmarked composition Red Riding Hood doll with jointed arms and painted side-glancing eyes, shoes, and socks. Her original box has a storybook inside. Courtesy Marge Meisinger.

❦ Cosmopolitan Toy Corporation ❦

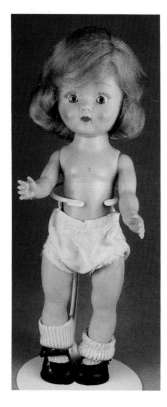

Ginger Type #1 c. 1954 with painted eyelashes; tight rolled wig (#1 usually had loose rolled wig).

Cosmopolitan Toy Corporation introduced Ginger, their 8" hard plastic toddler doll, in 1954, and launched an aggressive marketing campaign to promote the doll. Fortunately for collectors, much of this material is around today to document and identify the doll.

Cosmopolitan's founder, Kathryn Kay, had previously represented the Vogue Dolls Inc. Ginny doll until 1953, so she was well aware of the "hot" market for toddler dolls at the time she launched Ginger. Kay's toddler quickly became one of the best known mid-market '50s look-alike dolls. By the mid to late '50s, Cosmopolitan's line of small dolls also included 8" Cha Cha Heel Ginger, 8" Little Miss Ginger, 10½" Miss Ginger fashion dolls, and the 8" Baby Ginger vinyl drink n' wet doll.

While Ginger was well documented, her characteristics changed so much over time that identifying her can be challenging. Also, since Cosmopolitan sold unmarked Ginger bodies to their '50s competitors, it can be difficult to know which doll is which without the original box. A thorough study of Ginger's quality, eye size, and other characteristics by year helps with her identification. Note: Since so many competitors used the Ginger body, other chapters in this book frequently refer to "Ginger type dolls." This term indicates the common Ginger characteristics and/or specified eye sizes outlined below.

Toddler Dolls

Hard Plastic Ginger 7½" - 8"
Marks: Unmarked.
Boxes Marked: Cosmopolitan Doll and Toy Corporation, Made in USA.

TYPE #1: Painted Lashes c. 1954 – late 1950s
Doll Characteristics: The first 7½" hard plastic walking Ginger dolls had large sleep eyes with painted lashes above the eye and no molded lashes; head mold line through center of the ear; arms had separate fingers and distinctive C-shaped arm hooks squared off at the base (vs. competitor's 8" dolls C-shaped hooks set in a rounded base); straight walking legs that are set

wide apart with good toe detail; good quality plastic with a pleasing flesh color.
Dress Characteristics: See page 50.
Wig Characteristics: Wigs on these first dolls were coarse, and many were set in a side-part loose "flip" style, like primary competitor Ginny. *Wig Stitching & Style:* This first straight leg walking Ginger wigs had a single row of exposed stitching along the part, sewn to thin strip of stiffened backing. The backing could be tan vs. Ginny's white backing strip. Most were side-part flip styles. Wig colors were advertised as "platinum, honey blonde or brunette." *Wig Material:* No material was mentioned in the '54 brochure, but these early wigs appear to be Saran or poor quality Dynel compared to Ginny wigs.
Value: $55.00; MIB $125.00+.

TYPE #2: Small Eyes c. 1955
Doll Characteristics: Cosmopolitan changed Ginger's head mold around 1955, and Ginger now had smaller eyes with molded eyelashes. Other than the head, she had the same characteristics as the '54 straight leg walking and head-turning Ginger: Mold line through center of the ear; C-shaped arm hooks; separate fingers; and legs set wide apart with toe detail. Ginger's small red box brochure advertised: "The first 8-inch walking doll with moving eyes, plastic head... dressed in panties, shoes and socks." Note: Ginger's eyes varied by year, but Cosmopolitan sold the different versions simultaneously, using up old stock. There-

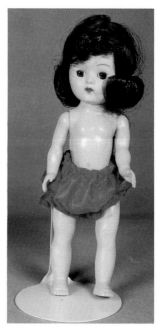

Ginger Type #2 c. 1954 with small eyes, molded eyelashes; tight rolled wig.

Ginger Type #2 c. 1954 – 55 with small eyes, molded eyelashes, and braids.

Ginger Type #3 c. 1955 with medium eyes, molded eyelashes.

Ginger Types #1-5: Ear mold line runs through the center of the ear on all types.

Ginger Type #4 c. 1955 with wide eyes; tightly rolled wig; original box, on Ginger stand; '56 Ginger brochure. Courtesy Mary Miskowiec.

Gingers Type #3 with medium eyes on right (in gown and in pink bodice dress) vs. (L to R) Type #1 in pink dress with sleep eyes with painted eyelashes; Ginger Type #2 in straw picture hat with molded lashes and small eyes.

Ginger Type #5 c. 1956 (far right) with molded lashes and medium eyes and jointed elbows and knees compared to Type #1 Ginger on left with painted eyelashes; at center, Type #2 Ginger center with molded lashes and small eyes.

fore, the '54 Ginger with painted eyelashes continued to be sold in '55 and later.

Dress Characteristics: See page 50.

Wig Characteristics: A better quality stitched Saran wig than '54; tightly rolled flip and braids (see Wigs below for details) and stitched Saran wig, that "can be wet, set, combed and curled...Available in pigtail or curl."

Value: $55.00; MIB $125.00+.

TYPE #3: Medium Eyes c. 1955 – 1956

Doll Characteristics: Same as Type #2 molded-lash Gingers, but now with slightly larger eyes called "medium eye" Ginger by most collectors.

Dress Characteristics: See page 50.

Wig Characteristics: A better quality stitched Saran wig than '54; tightly rolled flip and braids. (See Wigs, p.50, for details.)

Value: $50.00; MIB $100.00+.

TYPE #4: Large Eyes c. 1955

Doll & Wig Characteristics: Same as Type #3 but with even larger eyes. Collectors call them "wide eye" or "large eye" Gingers. They were apparently sold interchangeably in boxes. Note: Since eye sizes varied so much, some medium eye dolls border on large eye dolls. In any case, this is not a huge issue for identification since center ear mold and bodies remain consistent with Ginger characteristics.

Dress Characteristics: See page 50.

Value: $50.00; MIB $100.00+.

Ginger Type #5 with bent elbows, from the back.

Ginger Type #5 with bent elbows, from the front.

TYPE #5: Bending Knees &/or Elbows c. 1956
Doll Characteristics: Some medium eye Gingers had bending knees, and some even had bending elbows. Cosmopolitan's promotion for such Gingers is undocumented but remains a possibility. Labels on '56 "Pam" boxes promoted the doll's bending knees and elbows, and they used Ginger type dolls (see Fortune Dolls) as did other doll companies.
Dress Characteristics: See next column.
Wig Characteristics: Primarily loosely rolled "flip" styles (see Wigs at right).
Value: $55.00; MIB $125.00.

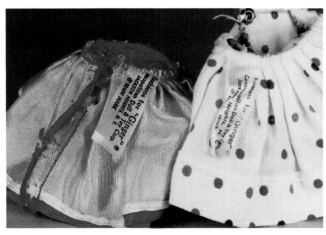

Ginger dresses were tagged and had a single unfinished back seam sewn closed below the dress opening. Some had attached slips, and finished waist seams were machine overcast stitched.

Ginger Dress Characteristics 1954 – 1956

Ginger's outfits stayed basically the same over the years:
Dress, Common Styles: *Quality:* Ginger dresses were tagged, well-made, and completely accessorized. *Necklines:* Mostly round or scoop, trimmed with lace or other trim. There were very few square necklines or attached collars. A few rolled collars are found. *Sleeves:* Except for a few puff sleeve styles with shoulder seams, most were cap sleeves with no shoulder seams. Longer sleeves were elasticized above or at the elbow or at the wrist. *Skirts:* Full gathered with tiny pleats sewn to waist seams. A single back seam was sewn closed below the dress opening. *Slips:* Most dressy styles had attached taffeta slips, but some cotton styles had no attached slips. *Pants:* Most sold on undressed dolls were straight cut cotton or taffeta with loose legs trimmed with lace. Pants on dressed dolls or in separate boxes had bloomer style pants from matching fabric. In both straight cut and bloomer style pants, the elastic was sewn onto the back of the fabric to gather at the waist and was unexposed from the outside.
Dress Finishes: Deep hems were turned and straight stitched to finish. The back seams were sewn closed below the dress opening, and the fabric edges were finished with industrial overcast stitching. Waist seams were also finished with industrial overcast stitching.
Dress Closures: Distinctive round metal or painted metal snap decorated with a circular "p" pattern. Also called "Greek key" pattern.

Ginger Wig Characteristics, Types #2-#5 c. 1955 – 1956

All of the early walking molded lash Gingers had the same type wigs.
Stitching & Styles: Wigs had a fully lined wig cap in two styles shown on their brochure cover. Flip styles were more tightly rolled

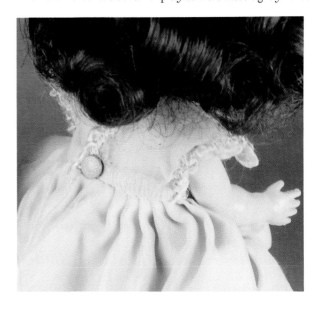

Ginger dress snaps were brass or painted round snaps with a circular "p" (or Greek key) pattern.

(i.e., hard flip) than Ginny's flip, and Ginger's even had tiny hairpins to hold it in place. It appears that the hair is folded over the part with no exposed stitching vs. Ginny with exposed stitching. While Cosmopolitan may have actually used soft flip wigs on some later Ginger dolls, the only advertised Ginger wig was the hard flip. Wigs can overlap on Ginger types as stock was used up. (Note: Since other companies bought the Ginger body to sell for their line, Gingers with soft flips are likely other dolls such as Jeanette by Fortune.) Ginger braids were chunky with two parallel rows of stitching along the center part with wig hair combed over the part vs. the exposed stitching on Ginny wigs.

Material: These wigs were advertised as Saran of good quality.

Ginger's wigs were in tightly rolled flip styles with full wig caps.

Ginger '54 brochure with red cover and pictures of Ginger's tightly rolled flip and chunky braids.

The first Ginger with painted eye lashes like this doll had poorer quality wigs that were hard to manage compared to later Ginger wigs.

Painted lash Ginger in a red taffeta dress similar to pink flowered taffeta dress closes with "p" pattern snap. Documenting the outfit numbers and colors is difficult since many Ginger dresses used this pattern, and brochures were black and white.

Ginger c. '54 with typical chunky braids.

Ginger Fashions

Painted Lash Ginger Type #1 c. 1954 wears tagged pink cotton dress with nylon overskirt, replaced hat. Hanging on left is 1956 Playtime Series #111 dotted cotton dress; bottom left is '54 Holiday Series #442 plaid cotton dress with lace trim; hanging in trunk: '54 School Series #224 dress with black velvet bodice and pink satin skirt with silver tread trim. All are tagged outfits.

Small eye Ginger Type #2 wears embroidered pink nylon outfit with lacy straw picture hat #665 from the Character Series c. 1954-55; separate outfit in box is plaid cotton dress with nylon blouse and red straw hat, '56 Playtime Series #112 (also came with plaid bow); four-drawer Ginger wardrobe trunk #1702.

Small eye Ginger Type #2 c. 1955 wears '54-'55 Playtime Series #116 printed cotton dress with pink bodice in her original box. Note her unrolled hair.

Small eye Ginger Type #2 c. '55 with chunky Saran braids advertised in catalog with 4-drawer trunk and outfits.

Medium eye Ginger Type #3 wears '54-'56 Gay Nineties Series #885 white organdy ruffled gown trimmed with red ribbon with a straw hat. The outfit number was #995 in '57.

Ginger 1954 Holiday Series #445 outfit with taffeta bloomers (#441 in '56) in separate box. The lacy weave lavender dress ensemble also had a black straw hat.

1957 Little Golden Book Ginger Paper Doll by Simon and Schuster illustrates Ginger on the cover wearing her '57 Playtime Series #112 lace trimmed plaid dress. Inside is a story and paper doll and clothes to cut out.

Ginger in 1954 Activity Series #556 in Mexican costume with black velvet pants and vest over white cotton blouse with black straw hat with pom poms. Missing satin waist sash. Courtesy Marge Meisinger.

Large eye Ginger Type #4 in '55 Playtime Series #116 tagged green nylon dress with pink taffeta slip.

Large eye brunette Ginger Type #4 in deluxe one-drawer trunk set wears 1956 lace and satin bridal gown #771 with lace veil. ($300.00). Realized prices courtesy Frasher's Doll Auctions.

Medium eye Ginger Type #3 Gift Box was advertised in the 1957 Montgomery Ward Christmas catalog with the doll and four outfits. Courtesy Carolyn Owen.

Ginger in Gift Box with lid on ($300.00). Price realized courtesy Frasher's Doll Auctions.

Medium eye Ginger Type #3 dressed in '56 Trousseau Series #773 gown with flocked tulle skirt over taffeta. Missing a straw picture hat. The '54 #773 gown version had ribbon bands trimming the tulle.

"Ginger Visits Mickey Mouse Club" costumes c. '55: Medium eye Ginger in Official Mickey Mouse Club outfit #S103 with knit "Ginger" top, blue pleated cotton skirt, vinyl Mickey Mouse mask, and Mickey Mouse patch on felt mouse-ear cap ($220.00); "Official Talent Roundup" blue cowgirl costume #S104 ($775.00); red "Mousekarade" costume with ears #S102 ($325.00). Courtesy Frasher's Doll Auctions.

Ginger Visits Adventure Land c. 1965: Top left: "Oriental Princess" gold striped tulle over red taffeta, black weskit, tall hat ($300.00); Right: Ginger Visits Fantasyland in Disneyland "Blue Fairy" c.'56 #1012 blue taffeta gown with tulle net-replaced crown and wand shown on Type #1 Ginger ($200.00). This Blue Fairy outfit was also the 1957 "Ginger Doll Dress-of-the-Month-Club" October "Halloween" outfit. Bottom left: Fantasyland "Dream Princess" in gold nylon over fuchsia taffeta, pointed gold and white hat with veil ($275.00); Right: Fantasyland "Cinderella" in white tulle and satin gown with silver glitter and trim, crown, and veil ($225.00). Prices realized courtesy Frasher's Doll Auctions.

Small eye Ginger Type #2 with original box for the Official Mickey Mouse Club costume with pamphlet. Courtesy Carolyn Owen.

Bent knee Ginger in "Official Mickey Mouse Club."

Fantasyland Dream Princess in gold nylon over fuchsia gown. Courtesy Jeanne Niswonger.

L to R: Small eye Ginger in Tomorrowland "Space Girl" #S1015 c. '56 red felt and gold satin outfit with black belt, cape, boots, and hat with gold antennae ($750 MIB); small eye ginger in Ballerina #553 c. '54 in white satin and tulle with red trim and slippers ($300.00 MIB); large eye Ginger in Majorette #555 from Activity Series c. '56 in white satin with gold trim and boots ($160.00). Prices realized courtesy Frasher's Doll Auctions.

(L) Wide eye Ginger as Tomorrowland "Sun Princess" #S1014 c. '56 gold satin gown with matching hat and fur cape ($450.00 MIB); (R) Wide eye Ginger as Adventureland "Cha Cha Senorita" #S10017 c.'56 in ivory satin body suit over dark gold ruffled gown and matching hat with fruit ($300.00). Prices realized courtesy Frasher's Doll Auctions.

Ginger bridal party: Small eye Ginger "Bride # 771" c. 1956-57 in white satin and tulle ($85.00); Bridesmaids #772 ($180.00) and #773 c. 1954 in white tulle over pink and lavender taffeta ($190.00). Prices realized courtesy Frasher's Doll Auctions.

Top left: Ginger in green coat ensemble with fur trim #960 c. '56 ($140.00); bottom left: Ginger wears Pioneer Girl #1010 from "Ginger Visits Frontierland in Disneyland" c. 1956, brown suedecloth pants and top; metal rifle, belt, and red boots; outfit also shown in the 1954 catalog as #1001 "Ginger as Davy Crockett," copyright to Disney ($240.00); bottom right: Ginger in Provincial outfit ($50.00); top right: Holiday series #443 cotton dress, green bodice ($140.00).

Large eye Ginger with bent elbows and knees wears a pink satin tagged dress with pink velvet waist tie c. 1956-57. This doll's documentation by company is hard to find.

Gingers may have been sold with pastel hair by Cosmopolitan, but there is no original documentation. Competitors may have used the Ginger mold for pastel hair dolls such as A&H and Kim dolls (see A&H and Kim sections).

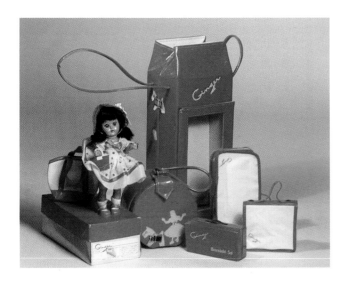

Cosmopolitan and other companies using the same mold sold black Gingers. A black Ginger is shown here with a full assortment of Ginger accessories (MIB black Ginger $400.00; accessories lot $200.00). Prices realized courtesy Frasher's Doll Auctions.

Ginger dolls were bought for use as advertising premiums, such as this medium eye Ginger sold as the Fab "Picture" premium doll.

"Ginger Doll-ers" c. 1957 were put into doll boxes and could be exchanged for a small die-cut doll.

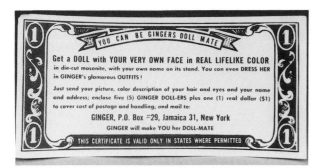

The back of a "Ginger Doll-er" explained the program.

Ginger "Make-Ur-Own Doll Kit" for 8" walking Ginger. Courtesy Vickie Glover.

Black Ginger: Medium and large eye black Ginger dolls are found today, and it is assumed Cosmopolitan sold them in the '50s. Shown with Ginger accessories including trunks, replacement wigs, fitted cases, etc.

Advertising Dolls: Other companies bought undressed Ginger dolls from Cosmopolitan and redressed them for premium and/ or advertising offers. While they may have looked like Ginger, many advertising dolls had lesser quality plastic, wigs, etc. which can confuse collectors. For clarification and descriptions of these advertising dolls with Ginger bodies, refer to the Advertising Dolls chapter.

Special Gingers 1955-60s

Colored Hair Gingers: Ginger dolls were reportedly sold with colored hair like Virga's Lolly Pop dolls. A number of Ginger dolls with purple and other color hair have been found on the secondary market. It is possible that Cosmopolitan sold them, but no original documentation has been found. It is assumed the colored hair Gingers are the Gigi dolls that A&H advertised with "pastel" wigs. Kim dolls have also been found with colored hair Gingers in the box. Other dolls companies may have sold Ginger type dolls with pastel wigs. (See A & H and Kim sections.)

Ginger Doll-er Certificate

A green "Ginger Doll-er" was included in each doll's box. Five Doll-ers plus $1 postage could be exchanged for a die-cut masonite doll "with your very own face" made from a photo also sent in.

"Make Your Own" Doll Kit: Cosmopolitan sold kits with all of the parts to make a 10" or 8" walking Ginger doll, along with glue and instructions for putting them together. "Perfect parts for perfect fit/The thrill of making you own doll." The kits were bubble-mounted on cards to hang on store racks.

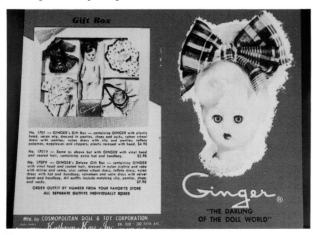

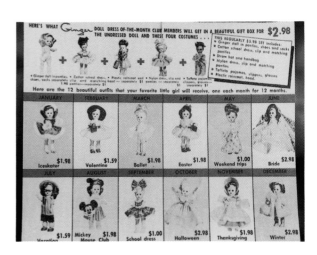

Front and back covers of brochure for vinyl head Ginger brochure with photographs with Gift Box #1701: two dress ensembles, pajamas, and a plastic hooded raincoat.

Flyer for vinyl head Ginger featured the "Dress-Of-The-Month-Club." Courtesy Marge Meisinger.

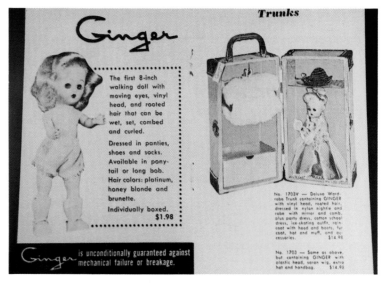

Inside Ginger brochure advertising "the first 8-inch walking doll with moving eyes, vinyl head, and rooted hair...;" also shown in trunk set #1703V.

Vinyl head dolls with hard plastic bodies marked "Ginger" on neck; doll on the left has slightly wider eyes. Doll on right has dye stain from clothing.

Ginger "Dress-Of-The-Month-Club"

Advertised in a flyer and in publications such as Breck's of Boston. The plan included a vinyl head doll and a different outfit received every month, 12 total, for $26.95. A basic set could also be bought including a doll in panties, socks, shoes, and four outfits for $5.98 or undressed doll only for $1.98.

Vinyl Head 8" Ginger 1957

Doll Mark: "Ginger" on neck.

Mark on Box: Unknown.

Doll Characteristics: Around 1957 Cosmopolitan sold an 8" Ginger doll with a vinyl head, rooted hair, a hard plastic walking, head-turning body, flat feet, and toe detail. Advertisements read, "The first 8-inch walking doll with moving eyes, vinyl head, and rooted hair that can be wet, set, combed and curled." Type #1 Gingers had a narrow vinyl head, poorly fitting sleep eyes that sometimes looked crossed, or fell into the head. Some had three lashes painted in the corner, but not all. Undressed dolls were sold in panties, shoes, and socks. Available in ponytail or long bob. Type #2 Gingers had wider vinyl heads with good working eyes. Rooted hair colors were advertised as "Platinum, honey blonde and brunette." Note: Type #1 was used by MEGO's "Lil Me Go Too."

Dress Characteristics: See Dresses on page 50.

Value: $50.00; MIB $75.00+.

High-Heel Dolls

In addition to the 10½" Miss Ginger vinyl fashion doll, Cosmopolitan sold two 8" dolls with high heels.

Cha Cha Heel, Vinyl Head 8" Ginger c. 1957

Doll Mark: Ginger on neck; Ginger on bottom of foot.

Mark on Box: Unknown.

continued on page 60

Vinyl headed Ginger c. 1956 marked "Ginger" on the neck, wearing '56 Playtime Series #110 red taffeta dress.

Vinyl head Ginger marked "Ginger" on neck, with original box. Note that her head appears wider than other vinyl head Gingers. Courtesy Marge Meisinger.

Ginger c.'57 with vinyl head and small eyes wears '57 skating outfit #443, a blue felt skirt with heart appliquè, a personalized knit shirt, matching tam, and suedecloth roller skates with metal wheels.

Vinyl head Gingers, both marked "Ginger" on the neck: (L) Cha Cha Heels Ginger c. '57 on the left vs. (R) flat feet Ginger on the right. Both marked "Ginger" on the neck.

Vinyl head Gingers c.'56–'56 in nylon ensemble #334 negligee over taffeta gown; red, white, and blue taffeta dress with straw picture hat; white nylon dress #225 with flocked hearts and red picot trim. Boxed outfits: '56 Holiday Series #442 purple and white taffeta dress, and boxed pink taffeta lounge outfit marked #1001 ($300.00 for 3 dolls; $60.00 two MIB outfits). Courtesy Frasher's Doll Auctions.

Doll Characteristics: Around 1957 Cosmopolitan sold an 8" Ginger doll with a vinyl head, rooted hair, a hard plastic walking, head-turning body, and cha cha heels with toe detail. Introduced in '57 and advertised as "Ginger Grows Up" and as "The First 8" Doll with the All New Cha Cha Heel."
Dress Characteristics: See Dresses, page 50.
Value: $50.00; MIB $75.00.

Little Miss Ginger 8" c. 1958

Cosmopolitan's 10½" Miss Ginger was introduced in 1957, and the 8" Little Miss Ginger was introduced the following year, adding to Cosmopolitan's line of fashion dolls.
Marks on Doll: "Ginger" on the head; "Little/Miss Ginger" on the back.
Boxes Marked: Little Miss Ginger /Cosmopolitan.
Doll Characteristics: A fully jointed 8" doll with vinyl head, sleep eyes with three lines painted in the corners, and molded lashes. Her body was hard vinyl, fully jointed at neck, legs, and shoulder, with molded breasts, 3rd and 4th fingers molded together with red painted fingernails and toes, and rooted hair. She had high-heel feet and looked very much like competitor 8" Miss Nancy Ann.
Clothing Characteristics: Same construction and closures as for 8" Ginger, all types with more adult styles. Boxed clothing could be purchased separately.
Wig Characteristics: Rooted Saran type hair in long bobs.
Value: $75.00; MIB $125.00+.

Baby Doll

Baby Ginger 8" c. 1956

Baby Ginger was the baby sister to Cosmopolitan's 8" Ginger toddler doll. Baby Ginger was a prime competitor to Vogue's 8" Ginnette baby doll. There were two Baby Ginger dolls c.1956.

Type #1 Painted Eye Baby Ginger: The first was an 8" soft vinyl baby with painted eyes and lashes on a baby body marked "Baby Ginger" on the neck. This is a rare doll to find today. Legs of Type #1 are straighter than those of Type #2.
Value: MIB $125.00+, rare.

Type #2 Rooted Hair Baby Ginger: A second 8" Baby Ginger was introduced as "The first and only 8" all vinyl fully jointed drink and wet baby doll, with rooted hair and moving eyes." Her distinguishing characteristics were rooted hair, painted lashes under the molded lash eyes, and straight fingers on both hands. The rooted hair Baby Ginger was a drink and wet doll and not always marked on the neck. She was also a premium doll for Kellogg's cereal box tops. (See Advertising Doll chapter.)
Value: $50.00; MIB $75.00+.

Zippy

Zippy was Ginger's playmate, introduced c. 1957. The 8"

Little Miss Ginger 8" blonde high-heel doll c. 1958 had sleep eyes with molded lashes with three lines painted at the corners. She wears a flowered taffeta dress with black trim. She resembled competitor Miss Nancy Ann.

Little Miss Ginger 8" brunette c. 1958 in white cotton dress with red buttons, and "Little Miss Ginger" handbag. Courtesy Marge Meisinger.

Ginger with her CBS TV star playmate 8" Zippy the Chimp c. 1957, an all-vinyl fully jointed toy with swivel head with sleep eyes. Zippy wears a red felt jacket and pants on the left ($325.00) and a taffeta button shirt and pants on the right ($275.00). Ginger in lavender Holiday Series #445 with black straw hat c. '54 ($120.00). Courtesy Frasher's Doll Auctions.

chimp was a CBS TV star, and the toy was an all vinyl, fully jointed chimp with swivel head and sleep eyes. Separate outfits were available for Zippy. Since he was produced for a short period of time, he is hard to find and very collectible.

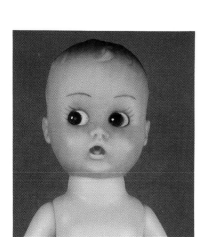

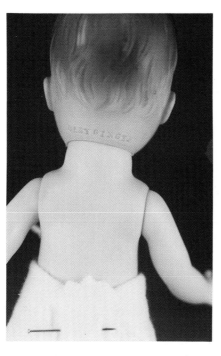

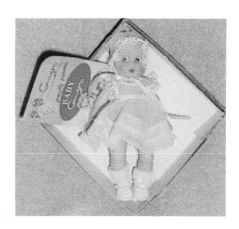

The first 8" Baby Ginger had painted eyes c. 1956, a very rare doll. Courtesy Marge Meisinger.

Baby Ginger c. 1956 with painted eyes, in her original box and wrist tag. Courtesy Kathy Hippensteel.

"Baby Ginger" mark on neck of painted eye baby doll.

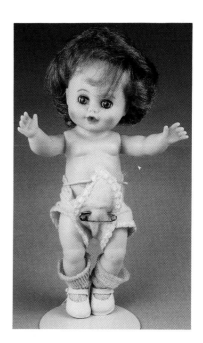

Cosmopolitan Baby Ginger large flyer featuring the 8" vinyl drink n' wet baby with rooted hair and sleep eyes with separate outfits. Note the vinyl head Ginger on the left and the special carrying case on the right. Courtesy Marge Meisinger.

Baby Ginger 8" vinyl doll with rooted hair, sleep eyes, molded lashes and lashes painted under, open mouth drink and wet doll, dimples on knees, and toe detail.

Separate Baby Ginger dotted blue nylon dress #631 with original separate box.

Baby Ginger's separate three-piece red print cotton sunsuit #613 with a terry-lined cape and matching bonnet, in original box.

Front and back covers of Baby Ginger small box brochure.

Close-up of Baby Ginger face with sleep eyes, molded lashes and lashes painted under the eyes, rooted hair, and open nursing mouth.

Inside Baby Ginger brochure showing separate outfits.

Ginger wears one of Zippy's outfits, a red and white felt outfit with matching cap trimmed in looped braid. This is a variation of Zippy's brochure outfit #4022 shown with a different braid. Courtesy Jeanne Niswonger.

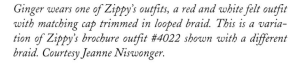

🍇 Doll Bodies, Inc. 🍇

Doll Bodies Inc., New York City, sold hard plastic dolls with their own label to the low-priced market in the '50s. Their hard plastic doll line included the popular 16" Mary-Lou Walker, a cute and affordable walking doll c. 1955. Doll Bodies' 18" walking dolls had many separate outfits and were also popular. Their line also included 7½" and larger inexpensive "dress me" dolls and "Dolls of Faraway Lands," with stapled-on gowns. One of Doll Bodies' most collectible dolls was the petite 7½" toddler Mary-Lu sold as a look-alike "dress me" doll or dressed with an assortment of separate outfits.

Display & "Dress Me" Dolls

Marks on Dolls: No mark on back, or "This is an original/Lingerie Lou/Doll, " or "Doll Bodies."
Boxes Marked: Some marked: "Lingerie Lou/With Removable Plastic Lingerie/ A Genuine Plastic/Dress-Me Doll/ Doll Bodies Inc. New York 10, N.Y."
Doll Characteristics: Doll Bodies advertised in *Playthings* magazine c. 1952, "Give a Girl a Doll She Can Dress," for their copyrighted "Lingerie Lou" campaign. The line included 7½" and 11" inch and other sized "dress me" display type dolls sold individually or in kits. (see page 269). They typically had sleep eyes with painted lashes, jointed head and arms, and molded feet with sharp corner bows (same bows as Duchess and A&H). They were also sold dressed as souvenir dolls.

DRESS KIT SET: The boxed set contained two display dolls in kits with stands, two patterns, and included a "Make Your Own Dresses For Your Doll Collection" booklet. The dolls were 7½" with sleep eyes, moving head and arms, fixed legs, and molded shoes with a sharp cornered bow, usually painted white. Their inexpensive wavy wig was glued to the head.

LINGERIE LOU: "Lingerie Lou with Removable Plastic Lingerie" was sold in several sizes. The smallest dolls were 7½" dolls packaged individually in folding blue window boxes, clad in removeable plastic lingerie. Their mouth paint has down-turned creases at the corners. The 7½" and larger dolls were also sold in acetate bags. Doll Bodies bought Lingerie Lou c. mid-'50s, and sponsored dress-me doll contests. (See Sewing Kit chapter.)

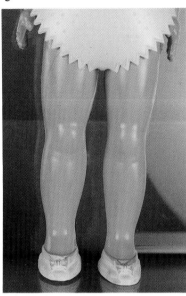

Molded shoes of the Lingerie Lou "dress me" dolls had bows with square corners.

Lingerie Lou doll c. 1952 "With Removable Plastic Lingerie/ A Genuine Plastic Dress-Me Doll" in her original box; a 7½" display type doll with painted molded shoes, moving head and arms, and sleep eyes.

Lingerie Lou's dressmaking kit c. 1952 included two 7½" sleep eye dolls, two heart-shaped pink stands, and two patterns, as well as a "Doll Collection" booklet.

Wig Characteristics: Wavy mohair glued to head.
Values: Dress Kit with 2 dolls: $65.00 – 75.00; individually boxed Lingerie Lou: $40.00.

Toddler Doll

Mary-Lu 7"-7½" c. 1955

Marks on Doll: Unmarked or some are marked on back "PRODUCT OF/DOLL/BODIES/ INC/ New York, N.Y."
Marks on Acetate Bag: An Original Mary-Lu Product.
Marks on Cardboard Overnight Bag: Mary Lu and her Overnight Bag/A Product of Doll Bodies, Inc., NYC.
Doll Characteristics: Mary-Lu was a strung 7½" hard plastic doll with sleep eyes, molded lashes, and lashes also painted under the eyes; ear mold line behind the ear. Most lashes and brows were painted rusty brown, but some were a dark brown. Despite reports, this writer has seen no examples of a walking 8" Mary-Lu. She had shoes with flat molded bows, usually painted white, and no toe detail. Arms had C-shaped hooks; fingers on her left hand were molded together but separate at tips; right hand had second and third fingers completely molded together. Her plastic is good quality, and mold lines are heavy along the outside of the legs. Note: This same doll was sold to other companies such as Roberta to dress and sell (see Roberta section).
Wig Characteristics: Wigs on the dolls sold in acetate bags appear to be Dynel as specified in the 1955 *Playthings* advertisement, but Mary-Lu's cardboard "Overnight Bag" specifies, "Genuine Saran hair," that you can "comb, curl, wave."
Clothes Characteristics: Dress waist seam is unfinished, and back seams are stitched closed under dress opening, and fasten with a hand-sewn metal snap; some dresses in cardboard case have circular metal donut snaps. The cardboard wardrobe is printed, "36 Asst. Styles," and "Matching Panties."
Value: Doll complete in overnight kit: $90.00; doll in bag: $40.00; dressed doll: $45.00.

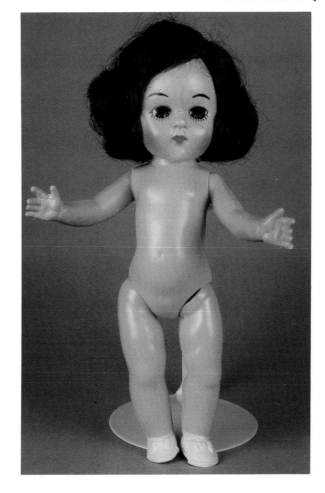

Doll Bodies' Mary-Lu, strung toddler, unmarked body with traits: eyelashes painted under eyes and flat molded bows on feet. Others dressed and sold the same doll (see Comparisons chapter).

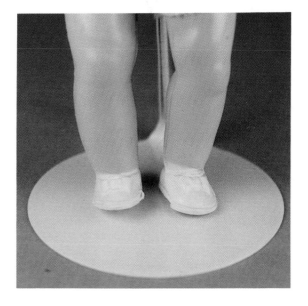

Doll Bodies' Mary-Lu distinctive display doll shoes with flat, molded bows, usually painted white.

Doll Bodies' 7½" strung toddler "Mary-Lu and Her Overnight Bag" c. 1955 included the doll with sleep eyes, molded lashes, painted lower lashes, and a Saran wig. Two extra dresses and matching panties were in the case. Courtesy Marge Meisinger.

Side panel of Mary-Lu's cardboard case. Courtesy Marge Meisinger.

Doll Bodies' 7½" Mary-Lu toddler doll stands outside her cardboard Overnight Bag. Courtesy Marge Meisinger.

This unmarked toddler with Mary-Lu characteristics has glued-on clothes. Since Doll Bodies' Mary-Lu's clothes were removeable, another company probably purchased the doll from Doll Bodies to dress.

An unmarked 7½" Mary-Lu with dark brunette wig wears a separate dress with metal snap which may not be original to the doll. Note painted white shoes with flat molded bows.

Mary-Lu 7½" toddler c. '55 was also sold in acetate bags printed, "Mary-Lu." These blonde and brunette wig dolls with original bags are 7½" strung dolls with flat molded shoes with bows painted white, and sleep eyes painted under molded lashes. Some Mary-Lu dolls found mint in bags are marked "Doll Bodies;" some are unmarked. Courtesy Mary Lu Paulett.

❦ Dollyana ❦

Dollyana, Passaic, New Jersey, was one of the small doll companies in the 1950s that bought dolls and/or parts to create their own doll. Dorrie dolls are not easy to identify without the box since they are a combination of parts from better known dolls. More than two dolls have been found in original boxes with the characteristics described below. However, since it was often the practice for small companies to substitute different types of dolls, there may be other types sold as Dorrie as well.

Dorrie Doll

Marks on Doll: Unmarked.
Boxes Marked: On front: "Dorrie;" on end: "Dollyana, Passaic, New Jersey."
Doll Characteristics: Dorrie is an 8" hard plastic, head-turning doll with sleep eyes and molded eye lashes; mouth painted with down-turned look at corners; mold line behind ear; arms with C-shaped arm hooks; straight walking legs with smooth flat feet and no shoe or toe detail. Hands have separate fingers on the right or 2nd and 3rd fingers molded together on left or they can be slightly separated depending on unmolding; prominent mold lines on arms. Note: Dorrie is identical in every part to A&H's Lisa, Gigi Type #1, and Linda Doll Co.'s Linda Type #1. (See Comparisons chapter.)
Wig Characteristics: Synthetic wig sewn to a backing strip and glued to the head.
Clothing Characteristics: Found in box undressed, with taffeta panties sewn to elastic and overcast stitched; legs finished by turning and straight stitching.
Value: $40.00 – 45.00 in box.

End flap of Dorrie's box reads: Dollyana, Passaic, New Jersey. Courtesy "On Maggy's Mantle."

Hard plastic 8" Dorrie walking doll with auburn wig undressed in original box. Courtesy "On Maggy's Mantle."

Hard plastic 8" Dorrie walking doll with blonde wig, undressed in red and white box; she has smooth feet, sleep eyes, mold line behind ear.

🍇 Dubell Products 🍇

Dubell's "little Princess" hard plastic doll was probably purchased from PMA (see Plastic Molded Arts section) based on her characteristics. It is not known what other dolls Dubell may have sold.

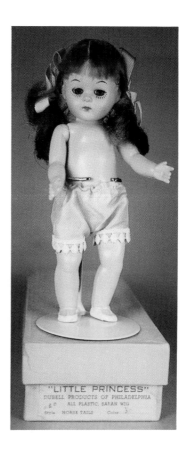

Little Princess 8"
Marks on Doll: Unmarked.
Box Marked: "Little Princess"/DUBELL PRODUCTS OF PHILADELPHIA/ALL PLASTIC. SARAN WIG/STYLE HORSE TAILS, COLOR: BR.
Doll Characteristics: The 8" hard plastic strung doll is unmarked with sleep eyes, molded lashes, and lashes painted under the eyes. Her plastic has a peach color, and the second and third fingers on her left hand are molded together; her feet have molded T-strap shoes painted white. Note: This unmarked doll is identical to dolls marked Plastic Molded Arts on the back (like Joanie Pigtails).
Wig Characteristics: The box label indicates the wig is Saran. It is stitched down the center to a backing strip and glued to the head. The long hair is not braided but is tied with pink ribbon bows in "Horse Tails" as indicated on the label.
Clothes Characteristics: Pink taffeta panties are gathered and stitched onto elastic and trimmed in braid.
Value: $55.00 in box.

Dubell Products of Philadelphia sold this 8" hard plastic strung doll in pants with white painted shoes. She has sleep eyes with lashes painted under the eyes. Here she is in her original box.

🍇 Duchess Dolls Corporation 🍇

Duchess Dolls Corporation of Jackson Heights, NY, was a major player in the late '40s and '50s small doll world. They specialized in "display" dressed characters or souvenir dolls, and they also sold undressed dolls for sewing projects (see Sewing Sets chapter). Their dolls were apparently also sold to other companies to dress. In 1955 Duchess entered the toddler look-alike market when they filed a patent for Randi, their only 8" toddler doll.

Display/Character Dolls
Dolls Marked: On back, Duchess Dolls Corp/Design Copyright/1948.
Marks on Boxes: Duchess Dolls Corp., Jackson Heights, NY. Square boxes had acetate window lids to display the dolls.
Doll Characteristics: 7½" hard plastic display dolls with "moving eyes, moving arms, moving heads" and fixed legs. These dolls had molded shoes with sharp corners on the molded bows.
Dress Characteristics: Stapled-on clothes in good quality silk,

satins, cotton, with stapled-on hats trimmed with felt, feathers, and bows. Their two most popular series were "Dolls of All Nations" and Disney characters such as Cinderella, Peter Pan, and Tinkerbell.
Wig Characteristics: Glued-on wavy mohair or synthetic wigs with no backing.
Values: Doll in box: $25.00; individual Disney characters: $35.00 – 45.00; Peter Pan/Tinkerbell set: $75.00+.

Dress Me Dolls
Dolls Marked: On back, Duchess Dolls Corp/Design Copyright/1948.
Marks on Boxes: Duchess Dolls Corp., Jackson Heights, NY. Plain brown-boxed Duchess dress-me dolls were sold at sewing and dime stores. Also sold in folded window boxes marked "Dress Fi-Fi" and "Dress Mi-Mi."
Doll Characteristics: Undressed 7½" hard plastic display dolls with painted eyes (Dress Mi-Mi) or with "moving eyes" (Dress Fi-Fi), moving arms, moving heads, and fixed legs. These dolls'

Duchess Dolls Corp. brochure cover advertising 7½" all plastic body dolls with moving eyes, arms, and head, c. 1940s.

Duchess "Copyright Walt Disney Productions" 7½" hard plastic Cinderella #737 doll with sleep eyes, moving head and arms, in white sparkle satin gown. Note that Duchess's Disney version of Cinderella has entirely different costume design.

Duchess Dolls of All Nations 7½" hard plastic #723 Gibson Girl with black skirt and white blouse; brochure on left was in the original box, c. 1940s.

Duchess Dolls of All Nations 7½" hard plastic #737 Cinderella with sleep eyes, heavy blush, moving head and arms, in white tulle gown; gold charm slipper tied to doll's wrist, c. 1940s.

molded shoes had sharp corners on the molded bows. They also made undressed 12½" dolls with moving legs sold as "Dress Lola."

Dress Characteristics: Fi-Fi and Mi-Mi dolls wore fabric bras and panties; others undressed.

Wig Characteristics: Glued-on wavy mohair or synthetic wigs with no backing.

Value: $35.00 in boxes.

Toddler Doll

Randi 7½"-8" c. 1955

Dolls Marked: Unmarked.

Marks on Box: RANDI/WALKING DOLL/WITH WASHABLE HAIR/THAT CURLS; Duchess Dolls Corp., Jackson Heights, NY.

Doll Characteristics:

TYPE #1: 7½" hard plastic walking doll with wide sleep eyes, painted lashes (no molded lashes); head mold line runs through center of the ear; arms have separate fingers and distinctive C-shaped arm hooks are squared off at the base; straight walking legs set wide apart with good toe detail. She had a good quality plastic with a pleasing flesh color. Note: Randi Type #1 is the same doll as Ginger Type #1 doll, indicating that dolls were probably bought from Ginger's maker, Cosmopolitan. Fortune also used the same doll for Ninette.

TYPE #2: Randi advertised by Davison's in Atlanta is an 8" Ginger #2 with small eyes and molded lashes. This Randi may have been one of Mego's "88-cent" doll promotions c. 1955 (see Mego section).

Dress Characteristics: Advertisements c. '55 showed good quality Randi outfits closed with round metal "p" (or Greek Key pattern) snaps, and constructed with unfinished back seams stitched closed below dress opening. Note: The interrelation of '50s doll companies can be seen from Randi's outfits which were almost identical to Fortune's Ninette dresses and for Fortune's '56 "Woolworth Pam" by fashion designer Michele Cartier (see Fortune section). However, Michele Cartier is not printed on the Randi boxes.

Wig Characteristics: Advertised as Saran wigs. They were stitched to a backing and glued onto the head. Most wigs were flip side-part styles.

Value: Doll: $45.00; in box: $65.00.

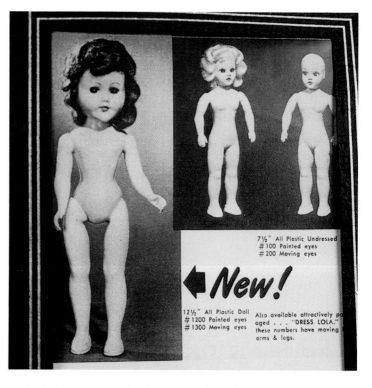

Duchess's 7½" undressed doll and 12½" "Dress Lola" dolls advertised in brochure.

Duchess 7½" sewing doll advertised in brochure, "All plastic undressed #100 painted eyes" in original cardboard box.

Randi Type #1 hard plastic 8" with painted eyelashes, in white "Tea Party Dress" #109 with black lace trim and straw hat; original box. Courtesy Tina Standish.

Randi Type #2 hard plastic 8" blonde with painted eyelashes, in white satin Bridal Gown #101; original box. Courtesy Marge Meisinger.

Randi Type #1 hard plastic 8" with painted eyelashes in "Gardening Outfit" #106 with denim pants and plaid shirt closed with "p" pattern metal snap. Came with yellow plastic rake.

Randi Type #2 hard plastic 8" brunette with molded eyelashes, in white satin Bridal Gown #101; original box. Courtesy Mary Van Buren Swasey.

Davison's of Atlanta newspaper advertisement c. 1955 for 8" hard plastic Randi Type #2 doll with molded lashes, showing undressed and dressed dolls with Ginger characteristics. These separate outfits appear to be the same as or similar to Fortune's Ninette doll. Courtesy Marge Meisinger.

🍇 Elite Creations 🍇

Elite Creations' delightful 8" hard plastic toddlers were named Vicki and Vicki-Lee in the 1950s. Vicki was a straight leg walking doll; later bent knees were added, and the last Vicki had a vinyl head. Fortunately Elite Creations produced a color brochure around the mid-'50s to help collectors identify some of Vicki's outfits but not all. Elite's inexpensive Vicki-Lee toddler and a Baby Vicki drink and wet doll are lesser-known dolls today. Since these dolls used many of the same doll parts as other companies, they can be tricky to identify without a box. Little Miss Tina was Elite's inexpensive display type walking doll.

Three 8" Elite dolls c. mid '50s L to R: Vicki Type #1 with straight legs and molded T-strap shoes, peg arm hooks and separate fingers; Pam or Lucy type face with mold line behind ear. Type #2: Same as #1 but with bent knees and toe detail; Vicki-Lee on right with smooth painted feet.

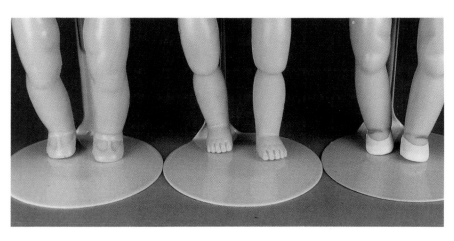

Foot detail on 8" Elite dolls (L to R): Type #1 walking Vicki, Type #2 bent knee Vicki, and Vicki-Lee.

Toddler Dolls

Vicki 8" c. mid-1950s

Marks on Doll: Unmarked.

Boxes Marked: VICKI THE WALKING DOLL/AN ELITE CREATION or VICKI WITH BENDING KNEE/ AN ELITE CREATION. The boxes were pink or blue and white with black print and had a window lid.

Doll Characteristics:

> **TYPE #1:** An 8" all hard plastic, fully jointed, straight leg walking doll; her head was virtually the same as Virga's Playmate doll with sleep eyes and molded lashes; head mold behind ear; molded t-strap shoes. Her arms had a "peg" arm hook and separate fingers like Fortune's Pam (see Fortune section). Arms were made of a lesser grade of plastic.

> **TYPE #2:** Same as Type #1 but with "bending knees" and toe detail (vs. T-strap molded shoes). Some have arms with C-shaped hooks, some with peg-shaped hooks.

Dress Characteristics: Vicki's outfits, including nurse and dungaree outfits, were simply made but very cute and were closed with a donut snap; styles varied for same number.

Wig Characteristics: Her wigs were of a Saran-type, in a flip or pigtails that were sometimes bound with brown string, not elastic.

Value: Doll (either type): $50.00; in box: $75.00.

Vicki, Vinyl Head 8" c. mid-1950s

Marks on Doll: "VICKI" on neck.

Boxes Marked: VICKI VINYL HEAD AND ROOTED HAIR/AN ELITE CREATION. Blue boxes with dark blue type and window lid.

Doll Characteristics:

Good quality 8" hard plastic body and vinyl head that turns, fully jointed, sleep eyes; molded lashes and three lines painted in corner of eyes; arms with C-shaped hooks and second and third fingers molded together; straight legs with molded T-strap shoes.

Dress Characteristics: White taffeta bride gown has regular button and button hole; other outfits close with donut-shaped snap.

Wig Characteristics: "Wash Vicki's hair, and brush it too-and style it's up to you!" printed on box.

Value: Doll: $50.00; MIB: $60.00.

Vicki-Lee 8" c. mid 1950s

Marks on Doll: Unmarked.

Boxes marked: Vicki-Lee/ An Elite Creation.

Doll Characteristics: Hard plastic, jointed doll; head does not turn; sleep

continued on page 75

Elite Vicki color brochure for 18 outfits, c. mid – 1950s.

8" Vicki Type #1 straight leg walker c. mid-'50s with molded T-strap shoes, and peg arm hooks wears "Pajamas" #408 outfit with yellow pants as shown in brochure. Courtesy Jo Barckley.

8" Vicki Type #1 straight leg walker doll with red braids wearing a blue and lavender plaid dress with white skirt trim; box marked "Alice." Courtesy Mary Britton.

8" Vicki Type #1 straight leg walker doll with blonde wig, in pink taffeta pinafore dress; box marked "Ruth." Courtesy Mary Britton.

8" Vicki Type #2 bent knee walker in cotton sundress and straw bonnet. Original box on right is marked "Sundress." Vicki Wardrobe cardboard wardrobe case on left.

8" Vicki Type #2 bent knee walker in original pink and white "Bending Knees" window box; marked "Blue Jeans" on end of box. The outfit with denim pants and plaid cotton shirt is #410 in Vicki brochure.

Reverse side of Vicki pink plaid and blue outfit box. Courtesy June Dove.

Folding pink and blue cardboard 7¾" x 10" window box has unique '50s graphic design; printed V-400/#410; contains plaid cotton flannel top closing with "donut" snap, denim pants, vinyl slip on shoes, and plastic glasses. Courtesy June Dove.

Reverse side of Vicki pink and blue cardboard outfit box. Courtesy June Dove.

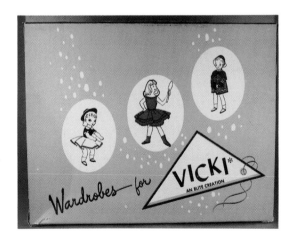

eyes with molded lashes; mold line behind the ear; mouth paint has a down-turned look; C-shaped arm hooks, fingertips on left hand separate but second and third fingers molded together on right; flat, smooth feet with no toes or shoes. Note: A&H's Lisa walker is the same doll, but the walking mechanism has been removed from Vicki-Lee so her head does not turn.

Wig Characteristics: Wavy hair not sewn to backing which is glued directly to head. Appears to be mohair.

Clothes Characteristics: Very inexpensively made unhemmed taffeta skirt gathered on elastic around waist and loose ribbon around neck and tucked into skirt to form top.

Value: Doll $30.00 – 35.00; in box $45.00.

Baby Doll

Baby Vicki 8" c. mid 1950s
Marks on Doll: Unmarked.
Boxes Marked: Baby Vicki Doll Boxes marked V-800.

Doll Box Type #1 Box: Acetate case with pink cardboard base and top, blue print.

Doll Box Type #2 Box: Pink and blue folding boxes with window display front. Baby Vicki Wardrobe Boxes marked V-900.

Outfit Box #1: Acetate top stapled onto a pink cardboard bottom, blue print

Outfit Box #2: Pink and blue cardboard box with window lid. Came in pink boxes or in pink and blue boxes. Outfit Boxes Marked: Baby Vicki Wardrobe/ An Elite Creation No. V800.

Doll Characteristics:

Doll in Box Type #1: Baby Vicki was an unmarked 8" vinyl jointed drink and wet baby with molded lash sleep eyes. She had a soft vinyl Ginnette type head mold with hard vinyl arms with straight fingers on both hands. Baby Vicki was the baby sister to Elite's 8" toddler Vicki.

Doll in Box Type #2: Same as above but with separate fingers on the left hand and second and third fingers bent, like Vogue's Ginnette.

Dress Characteristics: Cute cotton dress closed with a donut snap, waist seam unfinished, back seam below dress opening finished with an overcast stitch, fabric is cut along hem but not finished. The doll in the

case also wore a diaper and socks and carried a plastic baby bottle.

Wig Characteristics: Painted; some rooted hair.
Value: Doll: $35.00; in acetate case: $75.00.

8" Vicki bent knee walking doll with red braids, wearing a dress with horizontal pinstriped skirt and blue bodice; box marked "Heidi." Courtesy Mary Britton.

8" Vicki bent knee walking doll with red braids in "Dutch Girl" #414 blue plaid dress from the brochure, missing white Dutch cap.

"Wardrobe For Vicki" folding pink plaid and blue cardboard 7½" x 10" window box is "stitched" to look like Vicki's wardrobe case. This box is printed V–400/ #403, contains vinyl coat, plaid cotton pants, red vinyl purse, plastic glasses, and a vinyl hat with molded straw pattern. Note this is a different outfit than #403 on Vicki brochure.

8" Vicki with vinyl head and fair root-ed hair in original blue window box marked "Bride." The gown and head-piece appear different from catalog for hard plastic Vicki.

Elite Creations 8" Vicki-Lee strung doll in taffeta dress with white-painted smooth feet.

Baby Vicki Type #1 unmarked 8" vinyl drink n' wet doll wearing blue gingham dress, in original acetate case V-800. She has hard vinyl arms with straight fingers on both hands.

Baby Vicki Type #2 8" all vinyl baby doll with bent fingers on right hand; she sits with origi-nal pink and blue folding box with window front, marked #V-800 like the acetate doll cases. She wears a pink flannel two-piece sleep-er. Courtesy June Dove.

Baby Vicki outfit #905 in acetate box; two-piece, pink flannel print, footed pajamas. This is the same outfit as Baby Vicki in blue and pink cardboard box at left. Courtesy June Dove.

Baby Vicki Type #1 8" unmarked vinyl drink n' wet doll in acetate case #V-800; wears dot-ted yellow nylon dress with matching bonnet, yellow ribbon and lace trim; wears flannel diaper under dress and has a plastic bottle and knit socks. She has hard vinyl arms with straight fingers on both hands. Courtesy June Dove.

Side of Baby Vicki Wardrobe box for yellow print sundress, stamped #906 and "For 8" all vinyl baby doll."

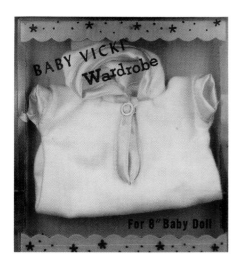

Baby Vicki white flannel bunting with pink satin trim, closing with a donut snap.

Baby Vicki outfit in 6" x 6" window box; inexpensive yellow print sundress made with unfinished hem and pinafore sleeve ruffles.

Baby Vicki outfits in 6" x 6" window box; pink and white melon slice print with turned and stitched hem but unfinished pinafore ruffles. Courtesy June Dove.

High-Heel Doll

Little Miss Tina
Marks on Doll: Unmarked.
Boxes Marked: Plastic case with blue bottom and clear plastic hinged lid; red and silver rectangular label, "Little Miss Tina/By Elite Creations."
Doll Characteristics: Little Miss Tina is an 8¼" slender display type doll with sleep eyes, molded lashes, turning head; strung arms with separate fingers on left hand and second and third fingers molded together on right hand; fixed legs with and high-heel feet and toe detail.
Clothing Characteristics: Stapled-on inexpensive outfits and hats; stapled-on white cotton panties; slip-on vinyl high-heel shoes.
Value: Doll: $25.00; in case: $35.00 – 40.00.

Elite's 8" Little Miss Tina walking doll with sleep eyes, fixed legs with high-heel feet, wears a stapled-on dress and red felt hat. She was sold in a plastic case with a blue bottom and clear top.

Baby Vicki outfit #902 in acetate lid box; pink cotton dress with stitched hem closes with a donut snap. Vinyl side-snap shoes and knit socks are in box. Courtesy June Dove.

❦ Eegee ❦

E. Goldberger was founded in 1917, and in the '20s they began to mark dolls Eegee. Their early dolls were imported bisque, composition, and cloth, but they are also well known for their good quality hard plastic and vinyl dolls beginning in the late '40s. Fortunately, the dolls were well marketed, so substantial printed information is available to learn about them. Their best-known dolls included the 17" hard plastic Susan Stroller and 13" Baby Gurglee with hard plastic head c. '53, and their 10" vinyl Little Miss Debutante c. '57. While they apparently did not enter the '50s toddler 8" hard plastic doll market, they did market a chubby 8" vinyl toddler doll and a 12" teen doll, both named Shelley. Some sources also name Eegee as the maker of the 8" Baby Susan, a Ginnette look-alike c. mid-1950s.

Shelley 8" c. 1957
Marks on Doll: On head: Eegee.
Boxes Marked: Unknown.
Doll Characteristics: Advertising states that Shelley, "Sits, kneels, sleeps. Washable Rooted hair. All vinyl." She had large sleep eyes with molded lashes.

Clothing Characteristic: Many changes of clothes were advertised including long gown, nurse costume, school dress, and ice-skating costume.
Wig Characteristics: Rooted, in bubble cuts and pony tail styles.
Value: $60.00.

Baby Susan, 10½", possibly 8" c. 1950s
Marks on Doll: On neck: Eegee.
Boxes Marked: Unknown.
Doll Characteristics: Pat Smith reports in *Modern Collector's Dolls I*, pg. 76, that Eegee sold an all vinyl 10½" "Baby Susan" doll with a nursing mouth. Smith and others also attribute the 8" vinyl "Ginnette-look-alike" doll marked "Baby Susan" on her neck to Eegee, but this is not clearly documented. (See Hard Plastic & Vinyl Dolls, Miscellaneous, p. 113, and Marlon Creations section for more about 8" dolls marked "Baby Susan.")
Value: $35.00; MIB $45.00.

❦ Flagg Dolls ❦

Very little has been written about Flagg Dolls, the maker of 3½" - 7" flexible plastic dollhouse-sized dolls in the late '40s and '50s. Their bright and colorful dolls are as cute and collectible today as ever. What we know to date is mostly gathered from advertising and company brochures. This is the story they tell to date:

A company named AFCO Products from Lexington, Massachusetts, advertised 3" – 5" "flexible dolls" in the 1948 *House & Garden* and *Vogue* magazines. There were six family members in the line including Mother, Father, Boy, Girl, Grandmother, and Grandfather, and also maid, nurse, and "colored cook." Flagg introduced 7" dolls c. 1951, including a cowboy, cowgirl, ballerina and her partner, and advertised them in *House Beautiful* magazine under the new name of "Flexible Playdolls, Jamaica Plain, Mass." In 1952 the company added a Rumba dancer and partner to the line, advertised under the name "Flagg Flexible Dolls" at the same address in Jamaica Plain. So, it is assumed that this advertising reflects the route that the company took in the late '40s and early '50s.

New Flexible Play Dolls were continually added, and their 1955 flyer introduced an undressed "wardrobe doll," more dancing dolls, a Sports Series, and a small stage for the dolls' dancing. A baby doll was shown in advertising c. '56. In 1959 Flagg entered the teenage market with an 8" doll named "Campus Queen Wardrobe Doll" with "snap on washable costumes and set hair." Her hair was set in the popular teen pony tail style of the day. By 1963 Flagg even advertised TV night-lights, and their brochures and mailings continued into the '70s. They had an extensive mail order and direct mail business, but perhaps the dolls were sold retail to some extent as well. Over the years Flagg used several different boxes, but not enough is known to date them for sure by box type. Our special thanks to Vicki Johnson and to Shirley Bertrand of Shirley's Dollhouse, Wheeling, Illinois, for their Flagg Dolls and photos, and to Marge Meisinger for sharing her Flagg dolls, advertisements, and brochures, allowing us to track the company and its products.

Marks on Dolls: Unmarked.
Boxes Marked: Flagg Flexible Dolls/ Flagg & Co., Mfg., 91 Boylston St., Jamaica Plain, Mass. Box styles included lid boxes: plain; red and white striped; silver striped or dark or light orange with drawings of dancers. Decorative blue window

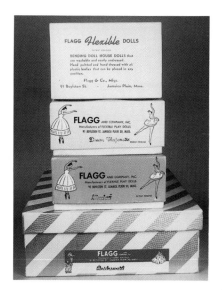

Flagg "Flexible Doll House Dolls" were originally advertised c.'48 by AFCO. Boxes shown c. '51-'52 are printed "Flagg & Co.": 3½" "Girl &, Boy;" 4½" "Father," "Mother." This set was also offered in a blue "Family Group" box with drawing of a house on front with each doll shown at a window. Courtesy Shirley's Dollhouse.

Flagg & Co. "Flexible Play Dolls" boxes. Top: Cardboard box for basic family play dolls; orange boxes for Dancing, Sports, and other series; silver and white striped for bridal party. Red and white striped boxes (not shown) were also used for Sports series. Courtesy Shirley's Dollhouse.

display boxes that looked like houses.

Doll Characteristics: Boxes printed "Bending doll house dolls that are washable, and easily undressed, hand painted and hand dressed with all plastic bodies that can be placed in any position." The dolls are one-piece bendable plastic; features are painted; fingers are molded together with separate thumb; hair is molded and painted-on, synthetic Dynel wigs are glued to the doll's heads.

Some dolls are offered as black dolls, such as "Baby Twins, White-Col."

Family sets of Mother, Father, Girl, and Boy dolls were also boxed together in sets. Female dancers can have either flat feet or high heels.

Series listed include:

Flexible Doll House Dolls (7") – Includes family sets, occupational dolls, bridal party, ballerina dolls.

Mother Goose Playhouse dolls 3½" – Includes Nursery Rhyme and Story themes.

Undressed dolls – 3½" Child (Boy or Girl), 4½" Adult (man or woman).

7" Flexible Playhouse dolls – Includes dancers, bridal party, Cinderella, Prince, Fairy Godmother, cowboy, girl, bathing beauty.

Clothing Characteristics: Early Flagg doll clothing was stapled onto the doll, but the '55 "wardrobe doll" and the '57 dancing dolls were advertised with removeable clothes. The fabric colors were bright and quite detailed for dollhouse dolls, particularly the dancers' costumes. Some dolls had high-heel feet with vinyl high-heel shoes that were removeable. Flat feet were painted to look like shoes.

Value: $25.00; MIB $50.00+.

Blue "Family Group" advertising c. '50s. The box has a doll shown at each dollhouse window. Courtesy Marge Meisinger.

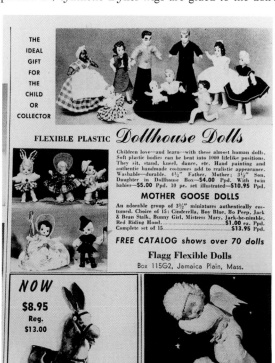

Advertising for flexible AFCO dolls beginning in '48 in Vogue magazine.

Flagg Bride doll 4½" in white satin gown stapled-on, in window display box. Courtesy Marge Meisinger.

Flagg Groom doll 4½" in tuxedo stapled-on, in window display box. Courtesy Marge Meisinger.

Flagg Dolls in original plain boxes (L to R): 3½" Bo Peep c. '55 in yellow taffeta dress with stapled-on felt hat. The dress came in three pastel colors; 3½" "Bunny Girl with Fuzzy Ears" c. '55 in red dotted cotton skirt, fleece jacket, and stapled-on hat with pink bunny ears. Dolls were packaged in window boxes. Courtesy Shirley's Dollhouse.

Flagg brochure c. '56 featuring Mother Goose Series 3½". Courtesy Marge Meisinger.

Three Flagg 7" dancers in bright costumes, with high-heel feet and painted toenails: right: "Rumba Dancer" c.'55 with pink ruffles and gold turban; center: Cancan dancer c. '55; left: Balinese dancer c.'59 with gold hat and magenta top. Courtesy Shirley's Dollhouse.

Flagg brochure cover c. 1955 featuring 7" Cancan dancer. Courtesy Marge Meisinger.

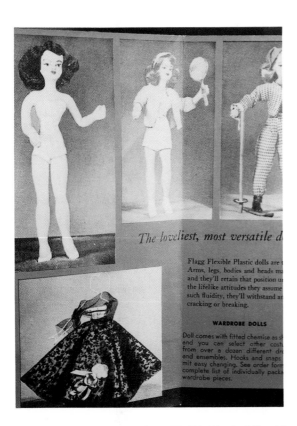

1955 brochure introducing Flagg Flexible Plastic dolls with removeable clothing that closed with hooks. Courtesy Marge Meisinger.

Flagg 7" "Cinderella" c. '55 with glued-on blonde wig, gold braid crown, blue satin gown, and flat silver painted shoes. Courtesy Shirley's Dollhouse.

Cinderella's flat silver painted shoes on 7" Flagg dolls.

Flagg 7" Bridesmaid c. '55 in pink satin gown with pink picture hat, original silver stripe box. Courtesy Shirley's Dollhouse.

Flagg 7" Bridesmaids c.'55 in pink and blue satin gown with picture hats; 3½" Flower Girl in blue gown. Courtesy Shirley's Dollhouse.

High-heel Bridesmaid feet with tulle ruffle on white cotton slip.

Flagg 7" "Majorette" c.'55 in original red stripe box, with painted blonde hair and white satin skirt, red top, and leatherette boots. Courtesy Sue Fay.

Flagg 7" Flexible Playdoll "Scottish Dancer" introduced c. '57 with original box; glued-on blonde wig, in plaid cotton kilt and scarf, painted socks.

Flagg 7" "Tap Dancer" c. '56 in original red and white stripe box with molded red hair wearing a gold sparkle jacket and hat, with green costume, flat painted black slippers. Courtesy Sue Fay.

Flagg 7" Female dolls c.'55 on right: Tennis Girl, Racket & Case, and Golf Girl, Clubs & Bag with (far right) 3½" bridesmaid in blue gown, blue window box; (L) Male Square Dancer doll c. '55 in denim pants, red check shirt, straw hat. Courtesy Vicki Johnson.

Flagg brochure c. 1956 with photos of tap dancer, other dancers, and family dolls. Courtesy Marge Meisinger.

Flagg unique 7" "outer space" dancer c. '59 with molded and painted blonde hair, wearing a black costume trimmed with gold, matching cuffs and turban, flat painted shoes. Courtesy Shirley's Dollhouse.

Flagg 7" "Gay 90s" dancer c. '59 with glued-on blonde wig, pink felt hat with net and bow, pink net skirt, garter on left leg, and high heels. Courtesy Shirley's Dollhouse.

Flagg 7" Flexible Play Doll in "Mexico" box c. '63 with glued-on black wig, wearing red cotton print skirt, white blouse trimmed with lace and braid, and white felt sombrero. Courtesy Shirley's Dollhouse.

Flagg 7" Flexible Play Doll "Irish Dancer" c. '59 with glued-on blonde wig, in white satin apron with shamrocks over green cotton skirt, cotton blouse trimmed with lace and lace mob cap; high-heel feet, black vinyl high-heel shoes.

Flagg 7" "Japanese" with a glued-on black wig in upsweep style and wearing a silk kimono. "Japanese" was introduced in '57, but this version is from '63.

The Wonderful World of Make-believe

Colonial doll house charms the hearts and dreams of little homemakers. Of colorful lithographed metal inside and out, the house has six rooms and sundeck. Outside, there are make-believe awnings and shutters, entrance light and landscape. Inside, 47 pieces of scaled-to-size plastic furniture decorate the rooms. Enjoying this comfortable home is a family of four plastic dolls (included). Easily assembled house measures 33x12x18¾ inches. Little girls delight at having their own home to care for. For ages 4 to 10.
151-0XB-10 .... $10.95*
Doll house family of five, for young doll lovers, is made of flexible plastic that bends in lifelike positions. Family wears clothing of felt and cotton. Father stands 4½ inches high. For doll house or regular play. 151-01-67...$5.25 (24¢)

Flagg 7" "England" doll c. 1970 in blue brocade gown with pink velvet bodice and side panels and black lace trim, faux fur sleeves trim, black turban. England was introduced in '63 without the black lace trim. Courtesy Shirley's Dollhouse.

Marshall Field's Chicago 1959 Christmas catalog advertised the basic set of 4½" Flagg dolls as "Doll house family of five."

Flagg brochure c. 1964 featuring color photos of nationality dolls. Courtesy Marge Meisinger.

Flagg brochure c. 1970 introducing new nationality dolls. Courtesy Marge Meisinger.

Flagg 7" Flexible Play Doll "Egyptian" c. '70 with original box, glued-on brunette wig, white satin costume with gold braid, high-heel feet with removeable white vinyl high heels. The doll was introduced in '55 with orange-trimmed sash at the waist.

Flagg 7" "Spanish" c. 1970 with original box, black wig, ruffled red net skirt with silver braid, gold fabric top; high-heel feet with black vinyl high heels. This doll was called "Bolero" in '59 with a silver gown, fitted below the knees. The name was changed to "Spanish" in '63; costume was changed to red net ruffles, as shown, in '70.

Flagg introduced 7" flexible Reneé in 1959 as the "Campus queen wardrobe doll" with separate out-fits. Courtesy Marge Meisinger.

❦ Fortune Toys, Inc. ❦

Fortune Toys, Inc., Brooklyn New York, was affiliated with Beehler Arts, also the parent company of Virga. The two companies used the same doll body parts for their 8" toddler dolls; hence, Fortune's best-known toddler doll "Pam" was very similar to Beehler's Virga Playmate "Lucy." Collectors are always trying to distinguish between the two. Fortune also sold other hard plastic toddler dolls including 8" Jeanette and 8" Ninette under patents filed in Fortune's name. Miss Pam was Fortune's 10½" high-heel fashion doll, and big sister to 8" Pam.

Toddler Dolls

Pam

TYPE #1: (With Virga characteristics) 8" c.'54-'55
Marks on Doll: Unmarked.
Boxes Marked: Only one Type #1 Pam has been found in a box, and it was a gold window box sleeve sliding over a blue cardboard bottom. Marked "My Name is Pam/ Fortune Toys Inc." Type #2 Pams with Ginger doll characteristics c. '56 are usually found in these boxes.

Doll Characteristics: Pam was an 8" unmarked, fully jointed hard plastic doll introduced in the mid 1950s, retailing for around $1.98, with outfits for 99¢. Pam's characteristics included head-turning walkers; sleep eyes with molded lashes; and head mold line behind the ear. Arms turned a lighter color plastic than the body on most dolls; separate fingers; peg-shaped arm hooks at the top of the arm post; molded-on T-strap shoes instead of toes; shoes unpainted. While most Pams have been found with more angular eyebrows than the other dolls, this is not always the case. Some Pam's eyes are slightly larger than other Pam's eyes, but no dating has been attributed to the two sizes.

Pam dolls have been found with pointed ballet toes, and/or with pastel hair. While there is no documentation for these dolls, it is assumed that Fortune, like fellow Beehler Arts affiliate Virga, also sold ballet and pastel color hair dolls. Other companies apparently used the Pam type dolls too.

Note: Pam's competitor Virga sold a line of "Playmates," 8" toddlers that were virtually identical to Fortune's Pam, except Virga dolls had C-shaped arm hooks. This is one of the only ways to distinguish the two dolls. (See Virga section.)

PMA's Joanie Walker was the same doll as Fortune's hard plastic walking 8" Pam with the same head, body, and legs with molded T-strap feet, and peg arm hook. However, many Joanie dolls had painted lashes under the eyes, or painted feet, or were marked, distinguishing her from Pam.

8" toddlers with Pam's characteristics were sold in pink and blue boxes marked "80W," a PMA box code. The manufacturer isn't marked on the box, so perhaps PMA or Fortune sold these dolls. (See Hard Plastic Doll section for information on "80W" dolls.)

Type #1 Pam's arms c. 1954 had separate fingers and a tube-shaped arm hook. Note that many of the first Pam dolls have lighter arms than the body, perhaps a change in the plastic material over time. She was like Virga's Playmate dolls except for arms.

Pam's wigs had a single row of stitching and were glued to the doll's head.

Pam's Type #1 distinctive peg-shaped arm hooks.

Pam's Type #1 eye size varied, and some dolls have been found with pastel hair.

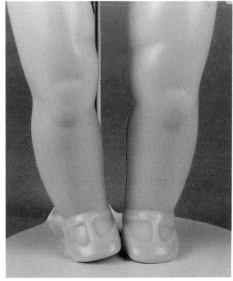

Pam's Type #1 molded T-strap shoes.

Dress Characteristics: Pam's clothing has Virga clothes characteristics. Pam's dresses used the same donut snap closures as Virga dresses.

Wig Characteristics: The glued-on wigs had two parallel rows of exposed stitching (sometimes very close) sewn along the part onto a single strip of stiffened backing vs. Ginny's wig with one row of stitching. Side-part wigs may have had one row of stitching. The backing strip color could be black for brunette dolls. Most styles were flips or braids with bangs, few if any side-part styles. It is assumed that Pam wigs were the same material as Virga's, advertised as Dynel wigs in '54, '56, and '57 brochures.

Value: $55.00+ doll; not enough examples in box seen for MIB price.

TYPE #2: (With Ginger characteristics) 8" c. 1956.

Doll Marks: Unmarked.

Marks on Box: Blue or gold boxes marked on lid and sides, "My Name is Pam, A Pretty Doll I Am, I stand up, I sit Down-I also walk around and around." The end of the box is marked Michele Cartier Presents Pam and her fabulous wardrobe/ Fortune Toys, Inc. Jackson Heights, NY.

Doll Characteristics: The Fortune 8" Pam dolls advertised in the 1956 Woolworth Christmas catalog were clearly not the well-known Type #1 Pams above. The '56 Woolworth Pams had Cosmopolitan's "Ginger" doll bodies and outfits by designer Michele Cartier! The hard plastic dolls had Ginger characteristics: small and/or medium sleep eyes with molded lashes, mold lines through the center of the ear; arms with C-shaped hooks and separate fingers; straight walking legs with toe detail. Fortune obviously used Ginger dolls for this specific line of Pams. Indeed, Ms. Jo Barckley, doll collector and researcher, has

Fortune's 8" Pam Type #1 in a checked sunsuit with straw bonnet.

Strung, hard plastic 8" black Pam Type #1 dolls were often used as souvenir dolls. This Pam type doll wears an undocumented Hawaiian costume with grass skirt. Paper lei around neck is stitched to the cotton sunsuit underneath. She wears a paper flower in her black wig (see Advertising Dolls).

Beginning c. 1956 the Pam Type #2 doll used Ginger doll bodies. She wears "Tea Party" with a nylon skirt trimmed with black lace over an attached taffeta slip, and a black straw hat as featured in the '56 Woolworth Christmas catalog.

1956 8" Pam Type #2 by Fortune in "Tea Party" costume in a blue Pam box. Note it is the same style as "Tea Party" Pam in gold box, but less elaborate without the nylon overskirt and attached slip, and with natural straw hat. Note that Pam Type #2 uses a Ginger doll head and body.

The 1956 Woolworth Christmas catalog featured Fortune "Pam", the walking fashion plate" and her outfits designed by Michele Cartier. The dolls shown were small eye Ginger with molded lashes, head-turning walker Type #2 Pam.

found small-eyed Ginger mold dolls MIB inside Fortune's Pam boxes, such as "Little Miss Muffet" Pam by Michele Carti-er. In yet another case, this writer has a MIB Pam box marked Michele Cartier, "Tea Time" containing a medium-eye Ginger mold doll. These are just two examples of many, confirming what the Woolworth ad shows.

Switching dolls was not uncommon in the '50s for the look-alike dolls. One explanation for "switching" the Pam doll for Wool-worth in '56 is that since Fortune also sold 8" Jeanette and 8" Ninette dolls, both Ginger mold dolls, perhaps switching Pam to Ginger bodies was a consolidation measure. Pam's "Tea Time" outfit designed by Michele Cartier is virtually identical to Ninette's "Tea Time" outfit, except for its less expensive fabric, indicating an economical move to target different markets. A third clue may come from the September 1956 patent application for the patent rights to the name and logo for Pam. Surprisingly, the filing was not by Fortune, Pam's maker printed on the box , but was by Cosmopolitan, Ginger's maker. So was there a new relationship between Cosmopolitan and Fortune at that point? Until further documentation surfaces, these are good guesses as to how and why two entirely different Pam dolls were marketed by Fortune in the '50s.

(L) Pam Type #2 (small eye Ginger body) by Fortune in deluxe gold box "Tea Party" dress, and (R) Pam (Larger eye Ginger body) by Fortune in less expensive blue box and less expensive version of "Tea Party."

The blue end of Pam's gold box c. 1956 featuring Michele Cartier designs. Note original price in pencil $1.98.

This is one of the only Pam Type #1 dolls found in a box. It is a gold box marked "Party Dress 8/29." Separately boxed outfits c. 1956 ($450.00 MIB doll; four gold boxed outfits $200.00; four gold boxed outfits and one blue boxed $220.00). Courtesy Frasher's Doll Auctions.

1956 8" Pam Type #2 by Fortune in "Miss Muffett" in green taffeta outfit with straw hat. Note she is in the gold box with blue end and rare "PAM" wrist tag on doll's arm. Courtesy Jo Barckley.

Dress Characteristics: Michele Cartier created dresses advertised in the '56 Woolworth catalog. They were constructed like Ginger dresses with unfinished back seams stitched closed below the dress opening and closed with painted round snaps stamped with "p" pattern. The Pam dolls in gold boxes had attached slips, and the Pams in blue boxes had no attached slips. Perhaps designated for different quality levels? Waist seams were finished with factory overcast stitching.

Wig Characteristics: Dynel wigs with a single row of exposed stitching along thin backing strip. Most were flip styles with side parts or bangs.

Value: $55.00+; 65.00+ in blue box; or $75.00+ in gold box. More for wrist tags, exceptional color.

Separate Fortune Pam "Smart Outfits" c. 1956, "Clown" in blue box and an unnamed cotton striped dress with black straw hat in the gold box. Both close with round metal snaps with "p" pattern. The unfinished back seam is stitched closed below dress opening, and waist seam is finished with factory overcast stitching.

Vinyl Head Pam (Flat Feet & Cha Cha Heels) 8" c. 1957

Doll Marked: PAM on back of neck; Ginger on bottom of foot.

Marks on Box: Pam with rooted hair/ Now with Cha-Cha heel.

Doll Characteristics: 8" Pam was a hard plastic, head-turning dolls with a vinyl head and rooted hair. Her feet were advertised as "The 8" walking doll with Cuban Heel shoes, vinyl head, rooted hair in assorted hair styles. Sleeping eyes and moving head." She is marked "Pam" on the neck but "Ginger" on the bottom of the foot. It is assumed they used the same hard plastic body as Cosmopolitan's 8" Cha Cha heel Ginger doll. Some unmarked dolls are found in Pam boxes with the same Cha Cha vinyl head but have flat feet.

Dress Characteristics: Her brochure showed 12 outfits. Unfinished back seams were stitched closed below dress opening with a "p" pattern snap. Shoes were slip-on vinyl. "Tea Party" and "Majorette" dresses are the same as Ninette's and Pam's dress by Michele Cartier, but the designer's name is not advertised. A strapless evening gown matches 10½" Miss Pam's evening gown.

Wig Characteristics: Rooted hair in bubble cuts, long flip styles, upswept, and ponytails.

Value: $55.00; $75.00 in box.

Fortune introduced Pam with vinyl head on the 1957 brochure cover.

Two 1957 vinyl head Pams with flat feet and marked "Pam" on the neck. Doll on left has curly hair and doll on right a flat bob.

Vinyl head Pams: Flat feet on left and Cha Cha heels on right.

Fortune's 8" vinyl head Pam c. 1957 with rooted hair and head-turning, walking body, marked "Cha Cha heel" on the box, "Pam" on the neck, and "Ginger" on the foot bottom.

Vinyl head Cha Cha heel Pam. From the front, she appears to have no neck.

8" Pam's Cha Cha feet have a slight high-heel curve.

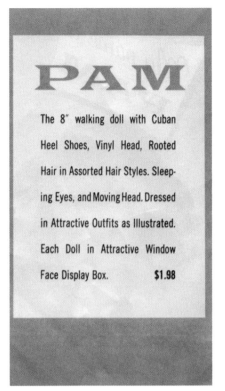

PAM

The 8" walking doll with Cuban Heel Shoes, Vinyl Head, Rooted Hair in Assorted Hair Styles. Sleeping Eyes, and Moving Head. Dressed in Attractive Outfits as Illustrated. Each Doll in Attractive Window Face Display Box.   **$1.98**

8/5 Bridal Gown   8/6 Ballet Costume   8/9 Evening Gown   8/10 School Dress

8/7 Blue Jeans & Jacket   8/8 Spring Outfit   8/11 Afternoon Dress   8/12 Outdoor Girl
Dressed as illustrated ..$1.98 Outfits only ....$1.00   Dressed as illustrated ..$1.98 Outfits only $1.0

Fortune's Pam with Cha Cha heels c. 1957, showed 12 outfits in her brochure.

Ninette 8" c. 1955

Ninette used first quality Ginger dolls with nice coloring and well-made costumes.

Doll Marked: Unmarked.

Marks on Box: White boxes: Ninette Walking Doll/By Fortune Toys, Inc, Brooklyn, NY Pink Boxes: Ninette Walking Doll/By Fortune Toys, Inc, Jackson Heights, NY.

Doll Characteristics:

TYPE #1: The 8" hard plastic dolls were walking, head-turning dolls. The first dolls used the same molds as Cosmopolitan's Ginger Type #1 dolls with painted lashes, mostly found in white boxes.

TYPE #2: The second Ninette dolls used the small eye Ginger #2 heads with molded lashes; mostly found in pink Ninette boxes. Both dolls had mold marks through the center of the ear, had C-shaped Ginger arm hooks with separate fingers, and legs with toe detail.

Wig Characteristics: The painted lash Ninette had a Dynel wig that was somewhat wiry. The Ninette with small eyes and molded lashes had a less wiry synthetic wig. Brochure advertised "Her Dynel hair can be combed and curled," and was basically the same wig as the '54 Ginger. *Stitching & Style:* A single row of exposed stitching along a thin strip of stiffened backing which could be tan vs. Ginny's white backing strip. Most were side-part flip styles.

Dress Characteristics: Brochure advertises, "Ninette has 24 beautiful outfits, designed exclusively for her by the famous fashion designer, Michele Cartier, Paris, New York." (Same designer as Pam advertised in Woolworth catalog above.) Her brochure had color photos of 19 of the outfits. They were sold in window lid boxes and constructed with unfinished back seams stitched closed below dress opening and round metal "p" pattern snaps. Note: Many of Ninette's outfits were advertised for Duchess' Randi dolls in '55. Ninette's "Tea Time" was advertised for "Little MeGo Too" dolls in '57. The sales were likely part of Mego's 88-cent doll promotions in '55 – '57. (See Hard Plastic & Vinyl and Mego sections).

Value: $55.00; $65.00 in box.

Fortune's 8" hard plastic Ninette Type #1 with painted lashes wears undocumented white printed taffeta dress with matching red straw hat, in original white box. Courtesy Jo Barckley.

Ninette Type #1 8" hard plastic doll with painted lashes wears #13/5 "School Outfit," black cotton print dress trimmed with lace, and a straw hat. Courtesy Jo Barckley.

Fortune's 8" hard plastic Ninette brochure cover c. '55 featured a Type #1 walking doll with sleep eyes and painted lashes, wearing the "Tea Party" white taffeta dress with black lace trim. Painted lash Ninette was the same hard plastic head and body used for competitor Ginger in '54 (see Cosmopolitan section).

Fortune's brochure for painted lash type #1 Ninette c. '55 with outfits.

Fortune's 8" hard plastic Ninette Type #1 walking doll, painted lashes in "Garden Outfit" #13/2.

Fortune's 8" hard plastic Ninette Type #2 wears green taffeta "Little Miss Muffet" outfit # 13/14 with straw hat, in original pink box. Courtesy Jo Barckley.

Fortune's 8" hard plastic Ninette Type #2 wears a red "Majorette" outfit # 13/16 in original pink box.

Pink box Ninette in "Lounging Ensemble."

Pink Ninette box showing "Michele Cartier" printed on the end.

Fortune's 8" Ninette Type #2 wears #14/9 "Rain Outfit" with green dress with blue rain cape in original box.

jeanette 8" doll

Adorable 8-inch walking doll, has moving arms, saran hair... **84¢**

jeanette clothes

Choose from many adorable costumes for your 8-inch jeanette doll..... **84¢**

Newspaper advertisement 4/24/58 for Jeanette 8" undressed doll and boxed outfits. Courtesy Marge Meisinger.

Fortune's 8" hard plastic Ninette walking doll with sleep eyes, painted lashes, and Dynel wig in original white box. This is a Ginger body doll. She wears red and white felt "Ski Outfit" #13/19.

Ward's catalog advertisement c. '55 for Ninette dressed in three costumes and 6 separate outfits from the line; note the center-snap shoes with each dress. Courtesy Tina Standish.

Jeanette 8" c. mid-1950s

Fortune marketed Jeanette, who was made from a lesser quality Ginger doll. Most of her clothes were not as well made as Fortune's Ninette or Pam.

Marks on Doll: Unmarked.

Boxes Marked: Doll box: "Jeanette/A Marcelle Boissier original/She walks, her hair can be curled and set in many hair styles." Outfit boxes: "A Marcelle Boissier Original Dress Outfit for Your 8" Doll."

Doll Characteristics: Jeanette was advertised c. 1957 – 58. She was a 7½" hard plastic doll with Ginger Types #2, #3, #4 characteristics (see Cosmopolitan) but of a lesser quality; molded lashes, large sleep eyes, walker, head-turning, C-shaped arm hook with separate fingers, and straight legs with toe detail. Also, the Jeanette dolls examined have different eyebrows from Ginger. Instead of being tapered on the ends, the brow is all the same thickness from end to end.

Dress Characteristics: Jeanette had cute outfits designed by Marcelle Boissier, but their quality was inconsistent. Some dresses were tied in the back with a ribbon and no other hooks or snaps. Others dresses had the round metal snap with

Fortune's 8" Jeanette separate dress "Birthday Party #106" taffeta dress trimmed with flowers, and straw hat. Dress ties closed with no snap.

Fortune's 8" Jeanette walking doll is a wide eye Ginger body and wears pink taffeta dress by Marcelle Boissier that closes with "p" pattern metal snap.

Fortune's 8" Jeanette "#102 Bridesmaid Outfit" box end label.

Fortune's 8" Jeanette separate dress "Bridesmaid Outfit #102" nylon trimmed with lace over dotted cotton, unfinished hem, and no snap.

Fortune's 9½" Pam (far right in red taffeta) compared to Fortune's 8" Pam (middle in black and white) and 8" Jeanette (far left in red dress). All three dolls wear dresses cut with Fortune's distinctive angular cap sleeves, and they close with "p" pattern snaps.

Fortune's 8" Jeanette wearing "Afternoon Dress #104," similar to other Fortune dresses and to competitor Ginger's dresses but not as well made.

Fortune's 8" Jeanette separate "Afternoon Dress #104" dotted red taffeta trimmed with braid finished hem, unfinished waist seam with round metal "p" pattern snap.

Close-up of 9½" Pam face showing differences from Virga's 9" Lucy on right. They have similar noses, but Pam's head and eyes are bigger, and mouth paint is different.

"p" pattern like Ginger's snaps. Waist seams were not finished, and some skirt edges were unhemmed and unfinished.

Wig Characteristics: Jeanette's wig is a "wiry" Saran-type, mostly in bangs, or side-part flip styles. Otherwise the doll is the same as Ginger.

Value: $40.00; $50.00 – 60.00 in box.

Pam 9½" c. 1950s

Marks on Doll: None.

Boxes Marked: Gold boxes marked on lid and sides, "My Name is Pam, I Walk!" The end of the box is marked Michele Cartier Presents Pam and her fabulous wardrobe/ Fortune Toys, Inc. Jackson Heights, NY. These are larger but the same design for Fortune's 8" Jeanette boxes.

Rare example of Fortune's MIB larger 9½" Pam c. 1956 with sleep eyes, regular jointed legs, and wearing dress like Fortune's 8" sized Jeanette.

Doll Characteristic: The only example of this rare doll found in the original box is a hard plastic, 9½" fully jointed doll with sleep eyes, molded lashes. She had regular leg joints and is not a pin-hipped walker like Virga's 9" walker. While the face and nose have similar characteristics to Virga's 9" Lucy, the 9½" Pam doll has a wider head and eyes than Virga's doll. Also, the Fortune's 9½" doll has two lines under the dimpled knees.

Wig Characteristics: Synthetic wig stitched to a backing strip. Bangs and wig are one piece.

Dress Characteristics: Dresses close in the back with a "p" pattern snap and are stitched closed below the dress opening. Note: Angular cap sleeve styles are common to all of these Fortune dolls: 9½" Pam red taffeta dress; 8" Jeanette #104 "Red Afternoon Dress;" and 8" Ninette #13/7 "Red Ensemble." The fabrics may vary, but they all use the same unique style, closing with a "p" pattern round metal snap. Fortune obviously interchanged styles for these dolls. Interestingly, competitor Duchess also used the same style for 8" Randi #102 "Red Ensemble." Since Cosmopolitan's Ginger appears to be the common denominator for all of these dolls' bodies and for the angular cap sleeve styles (as well as others), Cosmopolitan's mold was likely the original source for all of these competitors.

Value: $110.00 at Frasher's Auction.

Baby Doll

Baby Pamette 8"
Marks on Doll: PAMETTE on neck.
Box Marks: Unknown.
Doll Characteristics: Pamette was an 8" fully jointed all vinyl drink and wet baby with molded lash sleep eyes and unique with a deep loop forehead curl. Pamette was the '50s baby sister to Fortune's 8" hard plastic toddler Pam.
Clothing Characteristics: Unknown but possibly closes with circular donut snap like Pam's.
Value: $55.00+ doll only, more for wrist tag, exceptional color, etc. Not found in box to date.

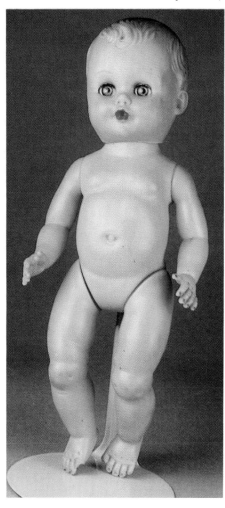

Fortune's 8" Pamette, an all vinyl drink and wet baby with molded lash sleep eyes with a deep loop in her unique molded forehead curl.

🍇 Grant Plastics 🍇

Grant Plastics of Townsend, Massachusetts, produced a line of inexpensive "Dress Me" dolls in sizes ranging from 6" to 20" tall in the 1950s. One of the dolls was an 8" toddler doll that they advertised as "Suzie." Suzie tags are the same design except for color.

Suzie 8" c. 1950s

Marks on Doll: Unmarked.

Boxes Marked: Plastic bags stapled to cardboard tops printed: Adorable/DRESS ME DOLLS/ 8" / 6-20"/ with moving eyes and moving/parts. New Style Coiffures/GRANT PLASTICS, INC./Townsend, Mass.

Doll Characteristics:

TYPE #1: Hard plastic 8" fully jointed, strung doll; sleep eyes and molded lashes; lashes also painted under eyes; heavy brown eyebrows; mold line behind ear; C-shaped arm hooks; straight legs with toes. Advertising showed the doll's toes painted white, but some dolls in bags did not have painted toes. Plastic on arms and legs have a more orange tone than body and head.

Very prominent mold lines along sides of legs and body. Note: This doll is often confused with others who have painted toes, like Midwestern's Mary Jean and Admiration's Carol-Sue. However, this doll has a different head, the mold line is behind the ear, and lashes are painted under the eyes. Type #1 Suzie tags are red and white. (See Comparisons chapter.)

TYPE #2: Hard plastic 8" fully jointed, strung doll with sleep eyes; molded lashes with lashes also painted under the eyes, mold line behind the ear; C-shaped arm hooks; feet with flat molded bows painted white. Note: This Suzie doll and her uniquely flat molded bow-feet have the same characteristics as Doll Bodies' 8" toddler doll. (See Doll Bodies section.) Type #2 Suzie tags are red and black.

Dress Characteristics: White cotton pants or undressed in the bag.

Wig Characteristics: Type #1 Suzie dolls had wavy mohair wigs glued directly to the head; Type #2 Suzie dolls may be bald with molded hair not painted.

Value: Types #1 or #2: $25.00; $45.00 in original sealed bag.

Grant Plastics' 8" Suzie Type #1 was an inexpensive "Dress Me" doll sold in plastic bags stapled to a cardboard label. This doll's toes are unpainted, but her feet are usually painted white. Suzie's head had molded lashes with handpainted lashes under the eyes. This doll is old store stock from a hardware store. Courtesy Marge Meisinger.

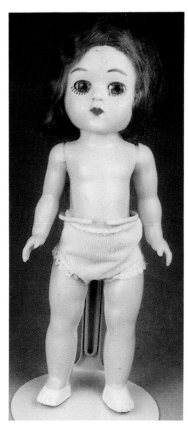

Grant Plastics' 8" Suzie Type #1 hard plastic strung doll with brunette mohair wig, and feet painted white.

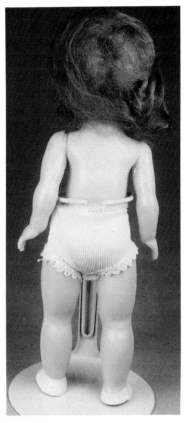

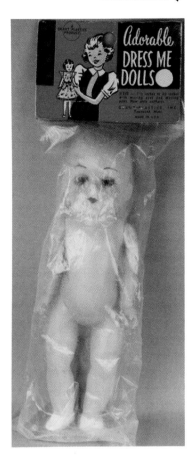

Close-up of Grant Plastics' Suzie Type #1 with toes. Note the heavy eyebrow and lash paint.

Back of Suzie Type #1. Note the thin inexpensive wavy mohair wig with no backing, glued directly to the doll's head, and toe detail.

Grant Plastics' Suzie Type #2 hard plastic 8" strung doll has white feet with flat molded bows.

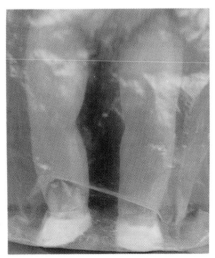

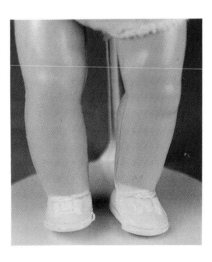

Suzie Type #2 in original bag with flat molded bows.

Type of foot for Suzie Type #2 without a bag (same as Doll Bodies).

Close-up of Grant Plastics' Suzie Type #2. Note the doll in her original sealed bag has a bald head with unpainted molded hair and no wig.

🍇 Happi-Time 🍇

In 1942 Sears, Roebuck and Co. filed a patent for the name "Happi-Time" for dolls and toys. Sears' Happi-Time products included small display dolls of various sizes as well as 8" look-alike Happi-Time toddler dolls.

Display Dolls

"Happi -Time" Miniature Dolls 7½"-8" c. 1940s-50s
The Sears line of display dolls included their patented, "Happi-Time Miniature Dolls for Young Collectors."
Marks on Dolls: Unmarked.
Boxes Marked: Happi-Time Dolls/Sears, Roebuck and Co.
Doll Characteristics: These 7½" -8" dolls had moving arms and fixed legs. Their heads had glassene eyes with painted lashes above the eye and either fixed necks or moving heads. The moving head dolls c.1950 were advertised as "lovely life-like plastic head turns and tilts-like yours, eyes open and close, rich details and decorations." The doll's feet had molded shoes with three incised lines for bows.
Dress Characteristics: Hang tags read, "Exquisite Costumes are Authentic and Designed Exclusively for Sears, Roebuck and Co.," and they included a great variety of character costumes. The stapled-on clothes and headpieces were of good quality satin, taffeta, cotton, felt, etc. Sears' 1954 Christmas catalog advertised that costumes included panties and a half-slip.
Wig Characteristics: Wavy mohair wigs glued directly to the head with no backing.
Value: $25.00; $35.00 in box.

Toddlers

Happi-Time Toddlers 8" c. 1950s
Marks on Doll: Unmarked.
Boxes Marked: Happi-Time.
Doll Characteristics: Hard plastic 8" fully jointed walkers; with sleep eyes with molded lashes, rigid vinyl arms with separate fingers, and peg-shaped arm hooks. They were first quality dolls with bright cheek blush and good coloring. Some dolls had straight legs with molded T-strap feet, and some dolls had legs with bent knees and toe detail. Note: The straight leg Happi-Time dolls are the same body as Fortune's Type #1 Pam dolls with peg-shaped arm hooks; no strung dolls found.
Dress Characteristics: Dresses were nicely made cotton dresses with a stitched and turned skirt hem, back seam left open with unfinished waist seams; dresses closed with a round

Sears, Roebuck and Co. Happi-Time Miniature doll wrist tag.

Inside of Happi-Time Miniature doll wrist tag.

handsewn metal snap, or closed with a ribbon or tie and no snap.

Wig Characteristics: Some dolls had synthetic Saran type wigs stitched to a backing strip and glued to head. Another type was a very soft, synthetic, and hard-to-manage wig with a dull finish, stitched to a backing strip and glued to the head.

Value: $45.00; $55.00+ in cardboard box; $75.00 in acetate container.

Note: Sears sold '50s toddlers in plain boxes. See boxes with "80W" code in photos on page 106.

Happi-Time Miniature doll box lid with Sears' trademarked brand graphics.

Happi-Time Miniature Bride, c. 1950s, 7½" hard plastic display doll with moving eyes, arms, and head with fixed legs, in white satin gown. Original box and hang tag.

8" hard plastic Happi-Time basic undressed girl doll c. 1950s with sleep eyes, molded lashes, rigid vinyl arms, bent knees with toe detail, and original cardboard box. Courtesy Marge Meisinger.

8" hard plastic Happi-Time basic girl doll c. 1950s with blonde wig, in panties, socks, and shoes. She has sleep eyes with molded lashes, rigid vinyl arms, and bent knees with toe detail in original cardboard box. Courtesy Bev Mitchell, photo by Patsy Moyer.

8" hard plastic Happi-Time head-turning toddler c. 1950s with rigid vinyl arms, walking legs with bent knees with toe detail; shown with her original and rare acetate box marked "Happi-Time." Her cotton print dress has organdy hem trim and matching apron, socks, pink vinyl slip-on shoes, and sunglasses. The dark line under her eyes is a stain from original elastic hair band that slipped down onto her face long ago.

8" hard plastic MIB Happi-Time girl doll c. 1950s with brunette wig, sleep eyes with molded lashes, rigid vinyl arms, and bent knees with toe detail. She wears a cotton dress, panties, and blue slip-on vinyl strap shoes; Note the original 98¢ sticker on the box side. Courtesy Jo Barckley.

9" hard plastic MIB Happi-Time girl c. 1950 with high cheek color, brunette wig, sleep eyes, and bent knees. Her cotton print dress has organdy hem trim and matching bib collar, socks, red vinyl slip-on shoes. The dark line under her eyes is a stain from original elastic hair band that slipped down onto her face. Courtesy Jeanne Niswonger.

🍇 Hard Plastic & Vinyl Dolls, Miscellaneous 🍇

Display Dolls 7" - 8"

"America" by Corrine: Brides of All Nations c. 1950s, 7"
unmarked sleep eye doll with painted lashes, jointed head and
arms, fixed legs with rectangular bows molded on feet. White
taffeta stapled-on gown and wrist tag marked "America." She
is one of 30 international brides by Mrs. Corrine Friedman,
Bronx, NY. MIB $40.00.

"St. Thomas" by Chiquita Trinkets of Miami, Florida c.
1951, 7½" unmarked doll with "St. Thomas" label on foot,
sleep eyes, painted lashes; strung arms and head; fixed legs
with rectangular bows molded on feet. MIB $25.00.

Chiquita Trinkets box with color photo of eight dolls: Melanie, Elaine, Lilly Langtree, Jenny Lind, Virginia Dare, Lillian Russell, Marquesa, and Dorothy Verdon.

Display Dolls 7" - 8"

Dream Girl, 7" doll c. 1950s with sleep eyes, strung head and arms; fixed legs with butterfly bow molded to toes; wearing a stapled-on blue taffeta gown. Note typical '50s era graphics on the lid. No manufacturer is printed on box. MIB $25.00.

"Cinderella" by House of Dolls, Chicago, c. 1950s, 7" sleep eye doll with printed lashes, strung head and arms; fixed legs with square corner bows molded to feet. No manufacturer is printed on box. Costumes varied and were stapled on. MIB $45.00; other styles MIB $25.00.

"Lady Hampshire," c. 1950s, 7" sleep eye doll with painted lashes, strung head and arms; fixed legs and parallel bowlines. No maker printed on box. MIB $40.00.

Note: Additional display dolls are described in the A&H, Doll Bodies, Duchess, Eugenia, Happi-Time, Hollywood, Nancy Ann Storybook, Plastic Molded Arts, and Virga sections.

"Canasta" 7" display doll with sleep eyes, painted lashes, strung head and arms; fixed legs with rectangular bows molded on feet; wearing stapled-on satin canasta print dress; unknown manufacturer. Dolls of All Nations by Duchess had a doll with the "Canasta" pattern gown, but different style so perhaps this is a variation Duchess Canasta doll. $25.00; MIB $40.00.

Unknown 7" painted eye doll with strung arms, fixed head and arms; painted-on black shoes with no bows. Her felt ensemble is very well made. This doll is the same doll sold undressed by International Doll Co., Mollye, dressed by Virga. Stamped in box: Faenza Coffee Shop Gift Wares; Allentown, PA. $25.00.

Small Dolls 5"- 6"

Unknown 5" Cinderella's hard plastic prince doll c. 1940s with paint-ed side-glancing eyes and fixed arms and legs. The bright storybook box with doll and a plastic coach toy has no maker. MIB $150.00.

Knickerbocker 5¼" Hawaiian molded hair, marked doll with halter and grass skirt, c. 1950s. $25.00.

Back of Knickerbocker 5¼" dolls, marked on the back, c. 1950s.

Knickerbocker Little 5¼" Hawaiian grass-skirted girl marked, "Knickerbocker/Plastic Co./Glendale, Calif./Des.Pat.Pend." on the back had side-glancing sleep eyes, fixed head and feet, strung arms. Other dolls were sold as souvenirs, such as the 1953 Ice Follies doll with mohair wig wearing a dotted Swiss dress and "skates" glued to the feet. $25.00.

Toddler Dolls 8" - 9" c. 1950s

End of pink and blue box; since "80W" is also a PMA box code, it is thought that they were bought from PMA or another maker.

Companies such as Sears, Roebuck & Co. often sold 8" unmarked toddler dolls in 1950s catalogs. They were sold in unmarked boxes or in boxes coded "80W" like this pink box with blue lid. Most dolls found in these boxes are Pam-like dolls with separate fingers and a peg arm hook (see Fortune section). MIB $55.00+.

Hard plastic 9" unmarked pin- hipped walking doll with toe detail c. 1950s with sleep eyes, wears a quality nylon dress tagged, "KRUEGER, N.Y.C." This is the same tag found on vintage '30s and '40s cloth dolls, clowns, etc.; it is assumed this is the same company well known for quality cloth dolls in that era. Note: This is the same doll used by Virga for 9" Lucy (see Virga section) and for 9" Marcie Daily Dolly (see A&H section and Comparisons chapter). $45.00 – 55.00.

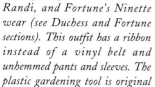

This Ginger type doll wears a long-sleeved version of the "Gardening Outfit" that Duchess's Randi, and Fortune's Ninette wear (see Duchess and Fortune sections). This outfit has a ribbon instead of a vinyl belt and unhemmed pants and sleeves. The plastic gardening tool is original to the outfit. $45.00.

Effanbee Fluffy Doll, 8½", introduced c. 1954, all-vinyl, sleep eyes, rooted hair; this doll marked Effanbee 1965 on neck; missing scarf. Also came dressed as Girl Scout and Bluebird. $75.00.

End flap for Colette doll.

Colette Doll boxed by "Madame Irene," an 8" hard plastic Ginger type toddler with painted lashes. She wears a blue felt ice skating costume with fur trim, matching hat, carrying bag, and slip-on ice skates. Courtesy Judy Cullen. MIB $75.00+.

Pastel hair doll on right, possibly Gigi #5 with pastel hair or BKW Virga wearing the same dress as a Virga Lolly-Pop doll. On left is Elite's Vicki in clown costume # 413. Courtesy Sandy Johnson Barts. $55.00+ each.

"Davy Crockett" 8" strung doll c. mid '50s, with sleep eyes and molded lashes, arms with C-shaped arm hook and 2nd and 3rd fingers molded together, T-strap molded feet painted black. Wears suede cloth costume with vinyl belt, metal gun, and faux fur cap; Virga type doll with distributor unknown. $45.00+.

This strung 8" toddler c. 1950s wears a fringed leather American Indian costume with beads sewn on front and attached matching headband. This is a Fortune type doll with a peg-shaped arm hook and molded T-strap shoes painted black. $45.00.

Back of red felt costume stapled at the neck to the doll's back; headband stapled to the head.

This strung 8" toddler c. 1950s wears a red felt American Indian painted design costume stapled to the doll's back; bead necklace; vinyl headband. This is a Fortune type doll with a peg arm hook, and molded T-strap shoes painted black. Virga Playmate dolls and Duchess type dolls were also dressed in similar costumes. $55.00.

Toddler Dolls International

Unmarked hard plastic doll, 8" strung sleep eye doll with molded lashes; mohair wig; toe detail, sewed-on felt Lapland costume. $45.00.

Close-up of Lapland doll's face.

8" light plastic Dutch doll with strung head, arms, and legs, sleep eyes, no lashes. Marked "Made in Italy" on the back; mohair braided wig. Cotton costume and lace cap are sewn-on, and black stockings are taped-on. $35.00.

Susan 8" unmarked, fully jointed inexpensive lightweight plastic doll c. '50s or '60s with sleep eyes, molded lashes, painted lashes below the eyes, and molded hair with a bow attached to the head. She was bought in Scotland in a sealed cellophane bag printed, "I'm Susan. I'm almost unbreakable because I'm made of super strength H.I. plastic/LINCOLN/An International Doll." No country of origin noted. Courtesy Lee Ann Beaumont. $50.00+.

Back of Susan 8" plastic doll with bow attached to head. Courtesy Lee Ann Beaumont.

Close-up of 8" Susan with molded lashes and lashes painted under eyes. Courtesy Lee Ann Beaumont.

Wrapper for Susan hard plastic 8" doll by Lincoln. Courtesy Lee Ann Beaumont.

Toddler Dolls c. 1960s – 1980s

Singer Crafts "Little Treasures," hard plastic 8" strung doll, sleep eyes with vinyl lashes and painted under eyes. She resembles an Alexander but is marked "Hong Kong" on her back; probably 1960s - 1970s. $55.00.

Tyrolean Ganda Dolls 8" vinyl dolls c. 1973, marked "Ganda Toys Ltd., 1973," sleep eyes and lashes painted under the eyes, and a stitched wig. She is often mistaken for a Madame Alexander Maggie Mixup with a watermelon smile. Dress is tagged "Tyrolean/Ganda Toys/1973." Courtesy of Mary Van Buren-Swasey. $55.00.

Tiara Dolls 8" hard plastic Playmates doll c. 1985 with braided wig and sleep eyes, often mistaken for an earlier Ginny type doll. Their blue and white window box is very similar to Ginny box c. 1977 Lesney era. This box is marked "Jackie." Courtesy Shirley's Dollhouse. MIB $45.00 – 55.00.

Lantern symbol is on the New Bright box and on the doll's back.

New Bright 8" vinyl dolls were made in Hong Kong and are fully jointed with sleep eyes, molded lashes, rooted hair, and are marked with a lantern symbol on the back.

The New Bright Industrial Company, Ltd. vinyl 8" dolls are often mistaken for vinyl Ginny dolls from the '60s and '70s. The "Bookcase Collectable Dolls" series of 12 dolls had costumes from around the world, closing with clear plastic snaps in back and slip-on vinyl shoes. $45.00 – 55.00.

Ganda Dolls plastic stand is marked Ganda Toys, Ltd. Courtesy of Mary Van Buren-Swasey.

Toddler Doll Advertisements

"Margie Marcher, The Walking Majorette Doll" c. 1956 advertisement for 8" hard plastic head-turning walker doll with sleep eyes and a Dynel wig. She came with costume, hat, baton, a "Midget dollhouse," and sheer nightie sold by Mrs. Lavalle, direct mail, NY. No manufacturer is named. Courtesy Marge Meisinger.

"Cuddlee Bride Walking Doll," with seven complete outfits advertisement c. 1956 in House Beautiful magazine. She is advertised as an 8" hard plastic head-turning walker doll with sleep eyes and a Dynel wig selling for $2.98 by Mrs. Lavalle, direct mail, NY; no manufacturer is named. Courtesy Marge Meisinger.

Toddler not shown: W.T. Grant Suzy, 8" vinyl doll advertised exclusively, sleep eyes and rooted hair, maker unknown.

"Famous Olympic Princess/Skating Ballerina & Walking Doll," with five complete outfits as advertised in the Chicago Sun Times, and in House & Garden, November 1956. She is a hard plastic head-turning walker doll with sleep eyes and a Dynel wig selling for $2.98 by Mrs. Lavalle, direct mail, NY. No height is given, but outfits are the same ones shown in Lavalle's 8" "Margie Marcher" advertisement; no manufacturer is named, but Smith's Modern Collector's Dolls 7th edition lists it as a Virga doll. Courtesy Marge Meisinger.

Bonnie Bride Walking Doll," advertisement c. 1966 for a 9" head-turning hard plastic doll in bride gown with six extra outfits by Thoresen's. The advertisement says, "She is the same doll that has been nationally advertised at $7.98," The manufacturer is unclear from drawings, but the address is the same as Lavalle's mail order advertisement. Courtesy Marge Meisinger.

Teen and High-Heel 8" - 9"

"I Am Joy" by Relco is a display type 8" doll with moving head, strung arms, and fixed legs with high-heel feet; inexpensive removeable clothing with two additional dresses in the box. MIB $25.00.

9" unmarked doll with vinyl head and blue hair, same head as Virga Go Go doll but different body: Vinyl body with fixed arms and high heels; in taffeta sheath with gilded net over, black vinyl high heels. $40.00 – 50.00.

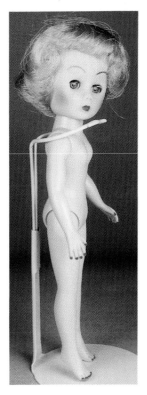

8" high-heel doll like Woolworth's Little Miss Marie without painted lashes; vinyl sleep eye head, hard plastic body with high-heel feet, unmarked. Rare; MIB $75.00+.

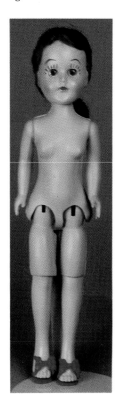

8" high-heel doll with sleep eyes and painted lashes, pin-hipped walker with jointed knees. Vinyl high-heel shoes, unmarked. $25.00.

Baby Dolls 8"

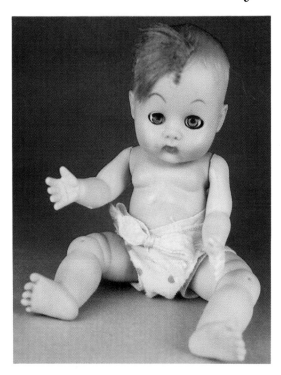

Unmarked all vinyl 8" fully jointed baby doll with rooted hair, manufacturer not known. Courtesy Marge Meisinger. $35.00.

Unmarked vinyl 8" fully jointed baby doll with hard plastic arms with straight fingers; one row of rooted forehead lock, by unknown maker. Virga's "Cookie" doll had a two-row forehead lock, so perhaps this is a version of Virga's doll. Courtesy Marge Meisinger. $35.00 – 45.00.

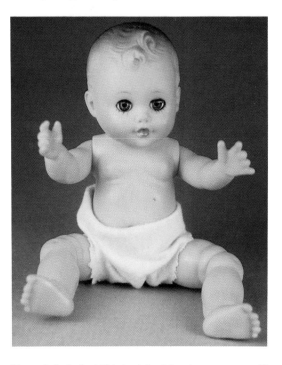

Unmarked all vinyl 8" baby doll with unique two top molded curls, bent fingers on right hand; maker unknown. Courtesy Marge Meisinger. $35.00.

Unmarked all vinyl 8" fully jointed baby doll with jointed head and painted side-glancing eyes; one-piece stuffed vinyl body; maker unknown. $35.00.

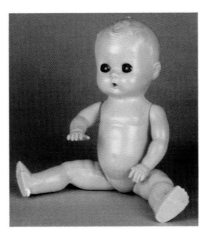

Unmarked all rigid vinyl 8" fully jointed baby doll with straight fingers on both hands, similar to Baby Susan but smaller head. $35.00.

Unmarked all rigid vinyl with fixed head, molded hair, jointed arms and legs, large sleep eyes; maker unknown. $35.00.

9" baby marked "U" (possibly Uneeda) on neck with sleep eyes and rooted hair, in Hawaiian grass skirt costume; shown on right 8" Madame Alexander Wendy c. 1966. Hawaiian baby: $55.00.

This 8" rigid vinyl baby is marked "Baby Susan" on the neck. She is a fully jointed baby with molded hair, sleep eyes, and molded lashes, and slightly bent legs with toe detail. Note: Eegee sold a marked 10½" vinyl nursing doll named "Baby Susan" (see Eegee section), but it is not clear if they also sold this 8" doll marked "Baby Susan" or if Marlon did. Note: See Baby Susan in Marlon section, page 123. Courtesy Toni Ferry. $45.00 - 55.00.

Back of 8" rigid vinyl doll marked "Baby Susan." Courtesy Toni Ferry.

Not Shown: Block Baby: An 8" Ginnette look-alike with lashes painted in corners of eyes; "A Block Doll Product" on back.
Purl: An 8" Fortune Pam type sold in acetate bag, "I'm Purl, Take me home, Make my out-fit."

This 8" soft vinyl, fully jointed baby is marked "Baby Susan" on the neck. She has molded hair, sleep eyes, and molded lashes with or without lashes painted under the eyes; slightly bent legs with toe detail. Her clothes fasten with circular donut snaps. Note: A soft vinyl baby marked "Baby Susan" has also been found in a box marked "Marlon Creations" (see Marlon Creations section.) $35.00; MIB $45.00.

❦ Hollywood Doll Mfg. Co. ❦

On Nov. 3, 1944 Domenick Ippolito of Glendale, California, (doing business as Hollywood Doll Mfg. Co.) filed a doll patent for "Hollywood Lucky Star." In 1946 and 1947 Ippolito filed approximately 27 more patents for doll and series names. Then in 1947 he personally filed a patent for "A Hollywood Doll in a five point star for dolls," and used it primarily for small storybook type dolls. According to mid 1940s advertisements, Hollywood's composition dolls ranged from 5" to 20". In the late 1940s Hollywood dolls made small hard plastic dolls with unique flat faces, and a 1947 brochure documents their "movable eyes, heads, arms and legs." Today collectors simply call them "Hollywood Dolls." At some point in the '50s, the company entered the market for hard plastic look-alike dolls with their 8" Toyland Series toddler dolls.

Hollywood Doll, Composition 5"-8" c. 1947
Marks on Doll: Unmarked or Hollywood Doll on back.
Marks on Box: "Hollywood Dolls" on boxes with various sized blue or red stars.
Doll Characteristics: Good quality, smooth composition dolls with a one-piece head and body, and strung arms; other composition dolls had a strung head, arms, and legs. All had hand-painted features, some with side-glancing eyes, and painted shoes. Most of the 5" Storybook type dolls had a distinct flat-faced, wide eye look. Series of composition dolls with moveable head arms and legs included 5" dolls: Little Friends, Playmates, Nursery Rhymes, Hollywood Book, Lucky Star, Princess; 8" dolls: Princess, Lucky Star, Nursery Rhymes, Playmates, Little Friends; 9" dolls: Bride Idyll Series, Garden Series, Toyland Series, Western, Punchinello.

Hollywood all hard plastic 5" "Queen For A Day" with original box; jointed head, arms, and legs, sleep eyes, painted white shoes; wavy blonde mohair wig. From the popular '40s radio and '50s T.V. shows of the same name. Courtesy Marge Meisinger.

Hollywood all composition 5" doll strung with jointed head, arms, and legs, painted features, flat face, wavy mohair wig, in Lady Lynette costume from the Princess Series c. 1947.

Hollywood 5" all hard plastic "Queen For A Day" fully jointed doll with a flat face, sleep eyes, wavy red mohair wig, and painted white shoes. From the popular radio and T.V. shows of the same name.

Hollywood all hard plastic 5" storybook doll with jointed arms, painted eyes, mohair wig, in a yellow taffeta gown.

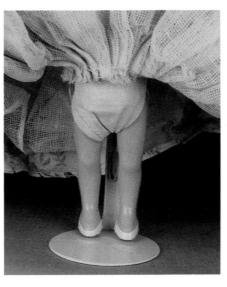

Hollywood all hard plastic 5" storybook doll with fixed legs and painted white shoes.

Close-up of 5" Hollywood hard plastic doll; note the distinctive flat nose and face.

Close-up of Hollywood hard plastic flat face design bride doll.

Hollywood fully jointed hard plastic dolls; original box "Princess Series/Bride".

Wig Characteristics: Wavy mohair glued to head.

Clothes Characteristics: Advertised as "Miniature dolls made and dressed in the latest Hollywood fashions." Well-made clothes with finished hems; panties sewed to body. Some with removable dresses closed with circular donut-shaped snaps.
Value: $45.00; $55.00 in box.

Queen For A Day, Hard Plastic, 5" c. 1947
Marks on Doll: On back, Star "Hollywood Dolls".
Marks on Box: Hollywood Dolls; glued-on fold wrist tag with company name.

Doll Characteristics: Hard plastic 5" fully jointed dolls with sleep eyes, lashes painted above eyes with no molded lashes, and a flat nose; arms with first 4 fingers molded together; shoes painted white.

Dress Characteristics: Good quality satin clothing closing with a donut snap; special Queen For a Day: gown with tulle, lace and velvet trim, finished hem, unfinished seams, stitched closed in the back below dress opening, metal donut-shaped snap. Velvet robe with real bunny fur trim. Cotton panties taped on; soft vinyl crown tied on head.

Wig characteristics: Wavy mohair glued on head with no backing.
Value: $45.00; $55.00 in box.

Toyland Series, 8" c. 1950s
Marks on Doll: On back, Hollywood Doll in star.
Marks on Boxes: A Hollywood Doll/ Toyland Series/HOLLYWOOD DOLL MFG.CO, GLENDALE CALIF; foil wrist tag glued on: Hollywood dolls, doll's name printed.
Doll Characteristics: Hard plastic fully jointed 8" non-walking dolls with sleep eyes and molded lashes, a seam line behind ear, an unusually thick neck, hands with separate fingers, and very thin legs with unusual flush fitting leg joints (possibly flanged), and toe detail. The doll's hands are unusually large in proportion to the body. Note: There may have been other series of 8" Hollywood dolls, but the only boxed examples found to date are from the Toyland Series.
Dress Characteristics: Good quality dresses with a finished hem, unfinished seams, stitched closed in the back below dress opening, and metal donut-shaped snaps. Matching

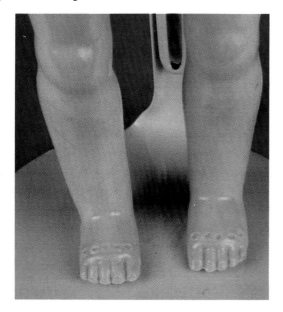

Hollywood 8" hard plastic doll, toe detail with dimples.

Hollywood 8" hard plastic doll in original window box with brochure; Toyland Series, Camellia.

Hollywood 8" hard plastic doll, from the back.

Hollywood 8" hard plastic doll, Toyland Series, Camellia, in lovely pink taffeta gown, tulle and lace trim; lacy straw hat trimmed with lace and flowers.

This undressed 8" Hollywood hard plastic doll from the Toyland Series shows characteristics: non-walker, jointed at head, arms, and legs, sleep eyes with molded lashes, unusual thin arms with large hands, separate fingers, thin legs with toe detail.

Hollywood label from Toyland Series Camellia, blue star trimmed box.

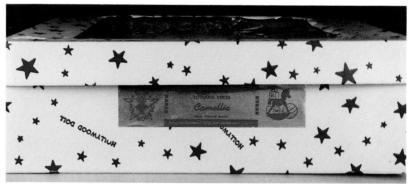

116

panties are sewn to elastic and lace-trimmed at the leg. Good quality straw hats and velveteen side-snap shoes, and socks complete the outfits.

Wig Characteristics: Long wavy synthetic wigs with bangs in blonde, auburn, or brunette were stitched along a backing strip and glued to the doll's head.

Value: $50.00; $60.00 in box.

Lullaby Baby Series 5" c. 1947

Marks on Doll: On back, Star "Hollywood Dolls".
Marks on Box: Hollywood Dolls.
Doll Characteristics: Hard plastic 5" baby with sleep eyes

and lashes painted above eyes (no molded lashes), flat nose; fully jointed, arms and hands with first 4 fingers molded together. Note: There were 12 dolls in the "Lullaby Series." There was also a "Little Baby Series."

Dress Characteristics: Baby Tim gown shown. Good quality pink taffeta gown with lace trim, finished hem, unfinished seams, stitched closed in the back below dress opening.

Wig Characteristics: Molded hair.
Value: $45.00; $55.00 in box.

Hollywood 8" hard plastic doll Toyland Series, Miss Hollywood, in pink-dotted nylon over taffeta gown, black-lace trim; lacy straw hat trimmed with black lace.

Hollywood all hard plastic 5" Baby Tim from Lullaby Baby Series, fully jointed with sleep eyes, molded hair, in pink taffeta gown trimmed with lace. Courtesy Marge Meisinger.

🍇 Ideal Toy Corporation 🍇

Ideal Toy Corporation was founded c. 1910, and quickly became a leader in the doll and toy market. In the late '40s and '50s, Ideal entered the post-war vinyl and hard plastic doll market, and the doll "hits" continued. The list of these dolls is great, but we can point out a few small dolls in their '50s line. The best source for complete information about all Ideal and all of their dolls is *The Collector's Guide to Ideal Dolls* by Judith Izen; First and Second Editions. These are just a few of Ideal's small '50s dolls, but probably the best know.

Lolly 9½" c. 1951 – 1955

One of Ideal's inexpensive, hard plastic play dolls was 9½" Lolly c. 1951, an undressed doll that was a staple in many playrooms.

Marks on Doll: IDEAL DOLL/9.

Boxes Marked: Sold in plastic bags with tag printed: LOLLY/IDEAL'S/WALKING DOLLY/ONLY 98 CENTS.

Doll Characteristics: Inexpensive 9½" hard plastic doll with molded hair, sleep eyes, straight walking legs with pin hip design.

Clothing Characteristics: Sold undressed with no panties in bag.

Wig Characteristics: Molded hair.

Value: $30.00.

Mary Hartline 7½" c. 1951

One of Ideal's lovelist dolls c. 1952 was Mary Hartline from the TV show "Super Circus," adapted from Ideal's Toni doll molds in 15" and up. However, Ideal also included Mary in a petite 7½" size c. 1951.

Marks on Doll: "Ideal" in oval on back.

Boxes Marked: Ideal's Official Mary Hartline Doll. Boxes are red with heart display lid, "Circus cut-outs inside."

Doll Characteristics: Hard plastic 7½" doll with fixed legs, strung head and arms, sleep eyes, Saran wig, and painted white boots.

Dress Characteristics: Mary Hartline wore a short red cotton costume with a music staff stenciled around the hem and "Mary" in a heart on the bodice; closes with buttons in back; matching pants. Note: There were at least two premium versions of Mary Hartline, some by Ideal (see Advertising chapter).

Wig Characteristics: Stiff Saran wig glued on.

Value: $45.00 – 55.00; $90.00+ in retail red cardboard box with heart opening.

Little Betsy Wetsy 8" c. 1957

Ideal specialized in baby dolls, and Betsy Wetsy was one of their most popular. She started out c. 1937 with a hard rubber

Ideal sold an 8" Little Betsy Wetsy only in 1957. She was a drink and wet baby with rooted curly Saran hair.

Ideal's Retail 7½" Mary Hartline doll had fixed legs, strung head and arms, and a Saran wig. Her box had a heart-shaped opening and cut-out figures of circus figures inside.

head and soft rubber body, and by 1954 had a hard plastic head and vinyl body with caracul wig, and by 1956 was an all vinyl toddler with rooted Saran hair from 11½" to 20". Ideal did offer Little Betsy Wetsy in 1957 only in an 8" size.

Marks on Doll: On head and back, IDEAL DOLLS/8; also IDEAL TOY CO./BW9-4.

Boxes Marked: Little Betsy Wetsy/She Drinks, She Wets. Closed boxes had white lids and pink sides, with Little Betsy Wetsy written in blue and pink script.

Doll Characteristics: Ideal offered an 8" Betsy Wetsy only in 1957. She was an all vinyl drinking and wetting doll, fully jointed, with sleep eyes and molded lashes, and 4 tiny painted lashes at corners; fingers closed on left hand, pointing finger on right hand; legs slightly bent with toe detail.

Clothing Characteristics: The basic doll was dressed in a tied-on flannel diaper, a plastic bottle, and white knit socks. Outfits were well, mid market garments mostly using cottons, flannel, knit, and lace; 12 outfits available in separate window boxes.

Wig Characteristics: Rooted curly Saran hair.

Value: $50.00; $60.00 MIB.

Tearie Dearie 9" c. 1963 – 1964

Marks on Doll: Ideal Toy Corporation.

Boxes Marked: Ideal Toy Corporation.

Doll Characteristics: 9" all vinyl jointed baby with sleep eyes, three painted lashes at eye corners, and open mouth nurser. She has rooted Saran hair, and the finger on her right index finger is pointing; legs are slightly bent with toe detail. This doll uses the body from the Betsy Wetsy doll '57.

Clothing Characteristics: Outfits were well-made, mid market garments mostly using cottons, flannel, knit, and lace.

Wig Characteristics: Rooted straight Saran hair.

Value: $40.00.

Ideal's 9" vinyl Tearie Dearie was advertised in 1964 with her plastic crib with folding legs and fitted top for $25. She wears her original nightie.

Ideal's 9" Tearie Dearie crib set included a cotton nightie, bottle, and accessories; shown without socks or shoes.

Ideal's Tearie Dearie c. 1963–67 was a darling vinyl drink and wet baby with sleep eyes and rooted straight Saran hair. She is wearing a cotton pajama set with matching bonnet.

🍇 Kim Dolls 🍇

Kim Dolls operated under the umbrella of Beehler Arts Ltd., and they listed the Beehler Arts address as their own. In 1957, "Kim Dolls, Beehler Arts, Ltd." filed for patent rights to the name "Kim." Interestingly, Kim Dolls sold two entirely different types dolls as "Kim." One was an 8" toddler and one was an 8½" Hi-Heel teen, yet they both used the same type of box in the same color. Further, three different types of doll bodies were used for the Kim toddler, all in the same type box. This is typical of '50s doll marketing in the "look-alike" category and can be confusing to collectors.

Toddlers

Kim Toddler 8" c. 1957

TYPE #1

Marks on Doll: None.

Boxes Marked: Kim (in an oval)/Ready to Dress/ Manufactured by Kim Dolls, 47 West St., New York City; on side of box: I sleep-I have washable hair. Kim doll boxes are the same color as the 1957 blue and gold Virga boxes, but they are thinner for a single undressed doll.

Doll Characteristics: An 8" hard plastic doll with sleep eyes and molded lashes; the mouth painting has a down-turned look at the corners; bent knee walker with toe detail; arms with C-shaped

arm hooks; 2nd and 3rd fingers molded together on the right hand and separate on the left. Note: This is the same doll as A&H's pin-hipped 8" Gigi doll (see A&H section).

Wig Characteristics: Synthetic wigs of good quality stitched to a backing and glued to the head.

TYPE #2

Marks on Doll: None.

Boxes Marked: Kim (in an oval)/Ready to Dress/ Manufactured by Kim Dolls, 47 West St., New York City; on side of box: I sleep-I have washable hair. Kim doll boxes are the same color as the 1957 blue and gold Virga boxes, but they are thinner for a single doll.

Doll Characteristics: Medium or large eyes with molded lashes, mold line through center of ear; arms with C-shaped hooks and separate fingers; bent knee walking legs. Note: This is the same doll as Cosmopolitan's wide eye Ginger doll.

Wig Characteristics: Synthetic wigs of good quality stitched to a backing and glued to the head. One Kim box has been found with a Kim (wide eye Ginger type) doll with a pink wig inside. This is one possibility for identification of the pink hair Ginger dolls found.

Value: Type #1 or #2 : $35.00 undressed; $45.00 in box.

Kim Vinyl Head c. 1956 – 1957

Marks on Doll: Unmarked.

Boxes Marked: KIM/ New! Rooted Hair-Vinyl Doll; Beehler Arts.

Doll Characteristics: 7½" -8" hard plastic doll with vinyl head and sleep eyes. Toe detail unconfirmed.

Kim 8" hard plastic Type #1 with down-turned mouth and ear mold behind the ear. Courtesy Mary Swasey Van Buren.

Kim 8" hard plastic Type #2 with bent knee, wide eye Ginger characteristics and ear mold through center of the ear.

Kim 8" hard plastic Type #2 bent knee doll with pink wig. Possibly sold undressed originally. Courtesy Tina Standish.

Pam and Polly Judd's *Hard Plastic Dolls II*, pg. 141, has a photo of the vinyl head Kim doll and box printed "Vinyl Doll;" appears to be the same as Virga.

Dress Characteristics: These dolls wore Virga doll clothing with donut-shaped snaps.

Wig Characteristics: Rooted hair.

Value: $35.00 undressed; $45.00 in box; $55.00 dressed in box.

Teen Doll

Kim Hi-Heel Teen 8½" c. 1956

Beehler Arts, Ltd., under their Kim Dolls entity, filed for the patented name "Hi-Heel Teen" in June, 1957 on the same day that they filed for the patented name "Kim."

Marks on Doll: Unmarked.

Boxes Marked: Kim/ Ready to Dress, 47 West Street, New York City, NY The folding boxes were blue and gold with a window front.

Doll Characteristics: Hard plastic 8½" tall doll with sleep eyes with molded lashes and high-heel feet. She was a head-turning walker with synthetic wig advertised as "washable hair," jointed at the head, arms, and above the knees; her second and third fingers are molded together. Kim teen had molded breasts but was thin compared with the competitor's 8" and 10½" fashion dolls (see page 218). Also, the lower leg is very thin. Note: Virga sold the identical 8½" high-heel doll in red and gold boxes marked "Hi-Heel Teen" (see Virga section). "Kim Dolls" and Virga were sister Beehler Arts companies.

Dress Characteristics: Stitched back seams closed with circular donut snaps.

Value: $35.00; $45.00 in box.

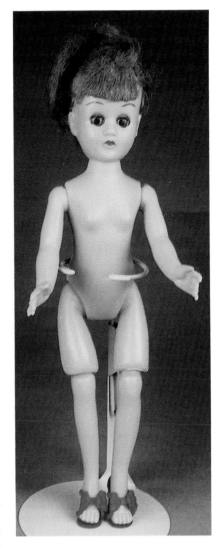

Undressed Kim 8" high-heel teen is the same doll as Virga's 8" "High Heel Teen." Note the thin lower legs characteristic of the Kim high-heel doll.

Kim 8" high-heel teen had the same box as the hard plastic 8" Kim toddler.

🍇 Linda Doll Co. 🍇

Linda Walking Doll 8", 1950s

Marks on Doll: None.

Boxes Marked: "Linda/Walking Doll/Manufactured by Linda Doll, New York City.

Doll Characteristics: Two types of MIB dolls have been found in boxes, but other dolls may have also been used.

TYPE #1: An 8" hard plastic head-turning walking doll with mold line behind ear, sleep eyes with molded lashes, high cheek color; arms with C-shaped arm hooks and 2nd and 3rd fingers molded together or can be slightly separated on left depending on unmolding; prominent mold lines on arms; straight legs with flat, smooth feet with no toe or shoe detail. Note: This is the same straight leg walking doll as A & H's Lisa doll.

TYPE #2: An 8" hard plastic head-turning walking doll with mold line through center of ear, sleep eyes with molded lashes, high cheek color; straight arms with C-shaped arm hooks and separate fingers; legs with bending knees and toe detail. Note: This is a bent knee wide eye Ginger Type #5 doll.

Clothes Characteristics: Sold undressed in box with lace trimmed panties.

Wig Characteristics: Wigs with stitched parts sewn to a strip backing and glued to head.

Value: $40.00 doll only; $55.00 – 65.00 in box.

Original pink folding window box is printed "Manufactured by Linda Doll, New York City," and marked, "L-100."

Straight leg walking Linda Type #1 by Linda Dolls, has sleep eyes and smooth feet with no shoe or toe detail.

Bending knee walking Linda Type #2 with sleep eyes and toe detail; dress may be original. Courtesy Linda Chervenka.

🍇 Marlon Creations 🍇

Very little is written about Marlon Creations, Long Island City, New York. One of their tagged dolls was an 11" musical newborn baby doll with vinyl head, hands, and feet with a key-wind music box playing Brahm's Lullaby. Research also shows that a company named "Marion Creations" (with an 'i'), also from Long Island City, NY, filed for a patent for the name "Newborn Baby" in 1961, so perhaps this is the same company. Another doll tagged "Marlon Creations" was an 8" vinyl '50s or '60s baby closely resembling Vogue's 8" Ginnette. This writer would welcome knowing about any other boxed examples of this doll and their marks.

8" Baby Doll

Marks on Doll: Unmarked doll; one identical doll marked "Baby Susan" on neck was found in a Marlon Creations box.

Boxes Marked: Pink folding window boxes and wrist tags are marked, "Marlon Creations, Inc.// Long Island City 1, NY". Doll's name not printed on box.

Doll Characteristics: This unmarked 8" all soft vinyl baby c. 1960s is a drink and wet doll with molded hair. The sleep eyes have molded eye lashes, and most also have lashes painted under the eyes. Her fingers are straight on both hands with 2nd and 3rd fingers molded together. Note: Marlon's unmarked baby doll is the same soft vinyl doll as those marked "Baby Susan" with or without lashes painted under the eyes (see Hard Plastic & Vinyl Dolls, pg. 113).

Since one soft vinyl "Baby Susan" has been found in a Marlon Creations box, this may indicate a relationship between the doll and that company.

Dress Characteristics: The printed nylon dress ties at the neck in back with no snap and has a matching bonnet. One cotton dress found has a thin rolled and stitched hem, ties at the neck in back, and closes at the waist with a plain metal snap.

Wig Characteristics: Molded hair.

Value: $45.00 doll only; $65.00 in box.

Note: Eegee sold a marked 10½" vinyl nursing doll named "Baby Susan" (see Eegee section), but it is not clear if they also sold this 8" doll marked "Baby Susan;" also see pg. 113, Hard Plastic & Vinyl Dolls section, for a rigid vinyl baby, marked "Baby Susan" on neck.

This 8" soft vinyl, fully jointed baby is unmarked in Marlon Creations box. She has molded hair, sleep eyes, and molded lashes with lashes painted under the eyes; slightly bent legs with toe detail. Her box is marked "#48/42 Flower Print Nylon Outfit."

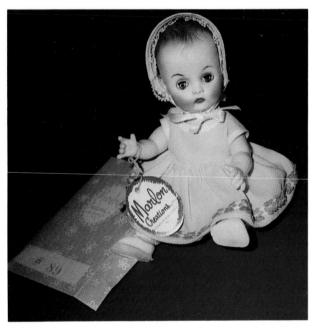

This soft vinyl 8" baby doll marked "Baby Susan" on the neck was found in a Marlon Creations box marked #89. Note that this doll has no lower lashes painted under her eyes. Her darling yellow dress closes with a plain metal snap at the waist and ties at the neck in back. Courtesy Linda Chervenka.

❦ Mayfair Products Ltd. ❦

Mayfair Products Ltd. of Ontario, Canada, made small mid-market dolls in the pre-Barbie '50s, but is not well known in the U.S. Here are two examples of Mayfair's small dolls.

Teen

Debbie 8" c. mid-1950s
Marks on Doll: Unmarked.
Boxes Marked: "Hi/I'm/ Debbie/Mayfair" on cardboard, "travel wardrobe-trunk" with carrying handle and clothes hangers.
Doll Characteristics: An 8" all vinyl, fully jointed 8" doll with wide sleep eyes and molded lashes, blushed cheeks; Saran rooted hair; arms with separate fingers with palms facing the body; high-heel feet; painted fingernails and toenails. She was a very stylish and petite teenage doll advertised as "Your teen doll by Mayfair," and also as "Canada's New Glamour Doll." She was "available at your favorite toy counter," and a competitor of Little Miss Revlon, Madame Alexander's Cissette, and other small U.S. and Canadian fashion dolls. Her equivalent in the U.S. would have been Little Miss Marie, or Little Miss Ginger, but her mold was unique.
Clothing Characteristics: The basic Debbie was dressed in "bra, crinoline, panty-girdle and high heel shoes." She had over 32 outfits pictured in her brochure/flyer, most had hats, some had handbags, all had vinyl high heels. Her mid-market clothes were well-made with hems and Mayfair labels. Taffeta gown closed with a smooth round painted snap; cotton clothes closed with a circular white donut-shaped snap. Slips were not attached. Mayfair also sold separately boxed shoes and underwear for Debbie.

Mayfair 8" Debbie in one-piece strapless gown with "rhinestone" on bodice and white vinyl high heels. Her matching white hat is trimmed with a flower and has white veil. This gown is tagged Mayfair but is not shown in the Debbie brochure/flyer.

Close-up of 8" Debbie high-heel doll's face.

Advertisement for Mayfair's 8" Debbie, Canada's high-heel glamour doll, and trunk.

Mayfair 8" Debbie in cardboard case marked "#800 Debbie/Honey" wearing taffeta half-slip and taffeta halter. "Mayfair's Debbie" is printed on the front of the half-slip in faint red lettering.

124

Mayfair's dress tag.

Mayfair's 8" Debbie in plaid corduroy Coat Ensemble #803 with matching pants, coat, and hat with black high heels; shown with original cardboard case. Courtesy Jo Barckley.

Mayfair's 8" Debbie in pink cotton check dress "Shopping #822" with straw hat trimmed with flowers.

Back of Debbie dress closing with circular donut snap.

Wig Characteristics: Saran rooted hair was in short or shoulder length bobs, and hair colors were primarily brunette or blonde.
Value: $45.00; $95.00+ in trunk all original.

Baby

Little Darling
Marks on Doll: Unmarked.
Boxes Marked: "Mayfair's/Little/Darling" printed on cardboard travel wardrobe-trunk with carrying handle.
Doll Characteristics: An 8" fully jointed baby doll with vinyl head and legs and rigid vinyl arms and body; open nursing mouth with wetting hole in the lower back; vinyl head had sleep eyes with molded lashes, molded hair; separate fingers on left hand, and 2nd and 3rd fingers on the right are molded up to tips which are separate; slightly curved baby legs with dimples on the knees and toe detail. She is a cute Ginnette look-alike baby doll.
Clothes Characteristics: Well-made mid-market outfits, with hems and back seams stitched below dress opening; circular metal donut-shaped snaps. Outfits included organdy dresses, cotton romper sets, flannel nightie sets, and velveteen overall sets.
Wig Characteristics: Molded hair.
Value: $40.00; $65.00 in trunk all original.

Mayfair's 8" Little Darling blue bassinet with outfits: pink cotton duster, blue organdy dress with lace and satin bow trim; blue check romper, plastic bottle in pink and blue vinyl holder. The swan hangers are original.

Nine outfits in Debbie brochure.

Eleven outfits in Debbie brochure.

Mayfair's 8" Little Darling vinyl baby with cardboard carrying trunk.

❦ Mego Corporation ❦

Mego was the well-known maker of small celebrity dolls and action figures such as Batman and Robin c. 1972 and many others in the '70s. However, Mego put together products and promotions as early as 1952, according to Marty Abrams, who led Mego through its heyday as president and chairman of the family business while in his '30s. Regarding the company's legendary name, Abrams recalls that "Mego Too" or similar wording, was the company's telex number in the '50s, hence the doll's name. Also, the founder's young son (Abrams father) would call out, "Me go too, Me go too" wherever the family went, hence the name Mego. Perhaps both are the case.

To explain why a '50s toddler doll would have the name Mego printed on the box, an item totally outside their famed product lines of the '60s and '70s, we turn to the company's history. Abrams explains that products Mego promoted in the early '50s included housewares as well as toys purchased from other companies. The toys were promoted through newspaper ads for "Boys Toys" and "Girls Toys" in large block newspaper ads featuring 50-70 different toys priced at 88 cents each. This writer has found at least three toddler dolls advertised by Mego in the '50s, well before their action figure stage. Understanding Mego's part in distributing these '50s toddler dolls and learning how the company mixed various toddler lines for sale is important. It will help toddler collectors to understand how Mego's packaging, outfitting, regrouping, and/or renaming of familiar dolls differed from their original manufacturer's line. The research on Mego toddler dolls is ongoing, but this is what is known to date.

Julie 8" c. 1958 – 1964

While Julie is not found among Mego's patented names, 8" toddler "Julie" dolls are found today in boxes marked "MEGO CORP-NEW YORK CITY." Mr. Abrams reports that Mego acted as Julie's distributor for A&H c. 1958. The Julie boxes marked MEGO use the same descriptive wording as Julie boxes marked A&H (see A&H section). This is one additional example of the often-confusing interrelationships between '50s doll companies that doll collectors are trying to sort out today.

Marks on Doll: Unmarked.

Boxes Marked: MEGO CORP- NEW YORK CITY. The yellow print on lavender box has an Easter Bunny and Easter egg design with printing: "I Am Julie/* I Walk/ * I Sit, * I Sleep/ * Dress Me/ * Curl My Hair." Note: This is the exact wording on A&H's "Julie" boxes. The Easter box design was part of Mego's Julie promotions.

Julie by Mego Type #1 with blonde Mindy type head and molded T-strap shoes in front of her special lavender and yellow Easter design box.

Close-up of face for Julie Type #1 by Mego. This is the same head (not body) used for Mindy Type #1.

Doll Characteristics:

TYPE #1: Medium or wide eye Mindy type heads with mold line behind the ear, C-shaped arm hooks and separate finger tips on left hand, and 2nd and 3rd molded together on the right. However, they have T-strap molded shoes instead of toe detail like Mindy. Note: Mego's Julie Type #1 has the same head and body as A&H's "pastel hair" Gigi dolls.

TYPE #2: Hard plastic toddler doll with 8" Ginger characteristics: Medium or wide eyes with molded lashes, straight leg walking doll with toe detail, C-shaped arm hook with separate fingers and mold line through center of the ear. Note:

Mego may have utilized other dolls for Julie as shown in Pat Smith's *Modern Collector's Dolls*, 7th Series, pg. 142.

Wig Characteristics: Synthetic wig sewn onto a thin backing strip and glued to the head; both shiny and dull style wigs are used.

Dress Characteristics: Undressed dolls sold in Mego's Easter boxes wore organdy or taffeta panties trimmed in picot. Separate dresses in Mego's "Julie's Easter Outfit" box were stitched closed below back dress opening, waist and back seams were factory finished with overcast stitching, and closed with a donut-shaped round metal snap painted white.

Two Julie boxes are marked Mego however, the dolls appear to be neither Type #1 or Type #2 Mego Julie, so possibly there was a third type of Julie. Courtesy Frasher's Doll Auction catalog.

End of box for Mego Julie printed: MEGO CORP. NEW YORK CITY.

Julie Type #2 brunette (on left) has Ginger characteristics with toe detail vs. Julie Type #1 (on right) with T-strap molded feet. Both came undressed in identical lavender and yellow Easter design boxes marked MEGO.

Close-ups of brunette Julie Type #2 (on left) with Ginger characteristics and mold line through center of ear vs. blonde Julie Type #1 (on right) with Mindy head and mold line behind the ear and mouth paint with down-turned corners.

Julie Type #2 in "English" outfit with cotton print skirt, and white organdy bodice, tie-on apron, lace-edged shawl, and mobcap with red bow. Unmarked side-snap vinyl shoes and socks are included. The dress is untagged and has a circular donut snap.

Julie's separate outfit in folding window "Easter Outfit" box is stamped "English." The box has a folding cardboard "handle" on top.

Little MeGo Too 8" hard plastic (Ginger type) doll with vinyl head and rooted hair in cellophane bag distributed by Mego (not printed on bag.)

Value: Doll $55.00; $75.00 mint in Mego Easter box, difficult to find. Separate boxed outfit $40.00 – $50.00, difficult to find.

"Little Mego Too" or Lil' Megotoo 8" c. 1955 – 1960

According to Mr. Abrams, Mego promoted an 8" vinyl headed (Ginger type) walking doll as "Little Mego Too." She was advertised for 88 cents in large block newspaper advertisements along with other toys and merchandise. These Ginger vinyl head dolls were probably purchased from Cosmopolitan,

and the outfits pictured were a mixture of dresses bought from other doll companies' first quality lines.

Marks on Doll: None.

Boxes Marked: Dolls were sold in cellophane bags attached to cardboard printed: 8" Plastic Doll/ "Little MeGo Too"/Vinyl Head-Rooted Hair. Other variations appear in advertising as "Lil' Megotoo, etc."

Doll Characteristics: These were inexpensive Ginger dolls, probably purchased from Cosmopolitan, with vinyl head and rooted hair. They were sold undressed.

Clothing Characteristics: A 1958 newspaper advertisement shows a collection of eight costumes. They are a mixture of outfits purchased from other companies, including Ninette's Tea Party costume.

Wig Characteristics: Rooted hair.

Value: $40.00 in bag.

Randi 8" c. 1955

An 8" hard plastic, straight leg Ginger type doll was advertised as "Randi" in large newspaper ads c. 1955. The large 88 cent blocks fit Mego's format, so it is assumed that they are Mego's ads. Mego reportedly bought and distributed these Randi dolls, so the outfits shown in the ad may vary from those Duchess offered for Randi. (See Duchess section for description under Randi Type #2.)

Value: $40.00.

Atlanta Journal Davison's advertisement, November, 1958 for "Little Mego Too" and eight costumes for 88 cents each. Aldens also sold this doll in their '58 mail order catalog. Similar ads offered Randi, an 8" hard plastic doll, for 88¢. Courtesy Marge Meisinger.

🍇 Midwestern Mfg. Co. 🍇

Display Dolls

Midwestern sold inexpensive hard plastic dolls in the 1950s. Among their early lines were 7" display dolls advertised on box flyers which listed several series: Twelve Little Ladies (12 dolls); Jean and Johnny; Pretty Girls That Tell a Story (19 dolls); Lovely Brides and their Bride-Maids dolls including Red Cross (8 and Nun); South of the Border; and Festivals (8 holiday dolls). Perhaps they sold other display dolls as well.

Mary Jean Snow Princess c. 1950s
Marks on Doll: Unmarked.
Boxes Marked: The Lovely Mary Jean Doll/Created in the/Junior Fashion Center of America of America/Midwestern Mfg. Co./St. Louis, MO./Originators of the Lovely Mary Jean Doll.
Doll Characteristics: Painted eye 7" hard plastic doll dolls with fixed head; legs with painted-on black shoes with no bow detail; painted side-glancing eyes, strung arms. Flyer in the box says, "Collect one after another and put them in the lovely Mary Jean Doll Collector Cabinet." Note: This is the same basic hard plastic, painted eye display doll that Virga boxed and sold in the '40s and '50s (see Virga section).
Dress Characteristics: Wavy mohair glued to the head.
Value: $25.00 in box.

Toddler Doll

Mary Jean 7½" c. 1950s
Marks on Doll: Unmarked.
Boxes Marked: Mary Jean/A Product of Midwestern Mfg. Co., St. Louis, MO. The folded dark pink and blue boxes had an acetate window display front.
Doll Characteristics: Mary Jean is a 7½" (box says 8") hard plastic doll with Ginger Type #4 characteristics including wide

Midwestern's 7" hard plastic "Snow Princess #551" display doll from the "Pretty Girls" series has strung arms, red wavy mohair wig, and a white satin gown trimmed in green with feather on front; she has a sparkle "snow ball" wired to her wrist. She is in her original box.

Feet with molded ring, no bow, painted black, c. 1950s.

Label from Midwestern Snow Princess, marked on end of box.

sleep eyes, molded lashes, mold seams through center of the ear, and C-shaped arm hooks with separate fingers. She apparently had a walker body, but Midwestern removed the walking mechanism (perhaps to lower cost), and she was strung through the hole in her neck that once held the walking rods. This arrangement gives her a "no neck" look, and legs swing but her head does not move. Her straight legs have toes that are painted white, a very good clue to the doll's identification.

Clothing Characteristics: Her clothes are removeable and inexpensively made. The skirt is made of cotton, turned and hemmed, stitched and gathered onto a ribbon; the fabric bodice has unfinished armholes, is stitched inside the skirt and under the waist band, closing with a handsewn square metal snap. She wears socks and vinyl unmarked side-snap shoes over her painted feet, and some Mary Jean dolls have stapled-on hair ribbons. Note: This 7½" doll is basically the same as Admiration's Carol Sue, but has removeable clothes instead of stapled-on clothes like Carol Sue.

Wig Characteristics: Wavy hair glued directly to the head, not stitched to a backing.

Value: $40.00 – 45.00 dressed doll only; $75.00 in box, hard to find.

Janie 8" c. 1950s

Midwestern sold a hard plastic 8" Janie doll in the '50, but at least one other doll marker also sold a Janie doll. That maker was Uneeda, and their Janie came in both a hard plastic and vinyl head version (see Uneeda section).

Marks on Doll: None.

Boxes Marked: Janie Walking Doll/A product of Midwestern Mfg. Co., St. Louis, MO./8" Walking Doll/Dynel Hair/To Comb and Wash. Boxes were red and white wide striped boxes with a window lid.

Janie, an 8" hard plastic Ginger type doll in window box labeled "Product of Midwestern Mfg. Co., St Louis, MO." Courtesy of Judy Cullen.

Midwestern's Mary Jean, 7½" hard plastic toddler doll c. 1954 in her original box; she is a jointed but non-walking doll with large eye Ginger characteristics. Her dress is removable, and her toes are painted white underneath socks and shoes.

Midwestern's Mary Jean 7½" hard plastic toddler doll c. '54 with painted white feet under her shoes and socks.

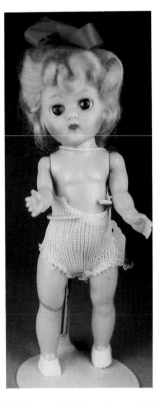

Midwestern's Mary Jean c. '54 wears inexpensive knit panties under her dress.

131

Doll Characteristics: The only example seen was an 8" hard plastic, small eye Ginger type doll with sleep eyes, molded lashes, C-shaped arm hooks, and feet with toe detail. Midwestern may have sold other dolls in Janie boxes.

Dress Characteristics: Inexpensively made dresses. One example was a ballerina with a pink lace ballerina dress.

Wig Characteristics: Dynel wigs in typical shoulder length bob.

Value: MIB $100.00+.

Junior Doll Fashions

Separate clothing cards are found today reading, "Junior Doll Fashions, Fits any 8 inch Doll/Product of Midwestern Mfg. Co., St. Louis, MO." They sold for 29 cents each. Cellophane bags were fastened to the card with dresses on individual plastic doll hangers. These were probably sold for Midwestern's Mary Jean dolls, but the inexpensive outfits would fit any Ginny look-alike.

Teen Doll

All American Girl Series 8"

Marks on Doll: Unmarked.

Marks on Box: "8" Walking Doll (on front)/All American Girl Series/A Product of/Midwestern Mfg., St. Louis, MO. (on bottom);" uses same shaped folding window box as Midwestern's Mary Jean.

Doll Characteristics: 8" hard plastic pin-hipped walker, thin doll with sleep eyes, painted lashes, and jointed head and arms; walking legs.

Dress Characteristics: Stapled-on and unfinished dresses; stapled-on felt hats or bows.

Value: $25.00 – 35.00 in box.

Label on 8" Janie Midwestern walking doll in red and white striped box printed "Janie." Courtesy Judy Cullen.

Box bottom of Midwestern's "All American Girl Series" 8" pin-hipped walking doll.

Janie, an 8" hard plastic Ginger type doll in window box labeled "Product of Midwestern Mfg. Co., St. Louis, Mo." Courtesy of Judy Cullen.

Midwestern's "All American Girl Series," 8" Walking Doll, a pin-hipped walker with sleep eyes and stapled-on clothes.

Close-up of "All American Girl" showing pin-hipped walker mechanism.

🍇 Nancy Ann Storybook Dolls 🍇

Nancy Ann Abbott created Nancy Ann Storybook (NASB) dolls c. 1936 with her business partner Leslie Rowland. By the 1950s the NASB hard plastic line included Storybook dolls, the Muffie and Lori-Ann toddler dolls, gorgeous fashion dolls, style show dolls, and others. The company was sold in 1966, but their dolls have a huge following today. We highlight here their small dolls of the '40s and '50s.

Storybook Dolls c. 1936

NASB tiny dolls lived up to the company's name with charming storybook themes as well as other popular series so loved over the years. The tiny 3" – 7" dolls were one of the most copied doll styles in the '40s and '50s.

Marks on Dolls: c. 1941: STORY/BOOKDOLL/U.S.A.
Later Dolls: STORYBOOK/DOLL/USA/PATENT/PEN.
Boxes Marked: Early boxes had pink, blue, red or white backgrounds, with silver or gold or white dots. Later dolls had white backgrounds with pink, blue, red or silver dots. Beginning in '48 the words "Nancy Ann Story Book" was printed around the dots. Foil box tags had outfit name and number and the NASB brochure in box. After 1940 the dolls had a round foil tag tied to the wrist with the company name on one side and name and number of the doll on the other.

Doll Characteristics: The first Storybook dolls were strung 3" – 7" bisque dolls with hand-painted faces. Most had fixed heads, but 7" dolls had bisque socket heads. Some had fixed legs, but others had jointed arms and legs. These dolls were cute but had the problem of breakage and peeling, and the sewn-on and glued-on clothes limited play value. Beginning in late c. 1948, hard plastic materials were phased into production for the 3½" – 4½" painted eye dolls with moveable heads and jointed arms and legs. They are often mistaken for bisque because of the paint color. All hard plastic 4½" – 6½" dolls with sleep eyes were introduced c. 1950 with moving heads, and jointed arms and legs. The plastic color varied widely from waxy to clear to yellowish. Hard plastic 3½" – 4½" baby dolls with sleep eyes and molded hair were introduced c. 1949 and made until c. '53.

Wig Characteristics: NASB bisque dolls had wavy mohair wigs sewn to a strip of cloth backing and glued to the head in blonde, brunette, and reddish colors.

Dress Characteristics: Early '40s dresses were sewn-on with pantaloons glued-on. In the '50s dresses were removeable with smooth round brass snaps.

Values: Storybook 1941-47: Child $75.00; Baby $140.00; Storybook, hard plastic after '47: Child $35.00 – 50.00; Baby $75.00+. More for special dolls such as black or special outfits.

Toddlers

Muffie 8" c. 1953

In 1953 NASB introduced an 8" hard plastic toddler doll to compete with Vogue's Ginny, Alexander's Wendy, and other look-alikes flooding the market. Muffie had a distinctive look and was very cute. *continued on page 139*

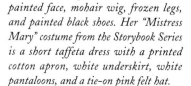

NASB 5½" bisque doll c. 1940s with painted face, mohair wig, frozen legs, and painted black shoes. Her "Mistress Mary" costume from the Storybook Series is a short taffeta dress with a printed cotton apron, white underskirt, white pantaloons, and a tie-on pink felt hat.

NASB 5½" bisque doll c. 1943 with painted face, mohair wig, frozen legs, and peeling face, a problem with poor storage. She is marked STORY-BOOK/DOLL/USA and wears "Tuesday's Child is Full of Grace" from the Dolls of the Day Series. Her pink dotted Swiss dress over taffeta is lace-trimmed with a felt tie-on bonnet.

NASB 5½" bisque doll c. 1940s with painted face, mohair wig with jointed arms and legs, painted black shoes, and mohair wig. Her "Queen of Hearts" #157 has a red taffeta bodice and white net skirt over taffeta. A large red felt heart accents the skirt and is stapled to the head for a hat. She has her original red dot box.

NASB 5½" doll c. 1940s in "Valentine Sweetheart" box that originally had a special die-cut heart insert. Taffeta dotted skirt has a felt heart trim at the hem. Original brochure in the box. Courtesy Marge Meisinger.

NASB 5½" hard plastic doll c. 1950 with jointed arms and legs, moveable head, and mohair wig, wearing "Bridesmaid" #87, a taffeta gown with tulle overskirt, from Family Series with sleep eyes, jointed arms and legs, and moveable head. Pearl barrette and original wrist tag.

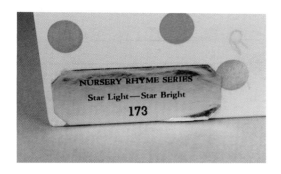

Star Light, Star Bright silver label on blue dotted box.

NASB 5½" hard plastic doll c. 1950 with mohair wig wears "Monday's Child," a printed yellow taffeta gown with blue lace trim, and blue felt hat.

NASB 5½" hard plastic doll Storybook Series "Star Light, Star Bright" #173 c. 1948 with painted eyes and wavy blonde mohair wig, coloring looks like bisque, has jointed arms and legs, and a moveable head. The long blue gown is dotted silver with wide lace, silver band trim around the hem, and a lace shawl. A wand with a star on top is tied to her wrist. A transitional bisque doll with plastic arms was also dressed in this outfit and can be confused with the all-plastic doll.

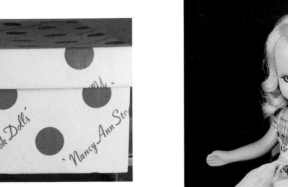

Original red dot box and label for NASB 5½" Valentine Sweetheart hard plastic doll.

NASB 5½" hard plastic "Alice Thru the Looking Glass" #119 from the Mother Goose series wears a long blue check dress, white organdy apron, and pink hair ribbon.

NASB 5½" hard plastic doll c. 1954 in "Valentine Sweetheart" box with special die-cut heart insert.

NASB 5½" hard plastic "Alice Thru the Looking Glass" #102 variation in a shorter blue dress, white organdy apron, and original hair ribbon in original box. Courtesy Marge Meisinger.

NASB 5½" hard plastic "Queen of Hearts" #157 doll with sleep eyes and mohair wig c. 1950s in taffeta heart print dress; original wrist tag.

NASB 6½" hard plastic "May" from Dolls of the Month Series wears a yellow flowered organdy skirt over taffeta trimmed with lace and a picture hat.

Original NASB red dot box with #401 label, 1950s.

NASB 6½" hard plastic "A Pretty Girl is Like a Melody" #401 from All Time Hit Parade Series, 1950s, with sleep eyes and mohair wig, wears a dotted pink organdy dress trimmed with pink satin ribbon and picture hat. Original brochure.

Back of "Pretty Girl" gown, showing the round metal NASB snap.

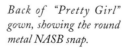

Close-up of "Pretty Girl," showing painted lashes over sleep eyes.

NASB 6½" hard plastic doll in original "When Irish Eyes Are Smiling" #404 wears a printed nylon gown over taffeta with wide lace and green satin ribbon trim, and picture hat. Original brochure, wrist tag, and red dot box, 1950s.

Close-up of "Irish Eyes" showing special molded lashes.

NASB 4½" hard plastic "First Birthday" c. 1950 organdy outfit with matching cap and white painted shoes. Courtesy Marge Meisinger.

NASB 3½" hard plastic baby with sleep eyes and molded hair, wearing #150 Christening Dress c. 1950s. Courtesy Marge Meisinger.

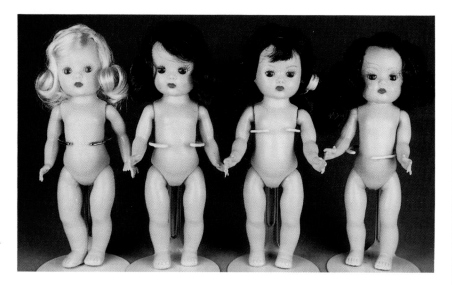

Muffie (L to R): Type #1: '53 strung blonde with no eyebrows. Type #2: '54 straight leg walking Muffie with no eyebrows. Type #3: '55-'56 straight leg walking Muffie with eyebrows. Not shown: Type #4 c. '56 was the same as #3 with or without bending knees. Type #5: '57 varied widely, this one is strung & unmarked; others walkers and marked.

Type #6: '68 International Series, hard plastic Muffie.

Muffie, close-up head photos (L to R): Type #1 strung with no brows, Type #2 walker with no brows, Type #3 walker with brows.

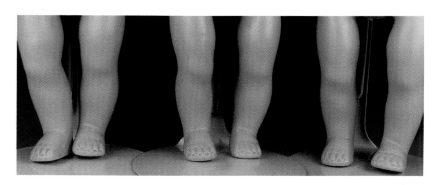

Muffie close-up of feet (L to R): Type #1, Type #2, Type #3. (Same type feet for Types # 4 & Type #5.) All have toe detail with dimples.

Type #6: '68 International Series Muffie face.

Doll Marks: On back: 1953-54-Storybook/Dolls/California; 1954 (some), '55-'56-Storybook/Dolls/California/Muffie. 1957 & after: Marked as '55-'56 and unmarked 1968 Int'l. Series-unmarked.

Marks on Boxes: White boxes with dots of pink, blue or red with "Nancy Ann Storybook Dolls" written between the dots.

Doll Characteristics: All dolls had hard plastic bodies with sleep eyes and toe detail. Her arms had separate fingers, and metal loops for stringing instead of plastic arm hooks. They had hard plastic heads until '56 when vinyl heads were introduced. Facial features and other characteristics also changed over time.

Type #1 '53: strung, straight legs, no eyebrows, lashes painted over eyes.

Type #2 '54: walker, straight legs, head turns, no eyebrows, lashes painted over eye & molded lashes (both).

Type #3 '55: walker, straight legs, head turns, painted eyebrows added, molded lashes and painted lashes (both).

Type #4 '56: walker, straight legs and bent knees, eyebrows painted & molded lashes. (Including pastel wig Muffies.)

Type #5 '57 on: varied widely, marked and unmarked, walkers and strung, etc.

Type #6 '68: International Series, "Muffie Around the World," walker, wide set straight legs, head turns, molded lashes & lashes painted under eyes.

Dress Characteristics (not including less well-made '68 International Series): *Dress Quality:* Muffie's high quality styles beginning in '53 used fine fabrics and trims like rick-rack and lace. Dresses were all tagged. *Necklines:* Round, scoop, square or with attached collars; square bibs were favorites. *Sleeves:* Mostly cap sleeves; a few elbow and wrist-length with no shoulder seams. *Skirts:* Full with tiny pleats for gathers, stitched with straight stitches at waist seams. The back skirt seam was left open. Most '53 dresses were mid-calf length. Later dresses were knee-length. *Slips:* Cotton, taffeta or organdy petticoats were attached on most styles, however some cotton dresses had no attached slips. *Pants:* Mostly taffeta straight-cut pants with lace-trimmed loose leg openings. Elastic at the waist was left exposed. *Finishes:* Deep hems were turned and sewn with straight stitching. The back skirt seam was left open with fabric edges turned and stitched to finish. The unfinished back seam edge at the hemline had a distinctive diagonal cut. Some dressy styles have the attached slips

sewn together in back seam. The waistline fabric edges were unfinished. *Closures:* 1953 & '54: Small, smooth brass snaps; 1955: Small, round painted snaps; 1956: Painted donut-shaped snaps.

Wig Characteristics: While the doll changed over time, the wigs remained basically the same through 1956 when rooted styles were also introduced. *continued on page 151*

Muffie dress closures were smooth round snaps in 1953 and 1954 like snap on the right and painted round snaps in '55. In 1956, circular donut-shaped snaps were added like snap on the left.

Inside Muffie dress: Back seam left open, turned back, stitched down with a diagonal cut at hem; unfinished waist seam; deep hem; with and without attached slip, tiny pleats for gathers.

Muffie wigs had a single row of stitching along a thin strip backing; both side part and center parts, curls or braids.

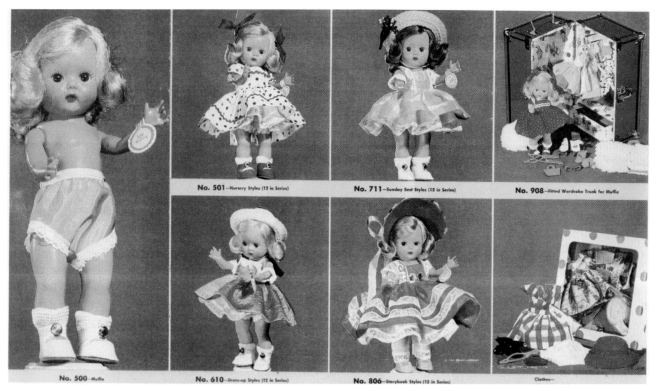

No. 501—Nursery Styles (12 in Series)

No. 711—Sunday Best Styles (12 in Series)

No. 908—Fitted Wardrobe Trunk for Muffie

No. 500—Muffie

No. 610—Dress-up Styles (12 in Series)

No. 806—Storybook Styles (12 in Series)

Clothes—

1953 brochure: Undressed strung Muffie #500; '53 Nursery Style dotted dress #501; Blue "DressUp" outfit #610; Muffie Sunday Best #711 gold dress and hat; #806 Storybook Style #806 pink lace-trimmed dress with pantalettes, matching bonnet; '53 boxed ensemble.

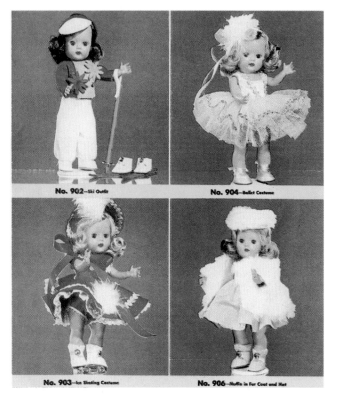

No. 902—Ski Outfit

No. 904—Ballet Costume

No. 903—Ice Skating Costume

No. 906—Muffie in Fur Coat and Hat

1953 Muffie brochure: Ski outfit #902, Ice Skating Costume #903, Fur coat and hat #906.

Strung Muffie in 1953 brochure: Special style #901, printed cotton sunsuit trimmed with blue braid. The doll came barefoot but originally had a tie-on felt bonnet and sunglasses.

1954 Muffie brochure, head turning walker dolls.

1954 Muffie brochure, head turning walker dolls.

#801 – 808 not shown.

muffie's special occasion styles

THEY WALK!

809   810   811   812   901   902   903

wardrobe chest and trunk

THEY WALK!

907   908

muffie's separate accessories

THEY WALK!

915   916   917   918   919   920   921   Undressed Muffie with some of her wardrobes

1954 Muffie brochure, head turning walker dolls.

Nancy Ann Storybook Dolls 🍇

(L) Muffie with light green hair c. 1956 ($675.00); (R) 1953 Muffie Storybook costume with wide red striped skirt, red bodice, and bonnet ($575.00). Prices realized courtesy Frasher's Doll Auctions.

Brunette Muffie with 1953 outfitted blue dotted cardboard chest #907 ($1100.00); (R) Brunette Muffie in pink taffeta dress ($270.00). Prices realized courtesy Frasher's Doll Auctions.

Muffie in 1953 Gay Cotton Prints #501, red lace-trimmed bodice with red print skirt. Courtesy Marge Meisinger.

Muffie in 1954 "Favorite Fashions" #607 red and white striped cotton with white collar with matching beret. Shoes were a center-snap style. Courtesy Marge Meisinger.

Muffie wears 1954 Dress-Up Style #707 white organdy over taffeta trimmed with embroidered braid, pink straw hat trimmed with satin ribbon, and pink center-snap shoes. Courtesy Shirley's Dollhouse.

Muffie Type #2 walker with no eyebrows, c. 1954, "Favorite Fashions" #608, flowered organdy dress trimmed with braid, ribbon, and lace with a blue straw bonnet trimmed with flowers. Shoes in brochure were center-snap style.

Muffie in variation of 1954 "Muffie's Dress-Up Style" #701 with magenta bodice, matching ruffled sleeves, and flowered print skirt. Separate blue geometric print fabric is from 1955 "Dress-Up Style" #703, but with red braid trim.

1954-56 Type #3 Muffie walkers with eyebrows, in original boxes. Courtesy McMasters Doll Auctions.

Undressed Type #3 Muffie walking doll c. 1955 with original box marked "Muffie Undressed/Auburn." This label type is typical of '55/'56 labels. Separate blue dot outfit in box. Muffie realized $425.00 at McMasters Auction.

Muffie Type #3 walker in brunette ponytail style wig wears 1955 "Favorite Fashions" #607, a dotted brown polished cotton dress trimmed with gold rick-rack with matching yellow straw hat. This is a matching outfit to big sister 10" Debbie.

Davy Crockett straight leg walking Muffie c. '55 (left) wears two-piece fringed suedecloth costume and cap closed with brown leather belt with belt, pin, gun, and transfers ($435.00); Davy Crockett Muffie (right) in brown fur cap and brown vinyl side-snap shoes, red dotted box marked Davy Crockett. Original red dot box marked "#940 Davy Crockett." ($240.00). Prices realized courtesy Frasher's Doll Auctions.

Muffie Valentine special doll in 1955 was presented in a special heart insert box. Muffie wears a white dress with red felt heart appliqué on bodice. Courtesy Marge Meisinger.

DRESS-UP STYLES

| 701 Dressed Doll 4.29 | 703 Dressed Doll 4.29 | 705 Dressed Doll 4.29 | 707 Dressed Doll 4.29 |
| 701X Outfit Only 2.50 | 703X Outfit Only 2.50 | 705X Outfit Only 2.50 | 707X Outfit Only 2.50 |

| 702 Dressed Doll 4.29 | 704 Dressed Doll 4.29 | 706 Dressed Doll 4.29 | 708 Dressed Doll 4.29 |
| 702X Outfit Only 2.50 | 704X Outfit Only 2.50 | 706X Outfit Only 2.50 | 708X Outfit Only 2.50 |

SPECIAL OCCASION STYLES

| 802 Dressed Doll 3.59 | 804 Dressed Doll 4.29 | 806 Dressed Doll 4.29 | 808 Dressed Doll 4.29 |
| 802X Outfit Only 1.98 | 804X Outfit Only 2.50 | 806X Outfit Only 2.50 | 808X Outfit Only 2.50 |

| 801 Dressed Doll 3.59 | 803 Dressed Doll 3.59 | 805 Dressed Doll 4.29 | 807 Dressed Doll 4.29 |
| 801X Outfit Only 1.98 | 803X Outfit Only 1.98 | 805X Outfit Only 2.50 | 807X Outfit Only 2.50 |

SPECIAL OCCASION STYLES

810 Dressed Doll 4.75
810X Outfit Only 2.98

812 Dressed Doll 5.98
812X Coat & Hat Only 2.98

809 Dressed Doll 4.75
809X Outfit Only 2.98

811 Dressed Doll 4.75
811X Outfit Only 2.98

White   Leopard

1956 Muffie brochure.

GAY COTTON PRINTS

501 Dressed Doll 3.29	503 Dressed Doll 3.29	505 Dressed Doll 3.29	507 Dressed Doll 3.29
501X Outfit Only 1.60	503X Outfit Only 1.60	505X Outfit Only 1.60	507X Outfit Only 1.60
502 Dressed Doll 3.29	504 Dressed Doll 3.29	506 Dressed Doll 3.29	508 Dressed Doll 3.29
502X Outfit Only 1.60	504X Outfit Only 1.60	506X Outfit Only 1.60	508X Outfit Only 1.60

FAVORITE FASHIONS

601 Dressed Doll 3.59	603 Dressed Doll 3.59	605 Dressed Doll 3.59	607 Dressed Doll 3.59
601X Outfit Only 1.98	603X Outfit Only 1.98	605X Outfit Only 1.98	607X Outfit Only 1.98
602 Dressed Doll 3.59	604 Dressed Doll 3.59	606 Dressed Doll 3.59	608 Dressed Doll 3.59
602X Outfit Only 1.98	604X Outfit Only 1.98	606X Outfit Only 1.98	608X Outfit Only 1.98

PINAFORE STYLES

652 Dressed Doll 3.59	654 Dressed Doll 3.59	656 Dressed Doll 3.59	658 Dressed Doll 3.59
652X Outfit Only 1.98	654X Outfit Only 1.98	656X Outfit Only 1.98	658X Outfit Doll 1.98
651 Dressed Doll 3.59	653 Dressed Doll 3.59	655 Dressed Doll 3.59	657 Dressed Doll 3.59
651X Outfit Only 1.98	653X Outfit Only 1.98	655X Outfit Only 1.98	657X Outfit Only 1.98

1956 Muffie brochure.

ACCESSORIES

(Top row—l. to r.)   (Bottom row—l. to r.)

915X Roller Skates	.50	919X Glasses (4)	1.00	923X Clothes Hangers	.25	926X Genuine Mink Muff	1.00
916X Shoes & Socks	.50	920X Suit Case	1.00	924X Separate Wig	1.00	927X Can-Can Petticoats (2)	1.00
917X Ice Skates	.50	921X Straw Hat	.79	925X Poodle Dog	1.25		
918X Plastic Raincoat	1.00	922X Doll Stand	.25				

WARDROBE SETS

957 Wardrobe Chest   5.98
Includes Muffie with shoes, socks, 2 dresses, hat
and other accessories.

958 Wardrobe Trunk   13.98
Includes Muffie with night gown and slippers,
red sleeper, 2 dresses, coat and hat, extra shoes
and socks and other accessories.

the sweetest dolls this side of heaven!

NANCY ANN *Storybook* DOLLS, INC.

1262 Post Street • San Francisco 9, California

1956 Muffie brochure.

Muffie 1956 "Bridal Party": (L to R) Bridesmaid #902 in blue nylon overskirt with flocked flowers; Bride #901 in white satin gown with wide lace trim; Groom #900 in black felt suit; Bridesmaid #902 in pink nylon overskirt. Courtesy Marge Meisinger.

Muffie 1956 "Santa" #914 in red wool knit jacket, pants, and cap with rabbit fur trim, black patent boots and belt. Courtesy Marge Meisinger.

Muffie hard plastic doll has special blue wiry Saran type ponytail style wig which is undocumented but thought to be from 1956, perhaps a holiday promotional doll. Also came in braids and other colors.

Muffie unmarked strung doll c. 1956 or later in yellow wide-striped dress with multicolored braid trim. The outfit is similar to 1953 Dress Up style #605 with white lace trim. The Muffie box for Margie #605 is from 1953. Courtesy Marge Meisinger.

Muffie's Pal poodle dog by Steiff with button in ear c. '56 sold as a separate accessory in white and black, in gray box marked "Muffie's Pal" ($710.00). Strung blonde Muffies: (L) Rose striped taffeta dress c. 1953 #712 Sunday Best with center-snap shoes ($450.00); (R) Printed dimity dress with blue braid ($500.00). Prices realized courtesy Frasher's Doll Auctions.

Muffie with side-part red wig wears 1956 white satin bridal gown #901 with lace trim; in case is #802 pink suedecloth skating costume, pants, and feather headband; 1955 red flannel sleeper #904; and red and white felt ski outfit #808. The blue case is not original to Muffie.

Muffie wears 1958 special red Valentine dress #5 to match Miss Nancy Ann.

(L to R): '53 Nursery Styles #501 polka dot cotton dress, straw hat added ($220.00); '56 Leopard coat and tam #812 ($250.00); cotton dress, pink skirt, blue bodice ($250.00); '55 Gay Cotton Print #506 red and aqua organdy dress & '54 #903 white fur coat, hat ($200.00); c.'57 Muffie Girl Scout ($225.00); '56 Aqua check and pink Pinafore Styles #652 ($190.00); Basic straight leg walking Muffie with blonde ponytail style in red dotted box ($550.00). Prices realized courtesy Frasher's Doll Auctions.

In 1968 Muffie Type #6 from "Around the World International Series," #611 Holland dress. Muffie has molded lashes and lashes painted below eyes and blonde Saran braids. (Type #6 described on pg. 139.)

Stitching & Styles: Muffie wigs through '56 were stitched like Ginny wigs with a single row of exposed stitching along the part sewn to a thin strip of stiffened cloth backing. Common styles were side-part flips; braids or ponytails both with separate piece bangs.

Materials:

Strung and straight leg walkers: 1953 -'54 – Dynel

Straight leg walkers: 1955 – Dynel & Saran

Straight leg and bent knee walkers: 1956 – Dynel and thin and coarse Saran

Colored hair Muffies: 1956 – Undocumented, coarse and wiry, in blue and green, 1956 perhaps Easter special dolls? Interestingly, later the International Series dolls using up Muffie parts c. '68 had Saran wigs with the hair combed over the stitching along parts.

Values: 1953-$350.00; '54- $180.00+; '55-'56-$170.00; '55 Davy Crockett $175.00; '68-International Series- $100.00.

Vinyl Head Muffie 8" c. 1956

Marks on Doll: On neck, NANCY ANN; on back, STORY-BOOK/DOLLS/CALIFORNIA/MUFFIE.

Boxes Marked: Nancy Ann Storybook.

Doll Characteristics: Muffie #500D hard plastic body, vinyl head, bent knee walking legs or Muffie #500C hard plastic body, vinyl head, straight leg walking legs.

They still sold simultaneously, the all hard plastic, bent knee walker #500B or straight leg walker #500.

Wigs Characteristics: Rooted Saran hair in bobs or ponytail styles.

Values: $165.00.

Lori-Ann 8" c. 1958

Lori-Ann is a difficult doll to study. The Lori-Ann marketing effort does not appear to have been a major effort, since so little advertising material is around compared with other NASB dolls. There were several types of Lori-Anns, and even some odd combinations are found today. One of the few NASB brochures for Lori-Ann c. 1958 advertises "New Lori-Ann" as an 8" all vinyl doll with long bobs or short Dutch cuts with 30 different outfits. However, according to dolls found in boxes, some Lori-Anns were all hard plastic or vinyl head, plastic body dolls.

There are explanations for the inconsistency of Lori-Ann dolls. According to the authoritative book on Muffie, *The Muffie Puzzle* by Roth and Maciak (see book resources), in the late '70s and '80s Lori Ann dolls with #500 Lori Ann wrist tags entered the market as a result of a purchase of factory stock. Also, in 1986 the Rothschild Doll Company purchased some of these Lori-Ann heads and advertised "Lori-Ann Muffies" by mail order. The following is the limited information that can be verified to date, but the Lori-Ann saga is ongoing since there is apparently still stock left to sell.

TYPE #1 Lori-Ann Hard Plastic c. 1958

Marks on Doll: Unmarked.

Boxes Marked: Lori- Ann/Nancy Ann Storybook.

Doll Characteristics: Hard plastic 8" unmarked walking dolls introduced with hard plastic Muffie heads.

Some had painted lashes above the eye, with or without molded lashes and/or eye brows

Wig Characteristics: The hard plastic doll's hair was glued on.

Value: $160.00.

TYPE #2 Vinyl Head Lori-Ann c. 1958

Marks on Doll: Nancy Ann on neck (very faint).

Boxes Marked: Lori-Ann/Nancy Ann Storybook.

Doll Characteristics: Hard plastic 8" walking dolls with vinyl heads.

Dress Characteristics: Most are open in back, closed with brass or donut snaps, using up old Muffie dress stock.

Wig Characteristics: Rooted wig and it is possible that some vinyl dolls may have had glued-on wigs (unusual for vinyl head dolls).

Value: $160.00.

TYPE #3 All Vinyl Lori-Ann c. 1958

Marks on Doll: Nancy Ann on neck (very faint or rubbed off).

Boxes Marked: Some marked Lori-Ann on lids.

Doll Characteristics: All vinyl 8" doll with straight leg, jointed body with rooted hair and large eyes. The faces seem thinner than the vinyl headed Lori-Ann and Muffie dolls.

Dress Characteristics: Most are open in back, closed with donut snaps. There was one flyer that showed 13 outfits for the dolls and a '58 brochure shows 30 outfitted Lori-Ann dolls.

1956 vinyl head bent knee Muffie marked Nancy Ann on head and back wears "Special Occasion Style" #802, dungarees with check shirt, vinyl print belt, and straw hat. Note she has both molded lashes and lashes painted above the eyes.

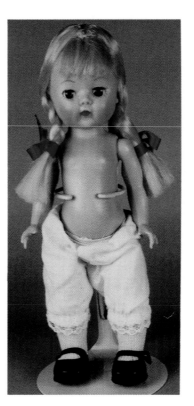

1956 Type #6 Muffie #611 in pantaloons under Holland dress.

Nancy Ann Storybook Dolls

Lori-Ann Type #2 c. 1958 with hard plastic body and vinyl head with blue eyes, and rooted blonde hair, wearing a riding outfit, red dotted cotton top and white pants, black boots. Note the original box and wrist tag #500.

Close-up of Lori-Ann Type #3.

Lori-Ann Type #3 all vinyl c. 1958 with brown eyes, molded lashes, and a rooted blonde Dutch cut, in blue cotton dress with donut snap.

Lori-Ann Type #3 c. 1958 all vinyl dolls with brown eyes and a rooted auburn Dutch cut wig. Note red clothing stains that transferred to the body. Courtesy Marge Meisinger.

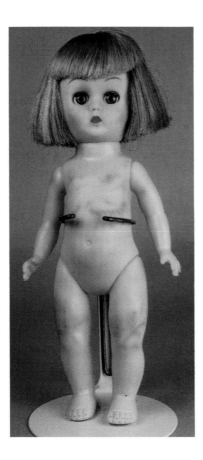

Lori-Ann dress closes with a circular donut-shaped snap.

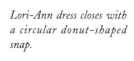

1989 Lori Ann/Muffies by Rothschild Doll Co. advertised c. '57 as "Mint in box condition...original," 8" Lori-Ann dolls with a vinyl Muffie head on a chubby plastic bent knee body.

152

Wig Characteristics: Rooted hair.
Values (Types 1, 2 & 3): $180.00+.

Lori-Ann/Muffies 8" c. 1989
Marks on Doll: Nancy Ann on neck.
Boxes Marked: Lori-Ann.
Doll Characteristics: 1989 Rothschild Doll Co. advertised a limited supply of "Mint in box condition...original," 8" Lori-Ann dolls c. 1957 by NASB. They had a vinyl Muffie head on a chubby plastic bent knee body.
Values $105.00.

Mystery Muffies c. 1957
Lillian Roth and Heather Maciak report in *The Muffie Puzzle* that there were a number of "mystery" Muffies. For example, NASB advertised Muffie outfits and dolls in blue striped boxes, but they were Ginger dolls, not Muffie dolls. The dolls wore Muffie panties and shoes. It was also reported that some boxes had a "City of Paris" label, a San Francisco department store. Lillian Roth shares that some of the outfits in the boxes were tagged NASB. For this reason we are putting this unusual doll in the Muffie section. Also, some bent knee Muffies are found in striped boxes marked "Muffie," and others are marked "Sally." The mystery is that there is no NASB mark on the box. These oddities are well worth collecting.
Value: MIB $150.00+ (higher at auction).

Little Miss Nancy Ann 8" c. 1959
Marks on Doll: Unmarked.
Boxes Marked: "Little Miss" on lid.
Doll Characteristics: A petite 8" vinyl head fashion doll with molded lashes and three lashes painted at corner of eyes; others have wider eyes without the painted lashes; hard plastic bodies with either rigid vinyl or soft vinyl arms; painted finger and toenails; high heel feet.
Dress Characteristics: Well-made dresses, some to match 10½" Miss Nancy Ann.
Values: $75.00 – 100.00 MIB.
Note: See pg. 150 for matching Muffie/Miss Nancy Ann outfit.

Muffie c. '56 with bent knees in blue and pink window box with "Muffie" label on them (Brunette $500.00 MIB; Blonde $400.00 MIB). Straight leg walking Muffie in yellow taffeta dress with red flocked design and black bow at neck ($210.00). Prices realized courtesy Frasher's Doll Auctions.

Ginger type bent knee and straight leg walker dolls were advertised by Nancy Ann Storybook c. 1957 in blue striped boxes wearing Muffie pants; tagged and untagged Muffie outfits also in the blue striped boxes. This brunette wigged hard plastic doll is a straight leg walker.

Muffie Doll with Ginger characteristics, wearing Muffie pants, with blonde hair and bent knees, in blue striped box. Courtesy Tina Standish.

"Muffie Pants" brunette Ginger doll in "Sally" box with "Fairy Tales Dolls, Inc. San Francisco" printed on end. Other dolls like this are found in boxes printed "Muffie" where Sally is printed. Courtesy Mary Miskowiec.

❦ Niresk Industries ❦

Niresk Industries of Chicago published an extensive mail order "Book of Gifts" filled with dolls and toys in the '50s. They also advertised in magazines and newspapers, making the incredible pledge, "Every item sold on a money-back guarantee." Niresk bought products from major dollmakers and resold them at prices competitive to the retail price. However, in most cases, Niresk usually didn't reveal the doll's recognized trade name. One such doll was Niresk's "Janie" 8" look-alike toddler doll that was virtually the same doll as PMA's "Joanie," (and likely bought from PMA), much to the confusion of collectors then and now.

Janie Pigtails 8" c. 1953 – 1954
Marks on Doll: None.
Boxes Marked: Unknown.
Doll Characteristics: A hard plastic 8" strung doll with sleep eyes, molded lashes, and lashes painted below eyes; arms with C-shaped hooks; molded T-strap shoes painted white. Note: Niresk advertised, "She's Made like a Big Expensive Doll." They were probably referring to Ginny, but, in fact, this is the same doll that Plastic Molded Arts sold as "Joanie Pigtails." (See PMA section.)
Clothing Characteristics: Niresk's basic 8" Janie Pigtails in nylon panties sold for $1.49; eight outfits were available separately at $1.00 – 1.98 each. One example found is the skating costume checked skirt that closed with a white button and buttonhole. Other outfit closures are unknown.
Wig Characteristic: Saran wig in pigtails, ponytails, or long bob styles. Note: Dubell sold this same strung doll with ponytails as "Little Princess" (see Dubell section).
Value: $35.00 – 45.00 undressed.

Janie Pigtails 9" c. 1955
Interestingly, Niresk substituted a 9" doll for the 8" doll in 1955, but still advertised her as Janie Pigtails.
Marks on Doll: None.
Boxes Marked: Unknown.
Doll Characteristics: All hard plastic 9" walking doll with sleep eyes, molded lashes, pin-hipped walking legs with toe detail. Note: This is the same 9" pin-hipped walking doll that Virga sold as "Lucy" and A&H sold as, "Marcie Daily Dolly."
Wig Characteristic: Saran wigs in pigtails, ponytails, or long bob styles.

In 1955 Niresk advertised 9" Janie Pigtails as a pin-hipped walking doll with toes for $1.49. Courtesy Marge Meisinger.

In 1953-54 Niresk advertised 8" Janie Pigtails as a strung doll with molded T-strap shoes for $1.49. Courtesy Marge Meisinger.

Clothing Characteristics: The basic doll was sold in nylon panties for $1.49; eight outfits were also available separately and appear to be identical as those sold for Niresk's 8" non-walking Joanie Pigtails doll for $1.00 – 1.98 each.
Value: $35.00 – 40.00 undressed; $45.00 dressed.

Janie Bride 8" c. 1956
Marks on Doll: None.
Boxes Marked: Unknown.
Doll Characteristics: All hard plastic 8" walking doll with sleep eyes, molded lashes, and lashes painted below eyes are shown in the advertisement; foot type not shown in ad. Note: This is likely the same 8" doll that Plastic Molded Arts sold as "Joanie Walker."
Wig Characteristic: Saran in pigtails, ponytails, or long bobs.
Clothing Characteristics: The doll was sold in bridal gown and tulle veil with six new outfits for $2.98.
Value: $45.00 dressed.

The color cover of Niresk's 1956 mail order book advertised, "Glamorous Janie Bride Walking Doll," an 8" hard plastic walking doll with seven "Paris-inspired" outfits for $2.98. Courtesy Marge Meisinger.

Niresk's 9" Janie Pigtails was advertised in 1955 with eight "custom made" outfits, including a pajama outfit "D" with robe, comb, brush, and a mirror. Courtesy Jeanne Niswonger.

In 1956 Niresk advertised 8" Janie Bride Walking Doll with six outfits for $2.98 in The Workbasket and other magazines. Courtesy Marge Meisinger.

❦ Norma Originals, Inc. ❦

Norma Originals sold display dolls in the early '50s in 7½" and 5½" sizes in international, sports, storybook, and an American series. However around '53 they also sold a toddler look-alike, Norma Playtime. This doll's body was virtually the same as 8" Lucy by Virga, but the face color was usually richer, and the clothes were better made (see Comparisons chapter).

Norma Playtown 8" c. 1953

Marks on Doll: Unmarked.

Boxes Marked: Boxes c. 1953 had nursery rhyme, A-B-C or other all-over design, and outfit name and number stamped on the box end; other boxes were turquoise, printed in white on the end, "Norma Playtown" and on the lid, "NORMA/Originals/New York 1, N.Y./You can wash, set and comb the hair of this doll;" round foil tags glued around the wrist are printed, "Norma Originals."

Doll Characteristics: A strung fully jointed 8" hard plastic doll with sleep eyes, mold line behind ear, molded lashes with or without lashes painted under the eyes; arms with C-shaped hooks and 2nd and 3rd fingers molded together; straight legs with molded T-strap shoes with soles painted white. This doll has bright cheek color. Note: This is the same doll as some of PMA's 8" toddlers and as Virga's 8" Lucy Playmate but with painted shoes and lashes (see PMA and Virga sections).

Dress Characteristics: Well-made clothes with finished hems, lace trims. Early dresses can have no closures and tie with a ribbon.

Wig Characteristics: Good quality Dynel or Saran wigs and some caracul lamb curly wool wigs in "poodle" cut styles.

Value: $45.00 undressed; $50.00 undressed w/wrist tag; $65.00 dressed; $75.00+ dressed w/wrist tag; $100.00+ w/box.

Hard plastic strung 8" Bride, with molded T-strap shoes, in white satin gown, tagged "Norma Originals" on the wrist. She has sleep eyes with molded lashes, but without painted lashes under the eyes. Courtesy Marge Meisinger.

Hard plastic strung 8" with molded lashes and painted lashes under the eyes, "Norma Originals" tag on the wrist, with molded T-strap shoes, with blonde caracul curly wig, in a plaid taffeta dress, red ribbon waist tie, and lacy straw hat. Tie-on shoes may not be original.

Hard plastic strung 8" with molded lashes and painted lashes under the eyes, molded T-strap shoes with painted soles, with blonde curly caracul wool wig, wearing a cotton dress. This doll and outfit are attributed to Norma dolls.

Doll with all the characteristics of Norma: hard plastic, strung 8" doll with molded lashes, molded T-strap shoes with painted white soles, wearing beautiful costume like Vogue Ginny's "Mary-Mary" outfit, but not as well made. The blue patterned original box is stamped "Gardener #2." The same doll has been found in the same type patterned box marked "#12 Lucy With Hat," and wearing a Ginny type pinafore dress with center-snap shoes. Not documented but possibly Norma Dolls.

Norma Playtown 8" hard plastic strung doll with original box marked #2011 Cowboy outfit. He has sleep eyes and a caracul wig and wears a cotton print top, ribbon scarf, felt vest and chap-style pants, red vinyl holster belt, metal gun, felt hat and red boots. Courtesy www.theriaults.com.

Blue Norma Playtown Doll lid. Courtesy Mary Van Buren Swasey.

Blue Norma doll box lid. Courtesy Mary Van Buren Swasey.

🍇 Ontario Plastics 🍇

According to most sources, Ontario Plastics both manufactured and sold their dolls on the '50s retail market. Reportedly they also sold their undressed dolls to companies like Beehler Arts, Inc. (see Virga and Fortune sections) and Plastic Molded Arts (PMA) to dress, relabel, and sell. Once again, with so many companies selling virtually the same doll under different names can be confusing to collectors. For example, we know that Ontario Plastics put their mark on a unique 8" toddler doll that they reportedly sold as "Paula Sue." While there is no original documentation to confirm that name, a 1953 *Playthings* magazine advertisement features Ontario's unmistakable 8" toddler as "Mademoiselle," represented by the A.H. Delfausse Company (per Pam and Polly Judd's *Hard Plastic Dolls II*, pg. 86). The same doll may have been sold under other names yet to be uncovered. In any case, she is charming and well worth collecting, despite any confusion about her name. A special thanks to the Henrietta Doll Lovers Club and their enthusiastic members

from the Henrietta and Rochester, NY area who have been so helpful in researching Ontario Plastics and their 8" doll, and for sharing their dolls for this chapter.

Paula Sue &/or Mademoiselle
Marks on Doll: Unmarked, or marked on back, ONTARIO PLASTICS INC./ ROCHESTER N.Y.
Boxes Marked: Unknown.
Doll Characteristics: Hard plastic, strung, 8" toddler doll with sleep eyes, molded lashes, and a deep crease under nose; some dolls have eyebrows, but some dolls have no eyebrows with pale plastic bodies; straight arms with 2nd and 3rd fingers molded together up to the tips which are separate; a metal ring arm hook like Ginny. Her legs are straight with toe detail. She is unique among the toddler dolls with her toddler "look."
Dress Characteristics: Well-made dresses with finished hems, unfinished inside seams, closed with circular Greek key

Undressed 8" strung Paula Sue marked "Ontario Plastics" on back c. 1953-54. Note her mohair braids, pronounced mold seams along the doll's side, and no eyebrows. Courtesy Carolyn Owen.

Close-up of Paula Sue's face with blonde Dynel wig, painted eyebrows, and pink plastic color. Note the pronounced crease below her nose. Courtesy Margaret Daggs, photograph by Dorothy Dailey.

Close-up of Paula Sue's face with Dynel brunette wig, painted eyebrows, and pink plastic color. Courtesy Sue Ring, photo by Dorothy Dailey.

Close-up of Paula Sue's face with red Dynel wig, painted eyebrows, and pink plastic color. Courtesy of Margaret Dagg, photo by Dorothy Dailey.

Close-up of Paula Sue's round metal dress snap with "p" pattern. Courtesy Dorothy Dailey.

Hard plastic 8" doll marked "Ontario Plastics" with blonde braids wears the blue cotton dress shown in the "Mademoiselle" advertisement c. 1953; straw hat with solid blue brim edge. Courtesy Mary Britton.

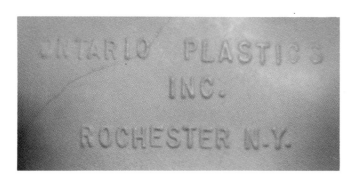

Mark on back of Paula Sue, "Ontario Plastics/Inc./Rochester N.Y." Courtesy Carolyn Owen.

("p" design) round silver, metal or brass snap. One source reports that Paula Sue dresses had circular donut-shaped snaps, but no such examples have been found for this study. Some pinafore sleeve dresses are less expensive versions of Ginny dresses in both style and construction. The "Mademoiselle" advertisement for the Ontario doll shows her wearing center-snap shoes with a pinafore dress and straw hat and prices her at $2.79 for dressed doll and $1.79 undressed.

Wig Characteristics: Mademoiselle dolls were advertised with Dynel wigs. One Paula Sue doll without eyebrows has been found with a braided mohair wig.

Value: $55.00 undressed doll with good color; $75.00+ for dressed doll; no boxed examples found to date.

Paula Sue marked "Ontario Plastics" c. '53-'54 in red pinafore dress trimmed with white with silver "p" pattern snap, and matching red visor tie-on hat. Courtesy Dorothy Dailey.

Paula Sue marked "Ontario Plastics" in blue cotton print dress with eyelet pinafore sleeves and skirt trim; straw hat brim is trimmed in matching cotton. Courtesy Margaret Daggs, photo by Dorothy Dailey.

This 8" strung, hard plastic doll was marked "Ontario Plastics" and advertised as "Mademoiselle" by A. H. Delfausse, in 1953. She is wearing the blue cotton dress with silver "p" pattern round snap advertised and styled like Ginny's Margie 1951 and '52 dress. Her straw hat is trimmed with printed pattern on the brim edge.

Paula Sue with blonde braids marked "Ontario Plastics" in red plaid dress with brass "p" pattern snap; black bodice with matching black and plaid cap. Outfit may be Virga. Courtesy Mary Britton.

❦ Plastic Molded Arts ❦

Plastic Molded Arts (PMA) sold dolls on the 1950s retail market in various sizes and price ranges. While PMA sold countless dolls, they are probably the best known for their inexpensive small toddler and dress me dolls. Interestingly, PMA was one of a number of '50s doll makers that also sold their undressed dolls (marked and unmarked) to competitors to dress and re-label for the retail doll market. Consequently, PMA's dolls can often be difficult to distinguish from competitors' dolls unless you have original boxes or tags. These are some of PMA's best-known small dolls on the '50s doll market.

Display Dolls – 1950s

PMA sold hard plastic "display" or "souvenir" type dolls in the '50s. Most had mohair wigs, painted eyes or sleep eyes, a jointed head and arms with fixed legs. Their molded shoes were usually painted black or white with three incised marks indicating bows. Many had storybook or seasonal themes, and some were created for special events such as PMA's 7½" - 8" Coronation Queen doll with sleep eyes in 1953. Some dolls were marked "Plastic Molded Arts" on back, and some were unmarked.
Value: $25.00 – 35.00 in box.

Nursery Rhyme Dolls 5½" c. 1950s

Marks on Doll: Plastic Molded Arts, Lic. New York.
Boxes Marked: Nursery Rhyme Doll/ Little Miss Muffet/ Manufactured by Plastic Molded Arts (or other character).
Doll Characteristics: 5½" hard plastic doll with fixed arms and legs, molded hair, side-glancing sleep eyes; molded T-strap shoes; strung arms with separate fingers on right, 2nd and 3rd fingers molded together on left.
Dress Characteristics: Cotton dress with ribbon tie at top stapled on.

Wig Characteristics: Painted-on hair.
Value: $25.00; $75.00 in original box (hard to find in original box).

Toddler Dolls

Joanie Pigtails was PMA's first 8" toddler doll competing with Vogue's 8" Ginny doll, the market leader. Joanie was marketed as a "lovable cuddler," and she is one of the cutest look-alikes. Competitor Niresk Industries sold the same dolls as, "Janie Pigtails," so the names can easily be confused (see Niresk section).

Joanie Pigtails (PMA) 8" c. 1953

Marks on Doll: Unmarked or some marked Plastic Molded Arts LIC/ N.Y.C.
Box Marked: Created by P.M.A. Dolls, Inc, L.I.C., N.Y.
Doll Characteristics: Joanie Pigtails was a strung, hard plastic doll with sleep eyes with molded lashes and lashes also painted under the eyes. Some report that lashes were also painted all around the eye on Joanies, but that is not substantiated. Also, her head mold line ran behind the ear; arms had C-shaped hooks and 2nd and 3rd fingers molded together; T-strap molded shoes with soles painted white or black on most but not all. The undressed Joanie Pigtails doll sold for $1.59 each. She was also sold in small hatbox cases as "Joanie the Wedding Belle" as advertised in *Playthings* magazine in 1953. Joanie Pigtails was also advertised for $2.98 in a cardboard "Wardrobe and Travel Case" in the 1954 Sears Christmas catalog.
Dress Characteristics: Dresses in the Joanie Pigtail "Travel Case" had back seams stitched closed below the dress opening

PMA 7½" bride "display" type doll c. '50-'53, marked "Plastic Molded Arts" on the back.

PMA 5½" Storybook Miss Muffet in display box wears a cotton stapled-on dress. She has sleep eyes and painted hair, fixed head and legs, and strung arms.

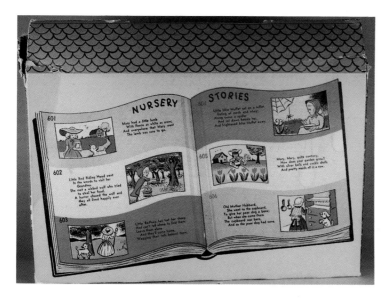

Back of PMA Storybook doll advertises others in the series, Mary Lamb, Little Red Riding Hood, Bo Peep, Mary-Mary, Old Mother Hubbard.

"Joannie Pigtails" with wardrobe

This pert, pigtailed playmate with wardrobe of custom-made clothes and accessories is sure to win the affections of your little girl. She wears her long, shimmering Saran tresses in two neat braids—her "mama" can comb, brush, dampen and set her hair in a variety of different styles. Lovable toddler is realistically molded of nearly-unbreakable plastic—has perfect "tiny tot" features; big, beautiful go-to-sleep eyes, accented by long curling eyelashes.

You can tell from the sizeable wardrobe she carries that she intends to make a long visit. It contains a pretty cotton frock with ribbon at waist, matching bonnet; pajama set with colorful nursery pattern; molded vinyl shoes. She wears panties. She carries her curlers, comb, brush and mirror. Doll has jointed arms, legs, turning head.

49 N 3049—8 inches tall. Shipping weight 1 lb. 4 oz. . . $2.79

$2.79

Bottom of 5½" Storybook box marked PMA Dolls, Inc.

Sears, Roebuck & Co. 1954 Christmas catalog advertised "Joanie Pigtails with wardrobe" for $2.79. Courtesy Marge Meisinger.

PMA's Joanie Pigtails c. 1953 in her Wardrobe and Travel Case, an 8" hard plastic, strung doll with sleep eyes, molded T-strap shoes painted white. Came with dress, pajamas, shoes, curlers, comb, mirror, and brush.

PMA 8" Joanie Pigtails c. 1953 in her Wardrobe and Travel Case.

Note the bright cheek color and lashes painted under the eyes of "Joanie the Wedding Belle" doll; she is a strung doll with molded T-strap shoes.

"Joanie the Wedding Belle" in her original brown simulated alligator case as advertised c. 1953. Packaged with Something Old (wedding veil), Something New (satin slippers), Something Borrowed (ring), and Something Blue (leg garter). The lavender dress on the lid has no closures; satin gown closes with a donut-shaped snap. Courtesy Judy Cullen.

with no hooks; some were tied with a ribbon or matching tie. Bloomers were gathered on exposed waist elastic with no leg gathers. Slip-on vinyl shoes had molded bows like Virga doll shoes. Pajama tops tied at the neck without hooks. Additional Joanie outfits were boxed and advertised separately.

Wig Characteristics: Joanie Pigtails had a Saran wig and advertising stated, "Her glamorous hair combs, curls and waves." Not all the dolls in Joanie Pigtails had braided wigs. Her "Wardrobe and Travel Case" was imprinted, "Joanie in Braids or Bob."

Value: $35.00 undressed; $45.00 – 65.00 dressed; $85.00+ in wardrobe box.

Joanie Walker 8" c. 1954

Marks on Doll: Unmarked.

Box Marked: Joanie Walker/P.M.A. Dolls, Inc. was either printed directly on a blue dotted box or on a gold foil sticker fixed to the box. Other boxes had a PMA pink graphic design with "Joanie Walker" printed in pink on the acetate lid.

Doll Characteristics: "Joanie Walker" was the same 8" hard plastic sleep eye doll as the strung "Joanie Pigtails" except her head turned as she walked. "I walk, sit, and turn my head," was printed on Joanie Walker's box. She had molded T-strap shoes, and most were left unpainted. Joanie Walker dolls had molded lashes, but some also had lashes painted under the eyes, perhaps phasing out old supplies; eye size may vary slightly; head mold mark was behind the ear. Also, Joanie Walker had either peg arm hooks and separate fingers, or C-shaped arm hooks and molded second and third fingers. Note: Joanie Walker was the same doll as Fortune's hard plastic walking 8" Pam with the same head, body, and legs with molded T-strap feet, and peg arm hook. However, many

Joanie dolls had painted lashes under the eyes, distinguishing her from Pam.

Dress Characteristics: Separate outfits were sold in boxes imprinted, "Time for Joanie/Fits all 8"/P.M.A" on acetate lids. These outfits closed in the back with square hand-sewn metal snaps or ties.

Wig Characteristics: The box indicates that Joanie Walker's wig was changed to Dynel, as her box was printed, "You can comb and curl my Dynel hair." Side-part wigs had one row of stitching on a backing strip, while center-part bobs and braided styles had two parallel rows of stitching sewn on a backing strip. Wigs were glued to Joanie's head.

Value: $35.00 undressed; $45.00 – 60.00 dressed; $65.00+ in box.

PMA 8" strung Joanie Pigtails c. 1953 also came with a bob hairstyle. Note the painted white T-strap molded shoes typical of PMA's version of the doll.

PMA 8" strung and walking dolls were often used for souvenir dolls such as this Indian with glued-on leather costume and black mohair wig. (See Hard Plastic section for other souvenir dolls.)

PMA 8" Joanie Walker c. 1955 was like Joanie Pigtails, but she was a head-turning walker. This Joanie wears a lavender nylon print dress and blue felt hat. Courtesy Marge Meisinger.

PMA Joanie Walker stands on her box c. 1955 with a blue dot pattern, solid lid, and sticker PMA label.

PMA undressed Joanie Walker in blue dot pattern box. Some had painted white feet.

PMA Joanie Walker in outfit #803, a white cotton print dress. Dynel hair was not the finest grade. Courtesy Jo Barckley.

Joanie Walker on her original box with foil label wears embroidered nylon dress tied with taffeta ribbon and a felt cap. Courtesy Jo Barckley.

Doll on right wears embroidered nylon PMA dress with square metal snap; doll on left wears PMA type dress with metal snap, but with attached tulle slip.

PMA's separate outfits for Joanie Walker c. mid '50s were marked "Time for Joanie"/ Fits All 8" Dolls. This outfit is a one-piece pink felt cowgirl outfit, felt hat, and boots and closes with a square metal snap.

PMA Joanie Walker box c. 1955 with "PMA" pattern on box and liner, with an acetate lid marked in pink at bottom, "Joanie Walker/PMA Dolls Inc." The head-turning walker wears a good quality Japanese robe style kimono over pants with flower in her hair. Note high cheek color.

PMA's Joanie Walker cardboard case c. mid '50s closes with a metal catch, has a place for a doll, metal clothes hanger, and a blue paper lining.

PMA "Time for Joanie" outfit c. mid '50s with red corduroy top, green felt pant, belt, and cap.

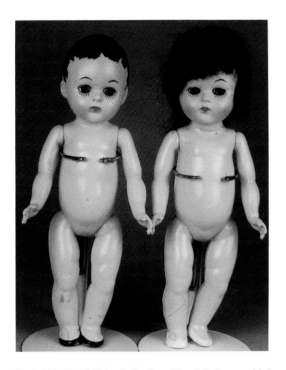

Early '50s PMA 8" hard plastic toddler dolls have molded lashes with painted lashes beneath the eye, prominent mold seams, and chubby bodies. Some of the molded T-strap shoes were painted white or black, others were not painted. Some were marked Plastic Molded Arts on the back, but others were unmarked. Note the coarse black synthetic wig on the girl and painted hair on the boy. These 8" dolls were probably bought by other companies to sell. They were also used as Premium dolls, like Nancy and Sluggo (see Advertising Dolls section.)

Original PMA graphic design box from mid '50s for a head-turning 8" hard plastic doll with separate fingers. Ballerina has flat feet. Box is marked "80W" on the end.

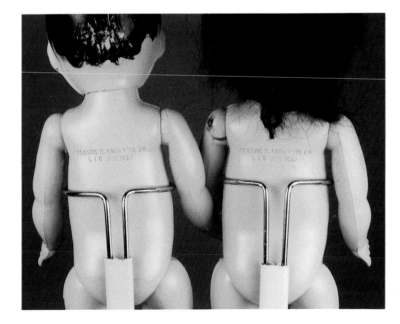

Boy and girl 8" toddlers marked Plastic Molded Arts Co/LIC New York on the back.

Girl marked Plastic Molded Arts on back with lashes painted under eyes, wearing an Alaskan costume.

This unique 10" pin-hipped hard plastic walker with sleep eyes c. mid '50s is marked Plastic Molded Arts on the back, has sleep eyes, and a Dynel wig. Outfits close with square metal snap.

Boy on right is marked PMA, two 8" identical dolls on left are not marked. Note that wigless doll on the left has molded hair under the wig. Courtesy Mary Van Buren Swasey.

PMA unmarked 8" doll with painted lashes under eye in queen costume with white taffeta gown, velvet robe, possibly from 1953 Queen Elizabeth coronation doll. Courtesy Mary Van Buren Swasey.

Vinyl head, head-turning 8" walking doll is marked PMA on the neck. She has molded feet and separate fingers, and her rooted hair is in a ponytail. Her dress closes with a circular donut snap.

"PMA" Toddler Dolls 8" c. 1954

PMA sold their "PMA" brand toddler dolls to the retail market in direct competition to their own "Joanie Pigtails" and "Joanie Walker" doll brands.

Marks on Doll: Unmarked or printed Plastic Molded Arts on back.

Box Marked: "PMA" pattern graphics on the box sides and/or lid and printed "80W" on the box end.

Doll Characteristics: These are the two primary types of "PMA" retail branded 8" hard plastic, strung dolls, and walking toddler dolls. Variations may be found in parts on dolls marked PMA, but this is what is found primarily:

TYPE #1: Painted lashes/molded lashes.

The first PMA brand toddlers were strung, fully jointed, non-walking dolls, with molded lashes and dark lashes painted beneath the eye; head mold marks run behind the ears. These dolls had C-shaped arm hooks with molded second and third fingers, and molded T-strap feet. They have prominent body seams and a shiny, peach-colored hard plastic. Note: Similar strung dolls are found in pink and blue boxes marked "80-W" but without the "PMA" printed on the box (see Hard Plastic & Vinyl, Misc. section).

Value: $45.00; MIB $60.00+.

TYPE # 2:

Some characteristics were the same as Type #1: Head mold behind the ears, molded T-strap shoes. However, new features included a walking mechanism, later walking dolls had bending knees, arms had peg-shaped hooks, separate fingers.

Dress Characteristics: Dresses have unfinished, stitched back seams closing with handsewn metal snaps.

Wig Characteristics: Side-part wigs had one row of stitching on a backing strip. Center-part and braids had two parallel rows of stitching sewn on a backing strip. They are synthetic, but appear coarser, mohair-like.

Value: $45.00; MIB $65.00+.

Joanie, Vinyl Head 8" c. mid-'50s

Marks on Doll: PMA on neck.

Box Marked: "Joanie Walker" on flat gift set box with window lid.

Doll Characteristics: Vinyl head-turning walker dolls with sleep eyes and molded lashes; rooted hair; arms with C-shaped hooks and second and third fingers molded together; straight legs with molded T-strap shoes.

Dress Characteristics: Dresses were closed with circular donut-shaped metal factory snaps; dresses resembled Virga dresses with pinafore sleeves. In 1957 a "vinyl head Joanie" was advertised in a boxed deluxe set with the doll and four outfits in a lidded box.

Wig Characteristics: Rooted hair, good quality.

Value: $35.00 undressed; $45.00 – 55.00 dressed; $65.00+ in box.

Sandy 10" c. 1950s

Marks on Doll: Plastic Molded Arts/Lic. N. Y. on back.

Box Marked: #1107 on box with PMA typical blue dot pattern all over box and lid.

Doll Characteristics: According to Pat Smith's *Modern Collector's Dolls, 4th Series*, this 10" hard plastic, pin-hipped walking doll marked Plastic Molded Arts was named Sandy. Her mold was unique on the '50s market. She has second and third fingers molded together, toe detail, sleep eyes with molded lashes, and lashes painted beneath the eyes.

Wig Characteristics: On box: You comb and curl my Dynel hair.

Dress Characteristics: Dresses have unfinished, stitched back seams, closed with handsewn metal snaps.

Value: MIB $100.00.

Baby

Joanette & PMA 8" Baby

Marks on Doll: Unmarked or some MIB examples are marked "A-E" on the neck.

Box Marked: Pink and gray PMA graphic pattern is over the doll box and lid. Second type of doll box has a plastic window with "PMA" pattern cardboard sides. PMA's 8" baby outfit boxes

Compare two PMA vinyl head, head-turning 8" walking dolls marked PMA on the neck, with molded feet and separate fingers, and rooted hair. The doll on the right has better color vinyl and smaller eyes.

Close-up of PMA vinyl head dolls marked "PMA" on neck, but doll on right has smaller eyes.

PMA's unmarked 8" baby c. mid '50s is in a PMA pattern box with vinyl head and body but hard plastic arms. She is a vinyl drinking and wetting Ginnette look-alike baby. She wears a cotton dress that closes with a square snap, with matching bloomers and tie-on bonnet.

Unknown '50s outfit marked "PMA Fashions for Peggy/Fits all 9-inch fashion dolls." Note the fluted snap at waist which is the same as for Vogue's Ginny and Jill, and for Ideal's Little Miss Revlon. Has original Walgreen's store label on the box.

PMA baby accessory packet with "Joanette" printed on the acetate lid, but "Joanie" printed on the foil sticker. Baby items includes shoes, plastic bottle, Ivory Soap bar, rattle, sponge, cotton, powder, and Q-tips.

A newspaper advertisement dated 11/29/56 for PMA's 8" Suzy Walker Teen, an inexpensive head-turning walker with stapled-on clothes, selling for 66 cents. Courtesy Marge Meisinger.

are marked "Joanette" in pink on acetate lid. Presumably PMA's baby was "Joanette," or perhaps Joanette was a second line.

Doll Characteristics: Joanette was an 8" Ginnette look-alike drink n' wet baby with sleep eyes and molded lashes. She has an open nursing mouth and hole in lower back. Her head, body, and bent baby legs are vinyl, but her arms are hard plastic with separate fingers. PMA's baby doll was undoubtedly sold to the same market as their 8" Joanie Pigtails and Joanie Walker dolls.

Wig Characteristics: Molded hair painted brown.

Dress Characteristics: Stitched unfinished back seams with handsewn square metal snaps; finished hems.

Value: $40.00; MIB $65.00.

Teen

Little Miss Joan c. 1957

Marks on Doll: Unknown.

Boxes Marked: Unknown.

Doll Characteristics: A 9" doll with a soft vinyl head with Saran rooted hair, hard plastic body with bending knees, and high heel feet. Note: PMA's advertisement for the 9" Little Miss Joan, 12" Miss Joan, and 20" vinyl high heel dolls in March 1957 *Toys and Novelties* are shown in Pam and Polly Judd's *Glamour Dolls of the 1950s and 1960s*, pg. 186.

Dress Characteristics: Sports and dress-up styles; ballet tutu; finishes and closures unknown.

Wig Characteristics: Rooted in upswept styles.

Value: $25.00 – 45.00; MIB $75.00+.

Suzy Walker c. 1956

Marks on Doll: Unknown

Boxes Marked: "Suzy Walker/She Sleeps/She Sits/She Moves Her Head" in folding rectangular window box.

Doll Characteristics: Inexpensive 8" display type doll with sleep eyes and painted lashes, head-turning walker with strung arms. Advertised for 66 cents in window box.

Dress Characteristics: Inexpensive stapled-on skirts and bodice.

Wig Characteristics: Glued-on mohair.

Value: $45.00 in box.

Fashions For Peggy

A separate boxed outfit "Fits all 9 inch high fashion dolls" is printed "Fashions for Peggy." Most PMA dolls are named "Joanie," and no PMA Peggy doll has been located to date. The outfit closes with a star gripper snap used for Vogue's Jill and for Ideal's Little Miss Revlon.

Value: $45.00 in box.

PMA's unmarked 8" baby in plastic window case is same vinyl doll as lid box with vinyl body and hard plastic arms. Courtesy Marge Meisinger.

❦ Reliable Toy Company, Limited ❦

Canada's Reliable Toy Company, Ltd. entered the doll business in the 1920s. By the 1950s Reliable was selling hard plastic dolls including Susie, a 9" pin-hipped walking doll c. 1957. Interestingly, in '59 they advertised the same doll as "Peggy the Walking Doll," and also as "Patsy the Walking Doll," undressed and without a wig.

Susie & Peggy & Patsy 9" c. 1957 – 1959
Marks on Doll: On back, "Reliable" (in script).
Marks on Box: Susie or Peggy or Patsy/Reliable.
Doll Characteristics: Hard plastic 9" walking doll with large sleep eyes and molded lashes, prominent cheeks; arms with separate fingers; straight pin-hipped walking legs with two dimples on the knees and toe detail.
Dress Characteristics: Taffeta dress with unfinished hem and seams, ties in back with a suedecloth top. Unfinished cotton panties are stapled on the back.
Wig Characteristics: Synthetic Saran wig in long or braided styles glued to the head.
Value: $50.00 – 65.00 US.

Eskimo Souvenir Doll 8" c. 1958
Marks on Doll: On back, "Reliable" (in script)/MADE IN CANADA/ PAT.1958.
Marks on Box: Unknown.
Doll Characteristics: Hard plastic 8" doll with jointed head, arms, and legs that swing in flanged joints, sleep eyes with molded lashes, closed mouth, straight arms with palms down and 2nd and 3rd fingers molded together. Toe detail with dimples over toes, angular arm hooks.
Wig Characteristics: Molded hair on this Eskimo.
Dress Characteristics: This same doll was undoubtedly costumed for other souvenir dolls including Canadian Mounties and others. Note: Reliable's doll with these same characteristics except for being an "open mouth nurser" is shown as Trudy in *Canadian Dolls*, Evelyn Robson Strahlendorf, 3rd edition.
Value: Fluctuates around $25.00 – 35.00; more with box.

Comparison of 9" dressed Reliable Susie c. 1957 on left and Reliable 8" Eskimo doll c. 1958. Courtesy Lee Ann Beaumont.

Reliable Doll Co. Susie 9" hard plastic doll c. 1957 with Saran hair and pin-hipped walking legs. She wears her original taffeta dress with suedecloth cape.

Reliable Doll Co. Peggy 9" hard plastic doll c. 1959 with pin-hipped walking legs, two dimples on the knees; dress not original.

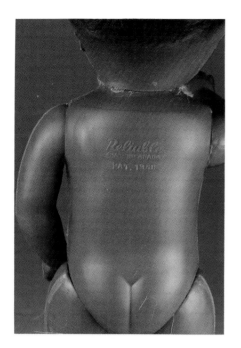

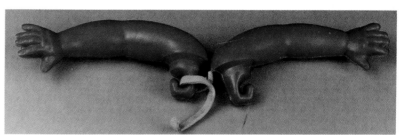

Arm hooks, Reliable's 8" doll c. 1958. Courtesy Lee Ann Beaumont.

Reliable's 8" souvenir Eskimo doll marked, "Reliable (Script) /MADE IN CANADA/PAT. 1958." Courtesy Lee Ann Beaumont.

Reliable 8" undressed Eskimo souvenir doll on right with flanged hips and Relible's 9" pin-hipped walker Peggy, also sold as Suzy. Courtesy Lee Ann Beaumont.

Reliable Doll Co. face of 8" Eskimo souvenir doll c. 1958. Courtesy Lee Ann Beaumont.

❧ Richwood Toy Company ❧

Richwood Toy Co. was founded by Ida H. Wood who sold dolls as early as 1940. At first Richwood dressed "display dolls" for sale, but by 1952 Wood sold a slim 8" non-walking hard plastic doll with flat feet and named her Sandra Sue. Later Sandra Sue dolls c. 1956 were walkers with arched feet, many consider to be a pre-teen alternative to "mature" figured dolls. Sandra Sue was truly unique and developed a following of her own.

Small Doll

Sandra Sue 8" c. 1952

Marks on Doll: "2" inside right arm and "0" inside left arm.
Boxes Marked: Sandra Sue/Richwood; wrist tag: Round The Clock Fashions/Sandra Sue.

Blue boxes had a silhouette in an oval on the lid marked "Sandra Sue" below.

Some separate outfits were sold in zippered plastic bags.

Doll Characteristics: The first 8" hard plastic Sandra Sue dolls were slim bodied dolls with a "tiny waistline." They had sleep

This doll is thought to be an early example of a Richwood "display" doll in a felt skating outfit, a style eventually used for Sandra Sue.

eyes with molded lashes and eyebrows and eyelashes painted in an unusual orange tone; arms had metal ring loops and 1st, 2nd, and 3rd fingers were molded together with a separate thumb; palms face the body; non-walking thin straight legs with flat feet. At first the feet had molded "soles" on the bottom of the feet without toe detail, but toe detail was added. Later Sandra Sues were walkers, and by 1956 she had arched feet.

Wig Characteristics: Saran wigs stitched to a backing and glued to the head.

Dress Characteristics: Well-made party dresses and sports outfits with finished hems and donut-shaped snap closures. Coats had fitted waists, and skirts were flared. Ida H. Wood, creator of Sandra Sue, introduced a collection of five dolls in costumes from Louisa May Alcott's *Little Women*, sold both as dressed dolls and separate outfits. Some dresses matched the company's 14" Cindy Lou marked "Made IN USA."

Value: Flat feet: $200.00; undressed doll: $150.00; arched feet: $150.00; undressed: $175.00 – 250.00.

Richwood 8" Sandra Sue in original outfit for Heidi c. 1950s, with box for Marmee. Courtesy Marge Meisinger.

introducing.... ## Sandra Sue

eight inch doll

Beautiful SANDRA SUE has more play and selling features than any other eight inch doll. She is shown here in her lovely slip and panties so that you may evaluate her top play features. A list of her features includes the following:

* SLENDER FIGURE
designed for stylish clothes

* BALL JOINTED
sits, stands, moves her head and arms

* WALKING DOLL
smooth all metal mechanism

* BEAUTIFUL FACE
created by a famous sculptor

* MOVING EYES
with tiny eyelashes

* HAND DECORATED FACE
individual expression on each doll

* SARAN WIG
stitchlocked, durable washable and combable

* PORCELAIN LIKE FINISH
specially processed on all parts

* HOSPITALIZATION POLICY
exclusive lifetime guarantee of unbreakability

Besides all these top play features, only SANDRA SUE has a playworld of clothes, furniture, accessories, and play equipment scaled just for her.

Brochure for Sandra Sue doll with flat feet.

Richwood's 8" Sandra Sue twins with flat feet, wearing full-length slips, panties, and tie shoes in original wide box. The dolls in slips were also boxed individually and as triplets for sale. Courtesy Marge Meisinger.

69 Checked taffeta suit with ruffled petticoat, separate jacket, and straw hat.

21 Blue jeans with plaid cuffs, matching plaid shirt and white sailor hat.

22 Pastel nightgown with wool and taffeta flare back robe and matching slippers.

54 Scotch Suit with authentic details. Wool jacket trimmed, plaid tartan and garters.

34 Nylon tulle ballerina with silver top, matching panties and ballerina slippers.

32 Bathing Suit of jersey with a satin panel. Beach hat and terry cloth beach jacket.

17 Two tone organdy party dress with lace trim and contrasting sash and flowers.

40 Velvet and gold tea dance dress with white taffeta petticoat and gold Juliet cap.

Inside Sandra Sue brochure.

Richwood 8" Sandra Sue with flat feet in original Sailor suit #23 with blue felt jacket, red tam, and white skirt. Courtesy Marge Meisinger.

Richwood 8" Sandra Sue with arched feet in original full-length slip c. 1956. Courtesy Marge Meisinger.

Sandra Sue, top (L to R): Brunette in #39 Gordon plaid cotton dress & yellow pinafore ($130.00 VG-Excl.); Red flannel PJs with eyelet trim ($120.00 Excl.); #23 Sailor suit wool jacket and beret & pleated skirt ($260.00 MIB); Oriental outfit, yellow, red, black striped jacket, black pants, and straw hat ($200.00 V. Excl.); Fur coat and hat ($120.00 VG). Bottom (L to R): Strapless pink and gold nylon over taffeta, black fur jacket, flat feet ($310.00 VG); High-heel feet Sandra Sue in blue nylon party dress in original blue box ($400.00 MIB); Pink felt coat and hat, white heels ($150.00). Courtesy Frasher's Doll Auctions.

Sandra Sue, top (L to R): Boxed brunette Sandra Sue with flat feet in cotton camisole ($400.00 Excl. in box); Sandra Sue Dolls in navy and cotton shirtwaist and in black camisole and pink and white striped skirt, high heels ($250.00 G-VG); twin auburn and brunette dolls in blue box ($270.00 Excl. in box); Bottom: Blonde in #21 blue jeans with red check shirt and cuffs, and brunette in Red Cross Nurse uniform ($120.00 VG.); Sandra Sue in green felt snowsuit with red trim and in red and white skating costume ($210.00 VG-Excl.); Blonde Sandra Sues in white camisole and pink straw hat, and pink felt coat and hat over pink organdy, black high heels ($180.00 Excl.). Courtesy Frasher's Doll Auctions.

🍇 Roberta Doll Company 🍇

The Roberta Doll Company is perhaps best known for two of their hard plastic walking celebrity dolls from the '50s Arthur Godfrey Show: 16" Lu Ann Simms and 18" Haleloke. The company also sold attractive 14" "Roberta Walker" dolls marked "Made in USA" on the back. However, they also sold small toddler dolls such as the two below.

Roberta Toddler, 7"-7½" c. 1955

Marks on Doll: Unmarked.

Doll Characteristics: Roberta reportedly bought Doll Bodies 7½" Mary-Lu doll to dress and sell with Roberta's label. She was a strung, hard plastic doll with sleep eyes, molded lashes, and lashes painted under the eyes; ear mold behind the ear. She had shoes with flat molded bows painted white and no toe detail. Arms had C-shaped hooks; fingers on her left hand were molded together to tips but separate at tips; right hand had 2nd and third fingers completely molded together, and left had separate fingers. Her plastic is good quality, and mold lines are heavy along outside of the legs. Note: As stated, Doll Bodies sold this same doll (see Doll Bodies section).

Wig Characteristics: Wigs on dolls appear to be Dynel but could have been another synthetic.

Value: $35.00 – 40.00.

Roberta Walker 8½" c. 1951

The most notable reference for this doll is in Judd's *Hard Plastic Dolls I*, pg. 218, and from the description and photo we learn the following characteristics. However her identification is still hard to definitely confirm.

Marks on Doll: Unmarked.

Marks on Boxes: Unknown.

Doll Characteristics: Hard plastic fully jointed 8½" head-turning walking dolls with sleep eyes and molded lashes, excellent toe and finger detail. Judd describes a painted "countersunk" pin hip.

Dress Characteristics: Unknown.

Wig Characteristics: Wigs stitched along a backing strip and glued to the doll's head, with molded hair under wig.

Value: $40.00.

This type of 7½" hard plastic toddler c. '55 with painted white shoes with flat molded bows was sold by Roberta Doll Co. It is the same doll as Doll Bodies' Mary Lu doll, and Roberta probably purchased the doll from Doll Bodies to dress. The outfit is '50s vintage but probably not original to the doll.

❧ Stashin Doll Company ❧

The Stashin Doll Company of Newark, New Jersey, is one of the least known doll companies from the '50s look-alike market. Since their dolls were unmarked and few of their outfits were tagged, identification can be difficult. Fortunately, printed material has surfaced to document Stashin's '40s display dolls and their "Andrea" and "Penny" '50s toddler dolls. Boxed Andrea and Penny outfits tagged with J.J. Newberry Co. price stickers place the line in the low-end '50s doll market. Research on Stashin Doll Company is ongoing, and the following is based on the best information obtained to date.

Display Dolls

Painted Eye Display dolls 5½"- 7½" c. 1940s – 1950s

Stashin's press photos and negatives for display type dolls place the company in West Orange, New Jersey, in the 1940s. Some of the dolls appear to be 5½" and 7½" composition dolls and a larger bride doll around 14"-15" with fixed legs and heads and jointed arms. The wigs appear to be mohair.

Value: No examples found, estimated MIB $20.00 – 30.00.

This "Colleen" doll appears to be a 7½" doll late '40s or '50s. A metal advertising plate describes the dolls as hard plastic with moving necks.

This vintage photo shows Stashin's painted eye dolls with fixed legs and heads. They appear to be 5½", 7½", and 14"-15" composition.

Stashin's sleep eye, hard plastic '40s WAC doll has pointed Duchess type bows.

Stashin's hard plastic, sleep eye "Mother-Daughter" dolls are Duchess type dolls c. '40s.

Doll Characteristics:

TYPE #1: Hard plastic 8" head-turning dolls with sleep eyes and painted lashes above eyes, mold line through center of the ear; arms with C-shaped hooks and separate fingers; straight walking legs with toe detail. Many of the Andreas have lashes and brows painted an unusual maroon color. Note: This is the same doll as Cosmopolitan's Ginger Type #1 with painted lashes and was also used for Duchess's Randi Type #1, and for Fortune's Ninette.

Wig Characteristics: Saran or Dynel stitched to a strip backing and glued to the head in long bob styles or braids.

Dress Characteristics: Well-made outfits open in back and closed with a round "p" pattern snap, some with attached slips, and finished hems. The box lid shows center-snap shoes, but dolls are also found with vinyl side-snap shoes. Flat felt circular hats with elastics seem to be a popular Andrea style. Some dresses are tagged "Andrea/Stashin Doll Co./Newark, NJ." *continued on page 183*

Character Dolls 7½" c. 1950s

Metal printer's plates for Stashin's display character dolls advertise "Stashin Proudly Presents...Its New Character Dolls. 7½" Plastic movable heads, stands alone, Utterly Enchanting...Outstanding color combinations...CHEAPER than the rest...You can now afford to undersell your competitors and offer a finer more saleable item. Money Back guarantee if these dolls are not all and more than we claim. You will now be dealing directly with the manufacturer with no middleman." Some of the hard plastic display dolls appear to have painted eyes, and some have sleep eyes. Based on the molded shoe bows with pointed corners on Stashin's sleep eye WAAC doll, Stashin probably purchased the dolls from Duchess Dolls, one found in window lid box marked "Gypsy."
Value: MIB $20.00 – 25.00.

Toddler Dolls

Andrea 8" c. mid-late 1950s

Two types of Stashin dolls have been found in outfits tagged "Andrea."
Marks on Doll: Unmarked.
Boxes Marked: Unmarked red and white diagonally striped boxes; also, a drawing for a colorful Andrea box lid is printed: "I'm Andrea/And I want to be your Dolly!!/Stashin Doll Co, Newark, N.J."

Stashin's Andrea 7½" brunette walking doll c. '50s has sleep eyes and painted lashes. She wears a pretty blue plaid nylon dress, open in back and closed with "p" pattern round metal snap; blue felt circle hat.

Stashin's Andrea Type #1, 7½" hard plastic walking doll c. '50s with sleep eyes. Note the maroon painted lashes. This is the same doll as Cosmopolitan's Ginger Type #1, Fortune's Ninette #1, and others.

Stashin's Andrea dress tag, "Andrea/Stashin Doll Co./Newark, NJ." Note the open back, attached slip, and round metal snap with "p" pattern. Courtesy Tina Standish.

Stashin Andrea 7½" blonde braided walking doll with sleep eyes and painted lashes in blue plaid nylon dress and original red and white stripe box. Courtesy Tina Standish.

Stunning Stashin Andrea skater in untagged pink costume with real fur trim, hat and muff, and skates with original box.

Andrea's open back costume closes with "p" pattern snap. Courtesy Tina Standish.

Close-up of skater Andrea's painted lashes and beautiful cheek color. Courtesy Tina Standish. Photo by Louie Laskowski.

Stashin's Andrea 8" walking doll with sleep eyes and painted lashed in a teal plaid taffeta dress with green felt tie-on hat.

Close-up of Stashin's Andrea in teal with painted lashes.

Stashin's 8" Andrea I doll in her satin and tulle bridal gown trimmed in lace.

Close-up of Stashin's separate boxed bridal gown, veil, panties, and paper flowers.

*Dress for Stashin's Andrea 8"
doll has plaid cotton skirt and
pink organdy top with ties
reminiscent of 1953 Ginny
outfits.*

*Inside of Stashin dress above
showing tag, "Andrea/Stashin
Doll Co./Newark, N.J." sewn in
the waist.*

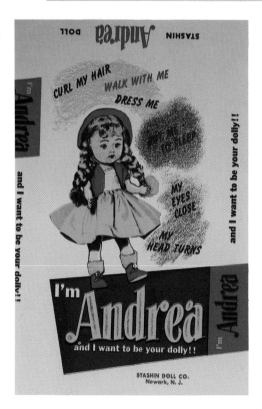

*Stashin's Andrea 8" walking doll c. '50s
with sleep eyes and painted lashes in a
pretty blue and gold striped nylon dress,
open in back and closed with "p" pattern
round metal snap. Matching blue felt
hat trimmed with gold braid.*

*The colorful printed sheet
for Stashin's Andrea doll
box lid shows the doll
and painted lash fea-
tures. An actual box with
the lid has not been
found.*

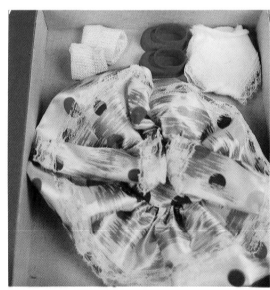

*A tagged Andrea dress, shoes, socks, and cotton knit panties
are boxed in a red and white diagonal striped box.*

Note: This is the same doll as Cosmopolitan's Ginger Type #1 with painted lashes and was also used for Duchess's Randi Type #1 and for Fortune's Ninette.
Value: $55.00 – 65.00 dressed; $75.00+ in box, hard to find.

TYPE # 2
Doll Characteristics: These dolls have the characteristics of Fortune's Pam. They are strung 8" hard plastic, head-turning dolls with sleep eyes and molded lashes, mold line behind ear; straight legs with molded T-strap shoes painted white. Note: Only one of this Type #2 has been found MIB. This is the same T-strap feet with "peg" arm hooks doll as Fortune's Pam but with shoes painted white.
Dress Characteristics: Same as Type #1 Andrea.
Value: #75.00+ in box. Only one example of Type #2 found MIB to date (see pg. 185).

Penny 8" c. 1959
Stashin's Penny doll has not been found to date in an original box or polyethylene bag as advertised. The following description is based entirely on Stashin's Penny photo and advertising copy.
Marks on Doll: Unmarked.
Boxes Marked: Dolls and outfits were placed into polyethylene bags and stapled onto cards marked "I'm Penny, And I want to be your dolly!!/Stashin Doll Co, Newark, N.J." Outfits are also found in unmarked red and white diagonally striped boxes.
Doll Characteristics: From the doll photo this doll appears to be the same as competitor Mary Lu by Doll Bodies. A hard plastic 7½" strung doll with sleep eyes with molded lashes and painted lashes below eyes, mold line behind ear; arms with C-shaped hooks; fingers on her left hand molded together up to tips; right hand 2nd and 3rd fingers molded together; shoes with flat molded bows painted white and no toe detail; mold lines are heavy along outside of the legs. Her brochure reads: "Yes, Penny's eyes, head, legs and arms move and she has Saran and Dynel hair, and her very own lace trimmed panties." Penny with one dress sold for 98 cents or doll only for 79 cents; individual outfits in bags for 39 cents. Note: This is the same doll as Doll Bodies Mary Lu, and Roberta's 8" girl doll (see Doll Bodies and Rober-

ta sections).
Dress Characteristics: Outfits are open in back with finished hems and unfinished waist seam; some closed with a round "p" pattern snap and some with regular handsewn metal snaps; some have attached slips. Some separate Penny outfits were boxed with a straw hat and with vinyl side-snap shoes not shown in the plastic bagged outfits, "Wardrobe of 30 dresses in assorted colors and styles." The round "p" pattern snap dresses are better made than the regular metal snap. No Penny dress tags have been found to date.
Wig Characteristics: Advertised, "Saran and Dynel braids;" other styles are not indicated on packaging; "Dress me-curl my hair-put me to sleep."
Value: $35.00 undressed; $55.00+ in bag; no examples found in original bags to date.

Stashin's "Penny" outfit box with red paisley cotton print dress, red straw hat, shoes, and socks. Note the hard-to-find red socks.

Stashin's "Penny" outfit box with pink taffeta sundress, pink straw hat, shoes, purse, and socks.

Stashin's "Penny" outfit box with blue flowered cotton dress, blue straw hat, blue vinyl side-snap shoes, purse, and socks; made the same as the red dress above.

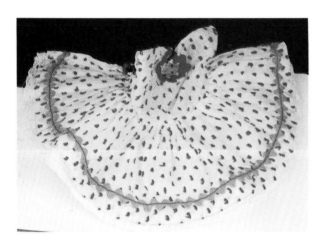

This dotted dress trimmed with rick-rack is advertised as sealed in a plastic bag with the Penny doll.

Packaged open back dotted dress from Penny advertisement has inexpensive square neckline trim.

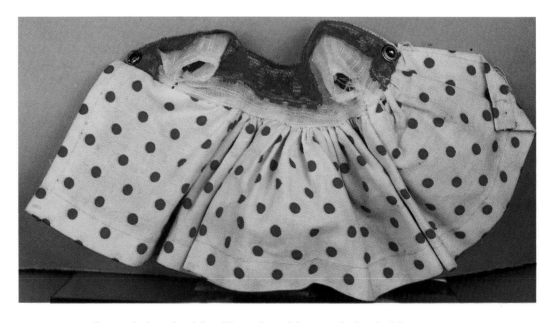

Inexpensively made red dotted Penny dress with an open back and a "p" pattern snap.

"J.J. Newberry Co./$1.00" label on Andrea's outfit box.

Stashin's Andrea Type #2 is an 8" hard plastic, strung doll with molded lashes, molded T-strap shoes painted white. She wears a dress tagged "Andrea" with a matching pink felt tam and has original red and white striped box. This is the only Type #2 Andrea found to date. Courtesy Deirdre Olson.

Stashin's Andrea window box lid for separate outfit.

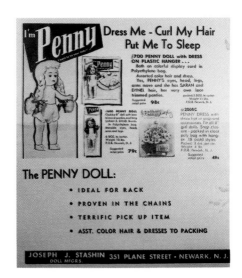

Advertisement for Stashin's 7½" "Penny" doll and her separate outfits. "Dress Me–Curl My Hair, Put Me to Sleep." She is probably a Doll Bodies strung doll with sleep eyes, a braided wig, and flat molded bows on feet. Her separate outfit shown at right is packaged in a polyethylene bag with either a "straw hat or soap." "1959" is written in pencil on the ad's backing.

Close-up of Stashin's advertised Penny doll has the characteristics of Mary Lu by Doll Bodies: Strung body with lashes painted under the eyes and flat bows molded to the feet. Ad calls her a "chubby 8" doll with lace trimmed panties, and long Saran & Dynel braids."

185

❦ Terri Lee Company ❦

Terri Lee was a popular 16" doll created and introduced c. 1948 by Violet Gradwohl. At first Terri Lee was made from composition and then in hard plastic, but her unique chunky body and wide set eyes never changed. Other Terri Lee dolls were added to the family, like 10" Tiny Terri Lee and unmarked 10" Linda Baby. These smaller dolls did not directly compete in the toddler or Ginnette look-alike market. However, c. 1956 Terri Lee Co. did introduce 8" toddler type Girl Scout and Brownie dolls using large eye, molded lash Ginger dolls purchased from Cosmopolitan. They were first-quality dolls with brunette or blonde Saran wigs set in fluffy, curled up styles. These dolls are very collectible today.

Toddlers

Terri Lee Girl Scout/Brownie 8" c. 1956 – 1958

Marks on Doll: Unmarked.

Boxes Marked: Official Brownie Scout Doll/Terri Lee Sales Corp. Boxes carried the official Scout trademarked insignia on the box in a striped design.

Doll Characteristics: Hard plastic 8" head-turning walker with sleep eyes and molded lashes; mold lines through center of the ear; straight arms with separate fingers and C-shaped hooks; straight legs with toe detail; some had bent knees. Note: This is the same doll body as wide or medium eye Ginger dolls (see Cosmopolitan section).

Dress Characteristics: Well-made cotton uniforms with plastic belts closed with a round flat brown or green metal snap, finished hems, round flat metal snaps up front of uniform. Girl Scout uniform had long sleeves; Brownie uniform had short sleeves with white hem stitching and double stitching trim on sleeves and across back; Terri Lee cloth tags inside felt beanie with Scout insignia on front; brown or green vinyl side-snap shoes and socks. Note: Since Cosmopolitan also sold Ginger herself in these Scout outfits, one of the best ways to tell which is which is by the tag inside the outfit.

Wig Characteristics: Well-made, glued-on Saran wigs. This particular Scout Doll usually had tiny ribbons pinned at the temples.

Value: $75.00 dressed; $100.00+ in box.

Tiny Terri Lee 10" c. 1955 – 1956

Marks on Doll: "C" in a circle on the neck.

Boxes Marked: Terri Lee.

Doll Characteristics: Hard plastic 10" doll, a head-turning walker, brown sleep eyes with heavy lashes; straight arms, 1st, 2nd, and 3rd fingers molded together with palms facing body. Note: There was also a 10" Tiny Jerri Lee doll from the same mold.

Dress Characteristics: Well-made, finished hems, regular buttons and snaps, and tagged Terri Lee. Some of her outfits matched Terri Lee and Jerri Lee.

Wig Characteristics: Well-made, glued-on wigs.

Value: $175.00 dressed; $225.00 in Girl Scout uniform.

Tiny Terri Lee c. 1955 hard plastic 10" walking doll in Majorette #3165 red and white satin costume with red felt hat with gold cord and feather. Courtesy Marge Meisinger.

Terri Lee 8" tagged Brownie uniform in original Terri Lee box with Brownie logo.

Terri Lee 8" tagged Girl Scout and Brownie (replaced belt) on right with separate Terri Lee packaged uniform. The Brownie on the left is Cosmopolitan's tagged Brownie Scout. All of these dolls are Ginger dolls. Courtesy Marge Meisinger.

Baby

Linda Baby 10" c. 1951

Marks on Doll: Unmarked.

Boxes Marked: Linda Baby.

Doll Characteristics: Terri Lee's 10" Linda Baby c. 1951 was a jointed "rose-petal vinyl" baby doll with molded hair. She was originally named Linda Lee after founder Mrs. Gradwohl's second daughter.

Dress Characteristics: Same as Tiny Terri Lee. Tags printed: "Linda Baby."

Wig Characteristics: Molded hair.

Value: $145.00.

The 1954 Toy Time advertises an undressed 10" Baby Linda doll with her Terri Lee sisters. Courtesy Marge Meisinger.

Tiny Terri Lee c. 1955 hard plastic 10" walking doll in red and white dotted costume with silver sandals and white straw hat trimmed with flowers with black velvet on the brim edge. Courtesy Marge Meisinger.

Tiny Terri Lee c. 1955 hard plastic 10" walking doll in brown leather cowgirl costume with brown felt hat with yellow cord tie and white boots. Courtesy Marge Meisinger.

❦ Tiny Town Dolls ❦

Very little is written about Tiny Town dolls, but they have become increasingly popular over the years. The "Tiny Town" for dolls patent was filed in 1949 by "Alma LeBlane doing business as Lenna Lee's Tiny Town Dolls." Box brochures are printed "Tiny Town Dolls, San Francisco."

Most of the dolls were 4", but 5" and 7" dolls are also found. All have felt faces with painted features, wide painted eyes with lashes, and mohair wigs. Their felt or cloth bodies are wrapped over wire armature for posing, and the thin arms have mitten-shaped hands. The painted metal shoes are attached to the legs for weight. Because of their size, it is assumed they were doll-house dolls as well as collectible shelf display dolls. They are quite unique in the '50s doll world. The dolls are not marked, but they have gold foil wrist tags with the company name on one side and doll's name on the other. Values range from $25.00 – 45.00; MIB $45.00 – 75.00.

Four series of dolls were listed in the box brochure: Series #1: Linda, Mary, Pat, Betty, Jean, Chickie, Honey, Blondie, School Girl, Mickey, Little Brother; Series #2: Cowgirl, Irish Colleen, China Girl, Lazy Daisy, Buttons & Bows, Little Peasant, Cowboy, Scotch Lass, China Boy, Outdoor Girl, Fiesta Girl, Little Artist; Series #3: Teacher and Pupils, red hair, brunette, blonde; Series #4: Family set, Mother, Father, Little Girl, Little Boy.

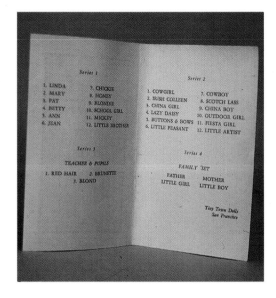

Tiny Town Dolls box flyer listing for series of the dolls. Courtesy Sandy Johnson Barts.

Tiny Town 4" boy with lollipop in original box with brochure. His felt face has painted eyes and features. Courtesy Sandy Johnson Barts.

Tiny Town 4" Mr. and Mrs. Claus figures with white wigs and red costumes. Courtesy Sandy Johnson Barts.

Tiny Town 4" Blondie with original box wears plaid skirt, felt jacket, and red tie-on hat. Courtesy Sandy Johnson Barts.

Tiny Town 4" Little Red Riding Hood with blue dotted dress and white apron. Courtesy Sandy Johnson Barts.

Tiny Town 4" doll dressed as Red Riding Hood. She wears a blue and white check dress with red cape. Original wrist tag and basket. Courtesy Marge Meisinger.

Tiny Town 4" dolls: (L) dressed as Linda in pink hat and blue check dress; (R) unmarked wears a red felt jacket and plaid skirt. Courtesy Marge Meisinger.

Tiny Town 4" dolls dressed as Hansel & Gretel. Costumes of cotton and felt with original wrist tags. Courtesy Marge Meisinger.

Tiny Town 4" Swiss Boy and Girl. Costumes of cotton and felt with original wrist tags. Courtesy Marge Meisinger.

❧ Totsy Manufacturing Company ❧

Totsy Manufacturing Company sold inexpensive dolls for the '50s doll market, and their 8" Little Miss Totsy was a look-alike competitor. A good photograph of the doll and box is in Pat Smith's *Modern Collector's Dolls Eighth Series*, pg. 261, and she has generously allowed me to print it here. Based on "Lovelee Little Doll Outfit" boxes, Totsy sold an 8" Ginnette look-alike doll too. Totsy filed a patent for the name "Sis-n-Me" in 1956 and for "Totsy-Teena" in 1957, but no boxed examples of these dolls have been found. Totsy research continues, and the following is based on information to date.

Toddler Dolls

Little Miss Totsy 8" c. mid 1950s
Marks on Doll: Unmarked.
Boxes Marked: Little Miss Totsy/The Walking Doll/Totsy Mfg. Co./Springfield, Mass.
Doll Characteristics: Hard plastic 8" doll, large sleep eyes with molded lashes, mold line through the center of the ear; straight arms with C-shaped hooks and separate fingers, straight legs with toe detail. Note: These are the same dolls as large eye Ginger dolls, purchased from Cosmopolitan (see Cosmopolitan).
Dress Characteristics: Undressed doll sold in Little Miss Totsy box, with panties, shoes, and socks. Separate Totsy outfits in blue "Lovelee Little Doll Outfit" boxes were surprisingly well made and closed with regular buttons or smooth round metal painted snaps. Most outfits came with socks and/or shoes.
Wig Characteristics: Saran wigs stitched to a backing and glued on.
Value: $35.00 undressed; $55.00 in box.

Doll Accessories

Young and Gay Doll Fashions
Boxes Marked: "Totsy Manufacturing Co., Springfield, Mass-Young and Gay Doll Fashions; Will fit all 8-inch dolls/(on sticker) Coat and Hat."
Value: MIP $15.00 – 25.00.

"Lovelee Little Doll" outfits for 8" dolls
Boxes Marked: Lovelee Little Doll Outfit/To Fit (blank circle to fill in) Inch dolls/By Totsy.
Value: MIP $15.00 – 25.00.

Wide eye Ginger doll found in Little Miss Totsy box. Photo courtesy Pat Smith's Modern Collector's Dolls Eighth Series; doll from the collection of Carl Jankech.

Totsy box for 8" undressed walking doll "Little Miss Totsy," a wide eye Ginger doll. Photo courtesy Pat Smith's Modern Collector's Dolls Eighth Series; doll from the collection of Carl Jankech.

"Young and Gay Doll Fashions" original box with blue cotton ensemble that closes with smooth, red, round snaps for an 8" doll. Twenty-four additional outfits listed on reverse side, c. 1950s.

"Lovelee Little Doll Outfit" MIB for 8" doll: A pink check sunsuit and jacket that closes with buttons for 8" toddler or baby doll; pink suedecloth slippers with white pompons are in the box.

"Lovelee Little Doll Outfit" MIB for 8" doll: Red and white ribbed knit pants, socks, and jacket closing with round white metal snap, for 8" baby doll.

"Lovelee Little Doll Outfit" MIB for 8" doll: Flannel pajama bottom closes with buttons for 8" toddler or baby doll. Vinyl side-snap shoes are in the box.

❦ Uneeda ❦

Uneeda dates back to the 1920s when they produced unique composition dolls. By the 1950s they had entered the hard plastic doll era, and one of their best-known dolls was Dollikins, a fully jointed 19" fashion doll with hard plastic head and vinyl body, even jointed at the ankles. They did produce a number of small dolls including a tiny 7" Little Miss Dollikins and a toddler doll look-alike, 8" Janie with a hard plastic body but vinyl head. Their best-known 8" dolls were licensed to be dressed in Girl Scout and Brownie uniforms.

Toddler

Janie & Janie Girl Scout c. 1959 – 1960
Marks on Doll: "U" on back of neck of vinyl dolls or none on hard plastic dolls.
Uneeda Boxes Marked: Unknown.
Uneeda Girls Scout Boxes Marked: "Girl Scouts/Official 8" Brownie Scout (or Girl Scout) Doll." Girl Scout boxes were green, and Brownie boxes were brown. According to Sydney Ann Sutton in *Scouting Dolls Through the Years*, Uneeda sold 8" vinyl head Scout dolls, but prior to that 8" hard plastic Scout dolls were sold in boxes marked "Beehler Arts" in tiny letters inside the box lid.
Doll Characteristics:
   TYPE #1: According to Ms. Sutton, the first official Girl Scout dolls were hard plastic "Lucy" dolls from Beehler Arts (see Virga) with sleep eyes, molded lashes.
   TYPE #2: Later vinyl head dolls with sleep eyes, molded lashes, and three lines painted in the corner of the eyes; arms with C-shaped arm hooks and 2nd and 3rd fingers molded together on both hands; hard plastic walking bodies; straight legs with smooth feet and no toe detail. "U" on neck. Note: This same vinyl head doll was sold as Gigi in plastic bell (see A & H section).
Dress Characteristics: Untagged (vs. Terri Lee and Ginger dresses that are tagged). Most have two fake buttons on the front of the dress and two round smooth metal snaps painted brown in the back, and vinyl belts. Early Brownie hats had a tan Brownie on front; later Uneeda hats had an orange Brownie.

Wig Characteristics: Brunette or blonde "Buster Brown" style cuts or bubble cuts.
Value: $45.00 undressed; $125.00 in Girl Scout uniform.

Teen

Uneeda is famous for its 10½" Suzette high-heel fashion doll with soft vinyl head and rigid vinyl body. Also popular was their unusually jointed 19" Dollikin doll with vinyl head and hard plastic body c. 1957, later all vinyl. The line also included an 11" fully jointed Dollikin c. 1968, and the following super-small 7" Little Miss Dollikin.

Uneeda's 8" vinyl head Janie Type #2; "U" mark on neck.

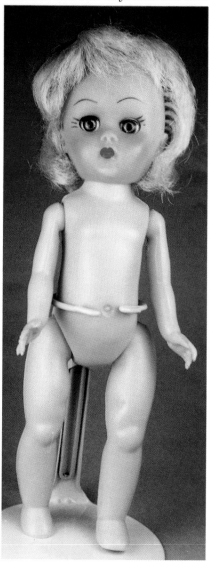

Uneeda's 8" vinyl head doll Janie, with sleep eyes, molded lashes, and three lashes painted at corners; arms with C-shaped hooks and 2nd and 3rd fingers molded together, and feet with no toe detail.

Little Miss Dollikins c. 1957
Marks on Doll: Little Miss/Dollikins/ US Pat/NO.3.101253/OTHER US AND FOREIGN PAT.PEND/MADE IN HONG KONG.
Boxes Marked: Uneeda.
Doll Characteristics: A 7" hard vinyl doll with soft vinyl head with painted eyes, no lashes; jointed at head, elbows, waist, hips, and knees; fingers molded together with separate thumb, high-heel feet.
Wig Characteristics: Rooted hair in long styles.
Value: $45.00 doll.

Uneeda untagged Brownie Scout uniform with fake buttons in front. The back closed with two smooth round metal snaps and also had a vinyl belt and felt beanie.

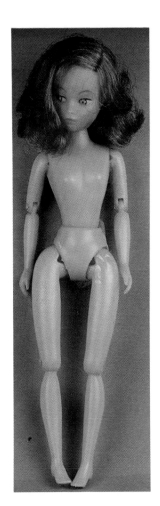

8" Uneeda Little Miss Dollikins c. 1957 hard vinyl doll with painted eyes, in knit hot pink outfit, and red vinyl high heels.

8" Uneeda Little Miss Dollikins doll with painted eyes, rooted hair, jointed at head, elbows, waist, knees, and hips; high-heel feet.

🍇 Unique 🍇

Unique is best known for their '60s low to mid quality blow molded dolls with rooted hair, including a 14" Alice in Wonderland type doll, and vinyl dolls like 12" Ellie May Clampett with painted eyes and rooted hair, both marked Unique. In the 1950s Unique sold a line of "dress me" dolls in plastic bags. Some of the dolls were display type dolls, including Duchess type dolls, and another was an 8" toddler doll named Jeanie sold in "dime" stores like J.J. Newberry.

Jeanie 8" c. 1950s

Marks on Doll: Unmarked.

Boxes Marked: Doll sold in polyethylene bags printed in red: ALL PLASTIC DOLL/ UNIQUE/ "JEANIE"/COMB AND SET MY HAIR/I WALK/I SIT.

Doll Characteristics: Hard plastic 8" doll with sleep eyes and molded lashes, mold line behind ear, mouth paint slightly turned down at corners; straight arms with C-shaped arm hook and separate finger tips on left hand and 2nd and 3rd fingers molded together on the right; straight pin-hipped walking legs with toe detail. Note: This is the same doll as A&H's Gigi #2 and Active's Mindy #1.

Dress Characteristics: This doll is sold in taffeta pants with elastic at the waist and overcast stitching at legs.

Wig Characteristics: Synthetic wig stitched to a backing strip and glued to the head.

Value: $45.00.

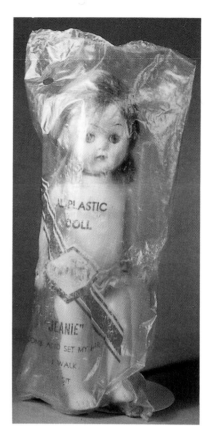

Unique's 8" Jeanie pin-hipped walking doll in plastic bag is dressed only in blue taffeta panties. The sticker on the bag is printed "J.J. Newberry/$1.00."

🍇 Virga Creations 🍇

Virga played an active role in the post-WWII doll world. Founded in the late '40s under the umbrella of Beehler Arts, Ltd., they were one of the first to sell hard plastic dolls to the low and mid-range markets. Founder "Rosemary Beehler, Creator of Virga Dolls," signed each brochure packed into doll boxes, and she undoubtedly participated in the company's 1950 filing for the "Virga" trademark, and for "A Virga Doll" later that year.

Virga's 8" Playmate toddler was one of the cutest 1950s look-alikes. As the momentum builds for Virga doll collecting, their prices are already starting to rise. However, they are still relatively affordable on the secondary market and will undoubtedly be sought out regardless of prices.

Display Dolls c. late 1940s – 1950s

Marks on Dolls: 5" hard plastic painted eye dolls: "Virga" on the back. 5" hard plastic sleep eye dolls and 7" – 7½" hard plastic sleep eye dolls: unmarked.

Boxes Marked: Manufactured by Beehler Arts Ltd., 47 West Street, New York City, NY.

Doll Characteristics: Virga creator Rosemary Beehler promised customers in her brochure c. 1951, "I will keep you pleasantly surprised with new characters from time to time." Indeed, she introduced a wealth of delightful dolls to collectors in the '50s. There is surprisingly little documentation on

continued on pg. 197

Two typical Virga boxes for 7"-7½" hard plastic display dolls. The box on the right is the typical pink Virga box and design. The light pink box with white lace pattern on the right for "Groom" doll and bridal party dolls is found less often.

"Gibson Girl" c. 1949 7" hard plastic painted eye doll with moving arms in pink Virga box wears a black organdy shirt with white lace-trimmed blouse; white felt hat tied with black ribbon.

"Valentine" c. 1949, 7" hard plastic painted eye doll with moving arms wears a red satin and tulle gown, in a pink Virga box.

"Majorette" 7½" c. 1949 hard plastic doll with bright cheek color, painted eyes, fixed head and legs, and moving arms, wears a felt costume with gold trim. Her white boots are painted on.

Bride #460 from "Virga World Series" (c. 1949-'50) 7½" hard plastic doll with "moving" eyes, arms, and head, wears a ruffled white satin gown, packed in a blue acetate window box.

Majorette c. 1949 hard plastic doll in original pink Virga box with acetate window insert, marked "A Virga Doll."

Virga's 7½" hard plastic Hobo #443 has jointed arms, legs, head with sleep eyes, and fixed legs. His clever costume has a felt jacket and hat, "patched" flannel pants, and a pack he carries on a stick.

Virga's 5" hard plastic "Tell Me A Story Series" c. 1949, advertising flyer features a series of 12 hard plastic dolls with side-glancing painted eyes, mohair wigs, and moving arms, marked "Virga" on the back; sold in square pink boxes with acetate window insert. Courtesy Jo Barckley.

Valentine 5" painted eye doll c. 1949 in gown with stenciled hearts, red satin ruffle, and a red felt heart stapled to her head.

Virga Bridesmaid #218 hard plastic painted eye 5" doll c. 1949, in yellow taffeta gown trimmed with nylon ruffle and pink satin ribbon. Note the unusual blue Virga marked box for the bridal series.

Virga's 5" "Little Bo Peep" # 203 from the "Tell Me A Story Series" c. 1949, in a lavender organdy dress stenciled with Bo Peep designs on the skirt and a blue felt hat stapled onto her head. This is the only braided style in the series.

Virga's 5" "Little Miss Muffet" #204 from the "Tell Me A Story Series" c. 1949, in a yellow organdy dress, stenciled Miss Muffet designs on the skirt, and a yellow felt hat stapled to her head.

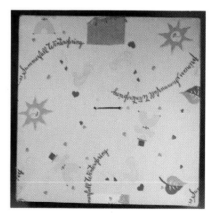

"Princess Summerfall Winterspring" hard plastic 8" jointed doll with sleep eyes from the "Howdy Doody" TV show c. 1950-51 has black braids and wears a "coronation gown," magic necklace, and 4-season tiara. Larger 14" and 18" Princess dolls came packed with Halo Shampoo, cape, and comb.

Virga wrist hang tag for 8" Princess Summerfall Winterspring hard plastic doll, moving eyes, c. 1950-51.

Unique Princess Summerfall Winterspring graphics on Virga's box, c. 1950-51.

early Virga Creations dolls, but the following photos show what has surfaced to date.

Virga introduced 5" plastic painted eye "display" or "costume" dolls c. 1949. They were jointed only at the arms and were marked "Virga" on the back. A 1949 *Playthings* magazine (per Pam and Polly Judd's *Hard Plastic Dolls II*) advertised the line with 12 different stapled-on costumes including nursery rhyme and storybook characters.

A brochure c. 1950 documents Virga's introduction of unmarked "moving eye" plastic display dolls in 5" and 7½" sizes with stapled-on clothes.
Value: $40.00 dressed; $55.00+ in box.

Playmate Strung Doll 8" c. 1954

Virga's look-alikes were among the cutest '50s toddlers with their button noses and sweet faces. Virga's 1954 dealer brochure named them "Playmate Dolls" distinguished from their earlier "display dolls."

Toddlers

TYPE #1
Marks on Dolls: Unmarked.
Boxes Marked: Manufactured by Beehler Arts Ltd., 47 West Street, New York City, NY.
Doll Characteristics: Playmate: Fully jointed, strung 8" hard

plastic head and body, non-walking; chubby bodies; sleep eyes with molded lashes; rare painted lashes below eyes; head mold line behind the ear; arms the same color as the body with 2nd and 3rd fingers molded together; C-shaped arm hooks; molded-on T-strap shoes instead of toes; shoes were usually unpainted vs. competitors like PMA painted Joanie doll feet (see PMA section). Most attribute manufacture to Ontario Plastics or to Plastic Molded Arts. Note: Virga's competitor, Fortune Dolls, sold the 8" Pam toddler with virtually the same head and body as Virga's toddler but with different arms (see Fortune section).
Wig Characteristics: *Stitching & Style:* The Dynel wigs in curls or braids that could be "shampooed, set, combed" according to advertisements. Two parallel rows of exposed stitching (sometimes very close) are sewn along the part onto a single strip of stiffened backing vs. Ginny's wig with one row of stitching. Also, the backing strip color could be black for brunette dolls unlike Ginny that had white backing strips in all cases. (Note: 1957 rooted styles obviously did not have these characteristics.) *Material:* Virga advertised Dynel wigs in the '54, '56, and '57 brochures, and they appear to be the same type for straight leg and bent knee Virga walkers.
Dress Construction 1954:
Quality: Virga dolls were mid to lower market dolls, and clothing lacked some of the detailing of higher quality dolls. None of the dresses were tagged.

In 1954 Virga's 7½" dolls were sold in "Acetate Wall Plaques" #702–#709.

Virga's 1954 "Acetate Wall Plaques" #710– #717.

Necklines: Round, square, or bib collar necklines were common.

Sleeves: Many high-waisted Virga dresses had pinafore sleeves gathered onto bias tape more crudely finished than Vogue styles. Dresses with regular waistlines were sleeveless or had cap sleeves with no shoulder seams. While some costumes (majorette, Girl Scout, Cowgirl, etc.) had long sleeves, regular dresses rarely did.

Skirts: Gathered with tiny pleats sewn to waist seam. Hems were deep, turned, and stitched with a straight chain type stitch. A single back seam was stitched closed below the dress opening.

Slips: Dresses did not have attached or separate slips.

Pants: Most were straight cut with bias-trimmed loose leg openings. The waistline elastic was stitched to the inside of the pants fabric and not exposed from outside.

Finishes and Closures: 1954: Virga dresses c. 1954 had round brass snaps with a circular "p" pattern like Ginger's snaps. Closed back seams were stitched unfinished below the dress opening. The waist seam was crudely cut, and left unfinished. 1955 on: Both walking and bent knee Virga dolls had circular donut snaps, and seams at the back and waist were stitched closed and overcast by machine.
Value: $45.00 – 65.00; MIB $100.00 – 150.00.

Playmate 1954 Dress Series

Virga had two lines of '54 toddler dolls, each with distinctive looking "removable clothes," and each costume was given a girl's name.

Regular Line Playmate Series 1954: An inexpensive series of twelve unmarked 8" dolls numbered P 801-812 wearing simply made dresses closed with either round brass snap or circular donut snaps. They wore inexpensive tie-on matching fabric hats.
Value: $55.00 – 65.00 dressed; MIB $75.00+.

Both Virga dresses have pleated waist gathers and deep hems turned and chain type straight stitch; left: Dress c. 1954 with a brass snap has a closed and unfinished back seam and an unfinished waist seam; right: Donut-snap dress c. 1955 has its waist seam and closed back seam finished with an overcast stitch.

Virga's "Birthday Party" #P-807 doll c. '56-'57 wears a flocked organdy dress with a square neck and cap sleeves. Lower left: '54 "Linda" #P-855 cotton dress with attached bib collar. Right: '56-57 #P-803 Luncheon Pinafore high-waisted dress with pinafore sleeves.

Comparison of two mid-1950s Dynel wigs: The wig type on the left was used by Virga's Lucy Playmate or Fortune's Pam with two lines of stitching at the parts. The wig on the right was used by Vogue's Ginny with one line of stitching. Both were stitched to a thin strip of stiffened fabric backing. Note that Virga's flips are not as tightly wound as Ginger's wig.

Left: Virga dress with donut snap phased in beginning 1954, and used from 1955 on; Virga dress on left c. 1954 has small, round brass "p" pattern snap.

DeLuxe Line Playmate 1954 Dress Series: Six DeLuxe strung dolls numbered P-851 to P-856 with straw hats and cute dresses, play clothes, and frilly pinafores. Some collectors have difficulty identifying Virga's '54 clothing today because of the similarities to competitors' clothing. For example, both Virga's and Cosmopolitan's Ginger had the small round brass or painted snaps with a circular "p" pattern. This can confuse collectors. Also, they are more familiar with Virga's later circular donut snap. Separately boxed 1954 outfits included Playmate DeLuxe Clothes Package including a straw hat; C 881-886 Fancy Costumes; Hat Box Assortment; Shoes & Socks; Roller Skate Shoes; and Ice Skate Shoes, along with 12 separate clothes assortments complete with accessories with tie-on hats, purse, pants and a felt jacket.
Value: $55.00 – 65.00 dressed; MIB $75.00+.

Type #2 Playmate Walker 8"
c. 1955

Marks on Dolls: Unmarked.

Boxes Marked: Manufactured by Beehler Arts Ltd., 47 West Street, New York City, NY.

Doll Characteristics: In 1955 Virga's 8" Playmate doll had the same unmarked head and body as the '54 doll except now the toddler walked! The dealer brochure advertised: "Heads move as they walk. They sit or stand." The Playmate line was increased from 12 to 18 dolls in '55.

Continued on page 203.

Note the early brass snap on "Mamie" P-811 used in 1954 and into '55, but changed to a donut snap in '55.

Virga's 1954 and 1955 Playmate Series- Mamie P-811 wears a dotted red dress with pinafore sleeves and matching tie-on hat and panties. Note: Hat shown is a replacement with a different dotted pattern.

8" Virga Playmate MIB with lashes painted under the eyes and with painted white feet (just as PMA's Joanie doll.) These dolls boxes are printed with "P-100" series numbers, and the dresses are sleeveless vs. the pinafore ruffled sleeves of the P-800 series.

1954 Virga brochure page for "Playmate Series;" strung 8" Virga dolls with sleep eyes, molded lashes, and molded T-strap feet.

Virga's 8" hard plastic "Playmates" tod-dler with sleep eyes sold as a Ginny look-alike c. 1954. Note the cute button nose, bright cheek color, and Dynel wig. She wears cute cotton dress "Ellen" P-802 with a pale blue cotton dress with pinafore sleeves, trimmed with braid embroidered with flowers along the skirt.

Virga's "Gloria" P-805 from the 1954 Playmate Series wears a crisp gold and white checked dress with matching tie-on hat. The strung '54 hard plastic dolls had bright cheek color and came in colorful Virga boxes.

Virga's Playmate "C" series outfits c. '54 were sold in acetate wrapped boxes lined with paper doily. This boxed "Toni" C-106 outfit includes dress with brass snap, bloomers, tie-on hat, and no shoes, a rare find today.

1954 "Toni" P-806 back with brass "p" pattern snap.

1954 "Toni", P-806, Virga Playmate doll.

Virga's 1954 Playmate Series "Amy" P-807, blue check dress, white pinafore sleeves, and matching tie-on bonnet. The red braid trim along the skirt hem is a variation on the check trim shown in the catalog sheet; dress closes with a brass snap.

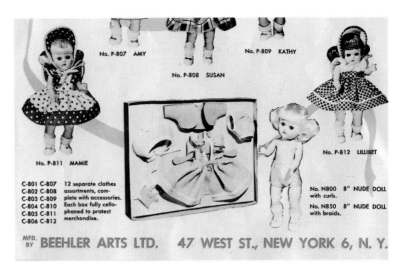

Virga's '54 catalog page showing P-811 Mamie, Susan #808, and P-812 Lillibet, and separate outfits from C series.

Virga's 1954 Playmate Series "Kathy" P-809 pale pink cotton dress with pinafore sleeves, lace or braid skirt trim, and matching tie-on pink bonnet; closes with a brass snap.

Virga's 1954 brochure advertised the DeLuxe Playmate Series. Clockwise: P-855 "Linda," P-851 "Cindy," P-853 "Peggy," P-853 "Nancy," P-854 "Betsy," P-856 "Kandy."

The 1954 DeLuxe Playmate Series, "Cindy" P-851 wears a crisp white pin striped taffeta dress with a pattern variation on skirt trim from catalog, and with no bodice trim. Her straw hat is trimmed with red and white stripe. The 1955 version of this outfit was very similar but with a different skirt trim pattern.

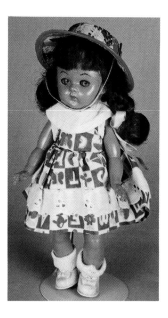

Virga's 1954 DeLuxe Playmate Series offered cute cotton dresses like this 8" "Linda" P-855 on a black Playmate doll. Note the colorful woven straw hat edged with red braid.

The 1954 DeLuxe Playmate Series 8" "Kandy" P-856 wears a crisp white cotton dress with blue fruit print on the skirt; pinafore sleeves and a straw hat. The 1955 version of this outfit added a cape.

Virga's 8" doll dressed in bride or first communion dress with white embossed taffeta with lace trim and a tulle veil closed with brass snaps c. '54; closed with a circular donut snap c. '55.

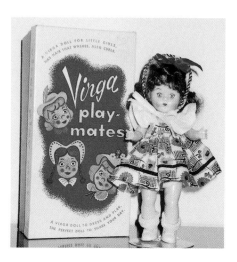

Virga Playmate 8" hard plastic '55 "Lillibet" P-812 wears a black and red print dress with white pinafore sleeves and tie-on hat. The '54 Lillibet dress had a checked pattern print. Courtesy Mary Britton.

Virga 8" strung doll wears an undocumented red satin pinafore dress trimmed with white lace with straw hat trimmed with red bow and flowers, assumed to be Valentine Special. Courtesy Amy Hirsch.

Virga's 6" "Bashful Angel" with moving eyes and feather wings in original acetate case.

Dress Characteristics: See '54 Playmate.

Playmate '55 Dress Series: The DeLuxe Playmate Series was increased from 6 to 12 dolls in '55. While the numbers and names of Virga's '54 dolls remained the same as for '53, some outfits had slight changes, and others changed entirely. One of the most notable outfit changes was for "P-806 Toni" who was dressed in a sweet little flowered dress in '54, and in '55 "P-806 Toni came in "Blue Jeans" (see pg. 200). Other new '55 outfits included a bridal gown and a nurse's uniform. Some of the '55 dolls retained first names, but others now had generic names by activity such as P-855 Sunday School Dress. Some of the outfits had the same round snap as '54, others had the circular donut snap used beginning in '55 and more familiar today. Despite the doll's variety of first names, one stuck when Virga printed "My Name Is Lucy/I Walk" on a plaid hinged travel case for the 8" and 9"

Virga's 8" hard plastic '55 "Susan" P-808 in "Playmate Costumes" box, originally cellophane covered. The purple cotton dress with a round brass snap has matching tie-on hat and pants with pink felt jacket and pink plastic purse. The same outfit in '54 had a different hem pattern.

Virga's 8" hard plastic "Judy" P-801 from 1955 Playmate Series wears a cotton purple print dress; missing felt Dutch style cap.

1954 Deluxe Playmate Series accessories included 6" Bashful Angel and 6" Baby Toddler.

Virga's 1954 catalog page shows the 8" Playmate doll in "Travel Case" #TC899 with accessories and dress ensemble. Note the diamond pattern case.

Virga's 8" undressed strung doll in a plaid travel case marked "My Name is Lucy/I Walk" with extra gold check dress P-805 "Gloria." Walking dolls also came in cases c. '55. Courtesy Marge Meisinger.

Virga's 8" hard plastic "Carol" P-803 from 1955 Playmate Series wears white cotton dotted dress and tie-on hat. Courtesy Billie Nelson Tyrrell.

Virga's 8" "Jane" P-804 from '55 Playmate Series, flowered yellow print dress; originally with a straw hat. '54 dress had different flowered pattern with tie hat.

dolls. Today many collectors simply refer to all of Virga's 8" dolls as "Lucy."

Wig Characteristics: Same as '54 Playmate.

Value: Dressed: $50.00 – 55.00; in box $75.00+.

Virga's 8" Lolly-Pop Playmate Dolls c. 1955

Marks on Doll: Unmarked.

Boxes Marked: Manufactured by Beehler Arts Ltd., 47 West Street, New York City, NY. There were two box lid designs. One had a balloon design; the other was the standard Playmate box with the words "Lolly-Pop" added.

Doll Characteristics: One of Virga's most colorful mid '50s series of dolls was called The Lolly-Pop Walking Doll. They used the unmarked bodies of the 8" Playmate Type #2 walking dolls, but they had bright wig colors and matching color taffeta dresses with pinafore sleeves. Lolly-Pop dolls are among the most collectible Playmates today. Other dolls had pastel colored wigs like NASB Muffie and A&H's Gigi, and Ginger reportedly had colored hair too. But Virga merchandised the colorful beauties better than any other company, so most think of Lolly-Pops as the colored hair dolls of the '50s.

Dress Characteristics: Lolly-Pop dolls wore distinctive taffeta dresses with pinafore sleeves with embroidered nylon trim around the skirt.

Wig Characteristics: Wigs were sewn onto strips of backing and glued to the head. Special colors for the series included, "Nile, pink, blue, maize, orchid, aqua, blonde, brunette, and redhead."

Value: Dressed doll $80.00; in box $110.00.

Virga's 8" hard plastic "Amy" P-807 from 1955 Playmate Series wears a blue check cotton dress and white felt Dutch style hat. The 1954 version of P-807 Amy had a matching tie-on hat with the blue check dress.

Virga's 8" hard plastic black doll "Topsy" P-813 was introduced in the 1955 Playmate Series wearing a cotton print dress with white piqué bib collar and red straw hat.

Virga's 8" hard plastic "Scotch Lass" P-818 from 1955 Playmate Series with a plaid cotton skirt and blue felt bodice with matching cap.

Virga's 1955 P-851 Cindy from the Deluxe Playmate series wears a pin striped taffeta dress very similar to the 1954 Cindy but with different skirt trim. Courtesy Jeanne Niswonger.

Type #3 Playmates, Bending Knees c. 1956 – 1960s

Marks on Dolls: Unmarked.

Boxes Marked: Manufactured by Beehler Arts Ltd., 47 West Street, New York City, NY. Boxes for the Playmates were simple with blue with gold trim and a separate window display lid. The larger boxes for the Candy 'n Spice series were deluxe with colorful interior graphics, a gate-fold interior closure, and a separate box top cover.

Doll Characteristics: Madame Alexander's 8" Wendy Alexander-Kin was "off and walking" around 1956 with uniquely designed bending knees, and Vogue's Ginny had bending knees of her own in 1957. Virga's 8" Play-Mate dolls (with their newly hyphenated name) were no exception.

The real surprise about Virga's bent knee dolls is that they are not the same dolls at all as the straight leg dolls, they even have a different head. Virga's '57 hard plastic bending knee dolls had sleep eyes and molded lashes, arms with the second and third fingers molded together, a Virga C-shaped arm hook, and feet with toe detail. The 8" bending knee dolls were also unmarked, so they are difficult to identify today.

Virga's use of Ginger type dolls with bending knees was confirmed only recently. Some previously dismissed mint Virga bending knee dolls as a Ginger doll in the wrong box because they didn't look like Virga's straight leg walkers. Fortunately this changed when Jo Barckley, who collects and researches dolls, acquired Virga's 1957 multi-page dealer brochure documenting 8" bending knee dolls with color photos showing the doll type. To some, the '57 brochure photos show that two different types of Virga bending knee dolls. Indeed, two different types of bending knee dolls wearing '57 catalog outfits have been found mint in Virga boxes today. One doll has mold lines behind the ear like the Active Doll Company's Mindy, and the other has a mold line through the ear's center like Cosmopolitan's Ginger dolls. In either case, the plastic was a reasonably good quality and has stood up well over the years.

The '57 catalog sheet shows 36 "Play-Mates With Bending Knees" and 18 "8" Candy 'n Spice Series With Bending Knees." One bending knee doll with accessories is shown with a "Bon Voyage traveling trunk" not marked Virga. The price list showed the bent knee and straight leg dolls sold simultaneously.

'57 Dress Characteristics: Dressed and undressed straight leg and bent knee hard plastic walking dolls were all sold in

Continued on page 214.

Lolly-Pop dolls in four of the nine different wig colors available and wearing the distinctive taffeta dress with nylon pinafore sleeves and skirt trim.

Virga Lolly-Pop dolls were sold in two different box styles. The hard-to-find box on the left has balloon graphics; on the right a standard Playmates series box with "Lolly-Pop" printed on the lid.

"Lolly-Pops," Virga's popular mid-'50s line had bright colored wigs including bright blue, pink, and also blue, green, and yellow.

Virga's 1957 catalog page showing 8" Play-Mates with Bending Knees #P-801 – #P-809. Courtesy Jo Barckley.

Virga's 1957 catalog page showing 8" Play-Mates with Bending Knees #P-810 – #P-818. Courtesy Jo Barckley.

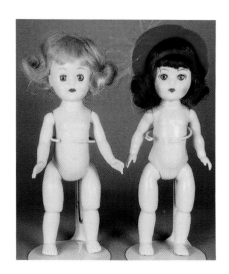

The 1957 bent knee walkers included the doll on the right, a wide-eyed Ginger, and also perhaps the doll on the left with Mindy type head.

1957 outfit P#803 Luncheon Pinafore, a chintz floral dress with organdy pinafore sleeves and attached apron, bow stapled onto the head.

In 1957 "Birthday Party" P-807 Virga Play-Mate doll sold as a bending knee or straight leg walker doll. She wears the original pink flocked organdy dress with matching hat.

In 1957 Virga phased in bent knee walking dolls and blue and gold window boxes like this with MIB P-810 "Coat, Hat, Slacks" red felt ensemble.

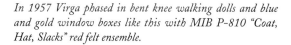

Virga's '56 or '57 straight leg walker MIB P-813 Virga Play-Mate in Riding Habit. Courtesy Jo Barckley.

Bent knee walker Virga doll c. 1957 wears "Blue Jeans" P-816.

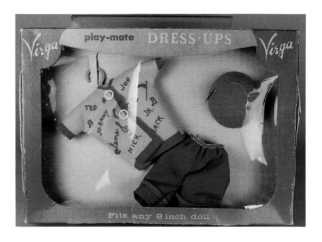

Virga's 1957 catalog page showing 8" Play-Mates with Bending Knees #P-828 – #P-836. Courtesy Jo Barckley.

Separate boxed outfit for 1957 "Blue Jeans" P-816 with cute red stenciled gold felt top and blue cotton pants.

Virga's 1957 catalog page showing 8" Play-Mates with Bending Knees #P-819 – #P-827. Courtesy Jo Barckley.

This 1957 "Artist" P-814 is one of the few outfits with "Virga" stenciled on the cotton smock pocket. The cotton pants and beret had different patterns.

Alternate "Artist" smock outfit. Courtesy Judy Cullen.

The 1957 "Traveling Suit" P-824 in original box is pink felt with matching hat on bent knee walker. Courtesy Mary Miskowiec.

Circular donut snap on embossed taffeta dress, possibly bride or first communion dress. Also came with brass snap c. '54.

This embossed taffeta dress is like Virga's 1957 P-819 "Bride" dress but with pinafore sleeves.

Virga's blue and gold box for 1957 outfits. Shown is the P-829 "Parasol Outfit" for Bending Knee doll.

The 1957 "Bridesmaid" P-821 in original box is blue organdy with pink satin trim, hat is a replacement of the white straw original hat.

The 1957 "Maid of Honor" P-820 is pink organdy trimmed with pink organdy and lace.

The 1957 P-829 "Parasol Doll" was shown in the catalog sheet without the rick-rack skirt trim. This variation has red rick-rack trim on white organdy skirt with printed cotton bodice and paper umbrella.

Reverse side of Virga's 1957 separate outfit box listing separate outfits available. Note they all have a "C" code vs. the dressed doll's "P" code for the same outfits.

Virga Play-Mates "Girl Scout" P-833 doll c. 1957 with bending knees, blue and gold window box. Note that the doll's Ginger head with wide eyes was different from the previous straight leg walking and strung dolls. Courtesy Dian Zillner.

Virga 1957 bent knee walker doll wears the "Picnic Outfit," P-831 yellow flowered cotton halter sundress with straw bonnet.

Candy n' Spice separately boxes outfit "Evening Gown" C-866, and embossed lace gown with pink velvet bodice over a pink taffeta underskirt.

Virga's 1957 catalog page showing 8" Candy n' Spice Series with Bending Knees #851 – #859. Courtesy Jo Barckley.

Virga's 1957 catalog page showing 8" Candy n' Spice Series with Bending Knees #860 – #868. Courtesy Jo Barckley.

The Candy n' Spice line c. 1997 had a deluxe gate-fold box with colorful graphics. This "Ski Outfit" P-859 is possibly from the 1956 line as the costume trim differs from the '57 catalog.

The Candy n' Spice "Gibson Girl" P-853 costume with black felt vest and checked skirt.

The Candy n' Spice P-856 "Visiting Outfit" with blue felt cape over white cotton dress. Original lid on the right fits over the gate-fold top. Courtesy Jo Barckley.

Virga 1957 Bent Knee Walker "Bride" P-864 wearing an embroidered nylon gown in a deluxe Tiny Twinkle box. Courtesy Marge Meisinger.

Virga's 1957 catalog page showing clothes display packages, Ballerina with box, and 8" doll with bending knees. Courtesy Jo Barckley.

The Virga ballerina box, outside gate-fold labeled "Tiny Twinkle." Brides and ballerinas were also sold in the blue and gold window boxes.

Tiny Twinkle Ballerina in special Virga DeLuxe gatefold box. Courtesy Judy Cullen.

Virga's "Tiny Twinkle" ballerina c. mid-1950s with pointed toes and deluxe box is a collector's favorite. This doll's wig is pink, but they also came in other colors.

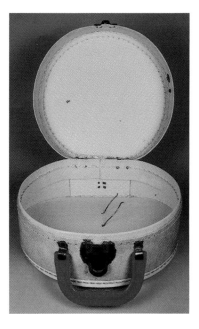

Virga's "Playmates/ School Breezaway" plaid cardboard hatbox case c. mid-1950s for 8" or 9" doll.

Virga's "Tiny Twinkle" ballerina c. 1957 with bright yellow hair, pointed toes, and deluxe box. Courtesy Marge Meisinger.

"School Breezaway" yellow-lined cardboard travel case with metal holder for one 8" or 9" doll with room for extra outfits c. mid-1950s.

Top of Virga dealer countertop display for their boxed separate outfits shown on catalog sheet c. 1957. Each unit contained 12 Virga clothes packages. Courtesy Mary Miskowiec.

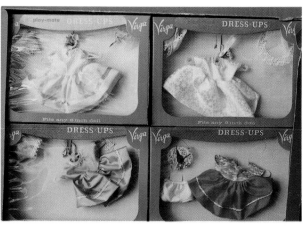

Inside '57 countertop display with one tier of four outfits with Lolly-Pop doll modeling in front. Courtesy Mary Miskowiec.

Inside countertop display with second tier of four outfits. Courtesy Mary Miskowiec.

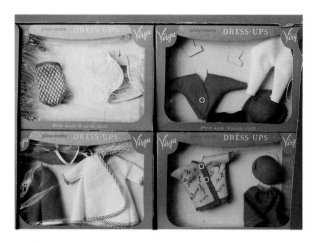

Top tier of countertop display with four outfits. Courtesy Mary Miskowiec.

Virga's Bon Voyage case came in several different colors, tan, blue, and red with a Playmate doll inside. Courtesy Jo Barckley.

The outside of case is printed, "Bon Voyage;" "Virga" is not printed on the exterior.

Virga's "Nurse Breezaway" red-lined cardboard case with metal holder for one 8" or 9" Playmate doll with room for outfits. Courtesy Toni Ferry.

Virga's Playmate 8" dia. x 4" deep "Nurse Breezaway" blue cardboard case c. mid-1950s. Courtesy Toni Ferry.

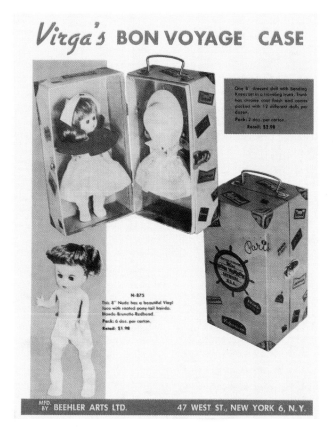

1997 Virga catalog pictures "Bon Voyage" case with "chrome coat finish," a bending knee doll, and extra outfits. Courtesy Jo Barckley.

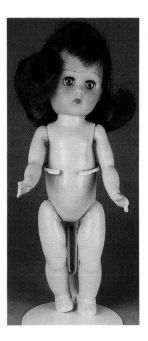

Virga's Bon Voyage case in red.

Vinyl head doll marked "Virga" on neck has slightly larger eyes than other marked "Virga" vinyl head dolls.

Undocumented red and blue "Little Traveler" case with Virga cardboard hangers and a walking doll inside. Courtesy Bunny Henckel.

Undocumented gold and black "Little Traveler" case.

Unusual Virga pink box for "vinyl face" dolls with rooted hair, hard plastic body, and molded T-strap shoes; marked Virga on neck.

'57. Virga's '57 Play-Mates and Candy 'n Spice series have the same "P" series numbers as Virga's 1955 De Luxe series plus six additional outfits, indicating a repositioning of that line. They no longer bore girls' names as some did in previous years. For example, '57 Play-Mates dolls had basic names like "Tea Party" and "Girl Scout." Only "Sunday School" and "Bride" dolls are found in both series but have different pattern designs. The cute but simply made outfits closed with circular snaps, had hats or hair bows of some type, and vinyl slip-on style shoes with either molded bows or fixed straps.
Value: Dressed doll: $50.00 – 55.00; in box $75.00.

Tiny Twinkle/Ballerina (photos, pgs. 210, 211)
Marks on Doll: None.
Box Marks: "Tiny Twinkle" printed on gate-fold lid.
Doll Characteristics: Virga sold a "P" series of boxed dolls as "Ballerina" (with pointed toes), and "Tiny Twinkle" dolls. Some ballerina dolls were hard plastic Playmate Type #2 dolls but with pointed toes. Others were vinyl head Playmate dolls with pointed toes. Tiny Twinkle dolls were featured in Virga's 1957 brochure with pointed ballerina toes, but they also put flat-footed Playmate dolls in the same boxes.
Wig Characteristics: Pastel color wigs in the same colors as the Lolly-Pop dolls; some had regular blonde, brunette, or redheaded wigs or rooted hair.
Value: $75.00 – 95.00 in box.

Counter Top Displays/Accessories (photos, pgs. 211, 212)
Dealers could also buy "C" series separate outfits in counter "display packages" for various lines: Play-Mate Regular, Deluxe, and Super Deluxe, Candy & Spice, and Ballerina Clothes in "Nine different colors...." Ms. Barckley's 1957 Virga catalog by Beehler Arts, Ltd. is the most comprehensive brochure examined to date.
Value:
    Individual boxed c. '54-doily box, $75.00.
    Individual boxed c. '55-56 acetate lid boxes, $50.00.
    Individual boxed c. '57 outfits, $45.00.

Virga's Playmate Vinyl Head Dolls 8" c. 1957 (photos, pg. 213)
Marks on Dolls: "VIRGA" on neck.
Boxes Marked: Manufactured by Beehler Arts Ltd., 47 West Street, New York City, NY. Boxes were blue and gold with window lids.
Doll Characteristics: In 1957 Virga offered vinyl headed, rooted hair, straight leg dolls with T-strap shoes that were marked "Virga" on the neck. Virga's 1957 price sheet lists, "8" Nudes, Vinyl Headed Rooted Ponytail Straight Leg." These vinyl headed dolls had the same molded T-strap feet as the all-hard plastic dolls, their second and third fingers were molded together, but their heads did not turn.
Dress Characteristics: See '57 bending knee Virga.
Wig characteristics: Advertised as "Rooted pony-tail hairdo. Blonde, brunette, or redhead." While the price lists straight leg "nudes" with ponytail styles, the dressed dolls had wigs set in flip styles also.
Value: $55.00; $75.00 in box.

Fashion Dolls

Schiaparelli Dolls 8" c. 1956
Madame Elsa Schiaparelli was a famous European fashion designer from the 1920s –1950s. In the early '50s she designed clothes for Effanbee's Honey doll, but around 1956 she designed three dolls for Beehler Arts through their Virga division: 12½" high-heel doll named Chi-Chi, an 8" doll named Go-Go (after Mme. Schiaparelli's daughter), and an 8" Tu-Tu ballerina. Virga's Schiaparelli dolls targeted the high end market and better department stores. We will concentrate on the two 8" dolls, Go-Go and Tu-Tu.

There is some discussion about the relationship between Virga and Schiaparelli since Virga's name does not appear as the manufacturer on the glossy pink and black Schiaparelli boxes. However, later dark pink cardboard Schiaparelli outfit boxes do list Virga's own street address for the Schiaparelli, evidence for the tie-in, or at least a copyright arrangement at that point. Thanks to collector/researcher Jo Barckley for sharing information about these special dolls.

Marks on Schiaparelli Doll: "Virga" on neck.
Boxes for Schiaparelli Dolls and Outfits Marked: "Go-Go" or "Tu-Tu" was printed on the glossy bright pink doll box lid with black box bottom. No manufacturer was marked on Schiaparelli's glossy pink and black boxes for either dolls or clothing. Hang tags on the doll: Schiaparelli Dolls, Ltd. New York, 10, NY.
Boxes for Virga's dark pink cardboard outfit box for Go-Go costumes marked: On box lid, VIRGA; On the box end, MFD BY SCHIAPARELLI DOLLS LTD., 47 WEST ST., NEW YORK 6, NY (Virga's address).
Doll Characteristics:
Go-Go
The 8" Go-Go hard plastic walker had a vinyl head with rooted hair in pink, henna, blonde, and other colors. The most prevalent style was a sophisticated upswept ponytail style, but they also had short bobs and flip styles. Go-Go had straight legs and was jointed at the head, arms, and hips and was marked "Virga" on the head. Interestingly, her flat feet were the same molded T-strap shoes as Virga's Playmate dolls. It appears that two different arm types were used for Go-Go, either peg hooks and separate fingers or C-shaped hooks and molded 2nd and third fingers.

Tu-Tu
Tu-Tu was the same vinyl headed doll as 8" Go-Go, but she had pointed toes instead of flat feet. She was dressed in leotards and ballet slippers. Her rooted hair was pink, green or other colors, and the most prevalent hairstyle was an upswept ponytail. Likewise, Tu-Tu apparently had, either peg hooks and separate fingers or "c" hooks and molded 2nd and 3rd fingers.
Dress Characteristics: Every Go-Go and Tu-Tu outfit found in the glossy pink and black boxes had a Schiaparelli label with regular metal handsewn square snap. Outfits included not only beautiful gown and party styles but also sports outfits, like a roller skater. Interestingly, Schiaparelli labeled outfits like "Rain Slicker Set Deluxe" and "Ice Follies Deluxe" the same as those outfits pictured in the '57 regular line as "Deluxe Candy n' Spice" outfits. Also, in later years Virga sold untagged separate outfits in dark pink and gold window boxes marked "Schiaparelli," with a factory applied fluted metal snap. Ms. Barckley notes that the fabric and design on these later costumes appear to be the same as earlier outfits, but the finishing touches were missing. For example, there were no labels, no handsewn square snap, and the cheaper looking box.
Value: Undressed Go-Go and Tu-Tu: $100.00 each; dressed: $125.00 each. Chi-Chi: MIB $125.00+.

Schiaparelli advertisement in the Chicago Tribune 6/56: Top: Riviera Beach Costume with red swimsuit, yellow terry robe, and straw pixie hat; bottom: Boxed outfit of white satin ice-skating costume lined with shocking pink with gold braid, shoe skates, and "Feather pyramid headdress." Separate costumes ranged from $3.00 – 5.00.

Virga's 8" Schiaparelli Go-Go head-turning walking doll with hard plastic body and vinyl head with pink rooted hair wears embroidered nylon gown with faux fur stole, in original box. Courtesy Jo Barckley.

Virga's 8" Schiaparelli Go-Go with original wrist tag in two-piece turquoise corduroy pants suit. Courtesy Jo Barckley.

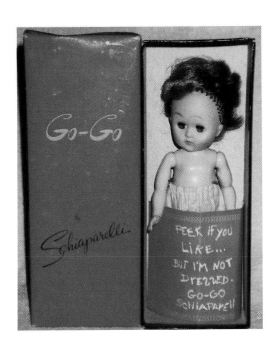

Virga's 8" Schiaparelli Go-Go head-turning walking doll with hard plastic body and vinyl head; sold undressed in original pink box. Courtesy Jo Barckley.

Virga's 8" Schiaparelli Go-Go head-turning walking doll with hard plastic body and vinyl head, wearing lavender nylon print dress and matching lavender straw hat. Schiaparelli tag (white rayon with woven deep pink/red script) sewn into back seam. Courtesy Jo Barckley.

This 8" bent knee Schiaparelli Go-Go doll has blonde rooted hair and wears a plaid-skirted dress with blue jacket and roller skates. Dolls ranged from $5.00 – 6.50. Courtesy Marge Meisinger.

Separately boxed Schiaparelli dress by Virga which was untagged and with metal snap. The original Schiaparelli outfits were tagged with square metal snaps. This box contained two outfits: a white gown, panties, tulle head scarf, and shoes; and blue gown ensemble.

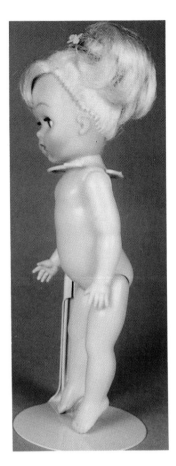

Virga's own version of a Schiaparelli outfit for 8" Go-Go doll with metal fluted snap and untagged. It was packaged in the box with a white gown.

Virga's 1954 dealer catalog offered 9" pin-hipped walking dolls. This is "Tiny Traveler" P-912 in a turquoise felt hat and coat ensemble over a pink dress. Note the distinctive red, white, and blue pin striped box with distinctive red lidded box design. Originally sold for $2.98 suggested retail.

Tu-Tu was Virga's 8" Schiaparelli doll with straight legs, pointed ballet feet, and hair set in an upswept hairstyle as shown on this undressed doll.

An 8" Tu-Tu wears a tagged Schiaparelli pink ballet costume.

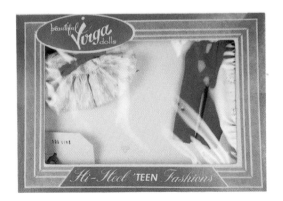

Virga sold "Hi-Heel Teen Fashions" in separate window boxes for their 8½" doll. This outfit is a slacks ensemble in original red and gold window box. Courtesy Marge Meisinger.

9" Virga "Connie Carnival" #912 c. 1954 in a print cotton dress with jacket and multicolored woven straw hat.

Virga's 1954 catalog page shows 9" Walking Dolls: #901 Sally Schooldays, #902 Patsy Party Time, #903 Betty Bed Time, and bottom row L to R #905 Debbie Dancer, #906 Barby Birthday, #907 Sunny Seaside, #908 Shirley Showers, #909 Sandra Shopper, #910 Terry Television, #911 Connie Carnival, #912 Tiny Traveler.

Virga's 1954 catalog page with 9" Walking Doll in diamond design "Play-Pal Travel Case" fitted with play clothes.

Toddler 9"

Virga's Pin-Hipped Walking Toddler 9" c. 1955 (photos, pgs. 216, 217)

Marks on Doll: Unmarked.

Boxes Marked: Manufactured by Beehler Arts Ltd., 47 West Street, New York City, NY.

Virga's 9" pin-hipped walker in plaid Lucy case. Note variation in the dotted dress with solid white skirt vs. previous plaid case shown below.

Virga's 9" pin-hipped walker was also sold in a plaid case marked "My name is Lucy, I walk." The case was the same one sold with Virga's 8" toddler doll. Note the wavy hair is glued to the head, while flip styles were shown in the advertising.

Doll Characteristics: In 1955 Virga also offered a 9" pin-hipped, sleep eye, head-turning walking toddler doll with toe detail. She was also sold in a plaid case marked "My Name Is Lucy/I Walk" the same as the 8" Lucy. It can confuse collectors that "Lucy" can be both an 8" head-turning walker and a 9" pin-hipped walker. She had separate fingers and a C-shaped arm hook. These dolls were in distinctive red boxes with a balloon design that reads, "A Virga Walking Doll/ I walk/My head turns when I walk/I sit/My hair combs/My hair washes/I stand/My clothes are removable." Competitors dressed these same dolls, and Colgate Palmolive frequently used them in premium offers. Without an original outfit or box, it is difficult to identify this doll as Virga's doll.

Dress Series and Characteristics: In '55 the 9" doll was offered in an unnamed series with 12 different outfits very similar to the 8" doll's wardrobe with straw or felt hats. They closed with circular donut-shaped snaps.

Wig Characteristics: Some of the 9" walking dolls had wavy hair glued right to the head, but others had lovely washable Dynel wigs set in a flip or braids.

Value: In plaid case, $95.00 – 125.00.

Teen

Virga's Hi Heel Teen Dolls c. 1956 (photos, pgs. 216, 217)
Marks on Doll: Unmarked.
Boxes Marked: Beautiful Virga Dolls/ Manufactured by Beehler Arts Ltd., 47 West Street, New York City, NY.
Doll Characteristics: Beehler Arts, Ltd. patented the name "Hi-Heel Teen" in June, 1957 but she was probably sold in 1956. "Hi-Heel Teen" was 8½" tall with sleep eyes with molded lashes and high-heel feet. She was a head-turning walker with synthetic wig advertised as "washable hair," jointed at the head, arms, and above the knees; her second and third fingers are molded together. Hi Heel Teen had molded breasts but was thin compared with the competitor's 8" and 10½" fashion dolls (see appendix Hi Heel Fashion dolls). Her outfits were sold separately in red boxes also marked Virga.
Dress Characteristics: Stitched back seams closed with circular donut snaps.
Virga's own "Hi Heel Teen" dolls were less expensive, much thinner, and had less stylish and more inexpensive clothes than Virga's Schiaparelli dolls.
Value: $75.00+ in box.

Baby

Cookie 8" Baby Doll
Marks on Doll: Unmarked.
Boxes Marked: Manufactured by Beehler Arts Ltd., 47 West Street, New York City, NY.
Doll Characteristics: Cookie was Virga's unmarked 8" jointed vinyl baby, curved legs and molded lash sleep eyes. She has a molded hair Ginnette type head (see Vogue section). However, Cookie is unique with two rows of rooted curly lock on her forehead and with hard plastic body. She was distributed by Beehler Arts LTD and wore flannel pajamas or a diaper with a plastic baby bottle in a window display box. Cookie was probably sold as a baby sister to the same market as Virga's toddler Playmate doll 8" Lucy.
Value: $45.00 – 55.00 doll only; $75.00 in box.

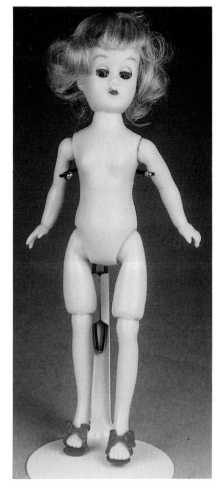

Virga's undressed Hi Heel Teen c. 1956 shows slim body and slender legs below knees. This is the same dolls used for the Kim high-heel doll (see Kim section).

Virga's unmarked Hi-Heel Teen c. 1956 was 8½" tall with sleep eyes and high-heel feet, wears a strapless gown with red velvet bodice and taffeta skirt with tulle ruffled over skirt trimmed in red edging. She was a head-turning walker sold in a red and gold box.

Cookie was Virga's unmarked 8" jointed vinyl baby, with curved legs and molded lash sleep eyes. She has a molded hair Ginnette type head. However, Cookie is unique with a rooted curly lock on her forehead and hard plastic body.

Close-up of Cookie face showing curly lock on forehead.

❦ Vogue Dolls, Inc. ❦

Vogue Dolls, Inc. was founded in 1922 by Jennie Graves, a talented doll costume designer. At first she named her company, "The Vogue Doll Shoppe," and she worked at home importing dolls to dress and sell to Boston area retailers. But by 1942, Vogue had outgrown Mrs. Graves's home, so she moved into offices in Somerville, Massachusetts, and she bought only U.S. made dolls. Among her cutest dolls were chubby composition 8" toddlers. She bought her first "Toddles" dolls in the 1930s from R&B and other dollmakers. Famed sculptor Bernard Lipfert later designed a Toddles exclusively for Vogue. Mrs. Graves's costume designs and ensembles became well-known in the doll world and were very popular.

When post-war hard plastics were available, Lipfert created a hard plastic toddler for Vogue in 1948 with painted eyes. Vogue's next toddler was Lipfert's famous sleep eye toddler introduced in 1950 and named "Ginny" in 1951 – the rest is history. Ginny was a wild mid-market success with her cute little face, lovely washable wig, and wonderful removable wardrobe available to buy separately. Ginny quickly became the standard by which other toddler dolls were judged. There were dozens of 8" look-alike dolls in the '50s, but Vogue gained notoriety as their pioneer by being first on the hard plastic market with the chubby little doll. Mrs. Graves and her daughter Virginia Graves Carlson, Vogue's chief designer, worked very hard to make Ginny the #1 "Fashion Leader in Doll Society." They created many promotional "firsts" that are still followed today in the doll world. Likewise, they created a

Back of 1930s Vogue outfit with stitched back seam and ties closed at neck.

Bottom of Vogue Toddles shoe marked "Goldilocks."

An 8" composition doll marked R&B on back, with single forehead curl under the mohair wig, but dressed by Vogue for Toddles line. Note that there are no painted lashes, also typical of R&B 8" dolls, and that the Goldilocks costume is undocumented.

Face of R&B's composition doll on left with distinctive molded forehead curl and no painted lashes vs. Vogue Toddles on right with mohair wig and painted lashes. Vogue sold both types as Toddles.

Early 1930s composition 8" R&B doll with straight arms with original box labeled "Vogue Doll Shoppe," with "Toddles/02BPink" hand-written.

little 8" baby sister for Ginny named Ginnette introduced in 1955, today's best known '50s baby. Baby brother Jimmy followed in 1958.

Happily, Ginny is still going strong after all these years. Vogue's sixth owner, the Vogue Doll Company, Inc., sells a darling Ginny in the best Vogue tradition. At the same time, avid collectors still seek out the original '50s doll. The *Collector's Encyclopedia of Vogue Dolls*, by Collector Books, co-authored by Carol Stover and Judith Izen, details all of Vogue's dolls sold since their 1922 founding. The basics about Vogue's '50s Ginny, Ginnette, and Jimmy are covered here, however, readers are referred to *Collector's Encyclopedia of Vogue Dolls* for complete details and additional Vogue dolls.

Vogue Toddles c. 1947 Debbie with original box and dress tag printed with Vogue's "Ink spot" design. Courtesy Barbara Rosplock-Van Orman.

Toddlers

TYPE #1

Toddles 8" c. 1937 – 1948

Marks on Doll: "R&B" on back or "Vogue" or "Doll Co." on head and/or back.

Boxes Marked: Vogue Dolls, Inc. Most boxes are solid light blue with lids.

Doll Characteristics: All composition 7½" -8" strung and fully jointed dolls with painted side-glancing eyes; two straight arms or bent right arm; straight legs with toe detail. The same doll with bent baby legs was called "Sunshine Baby."

Dress Characteristic: Well-made costumes, dresses, party or play outfits made with finished hems closed with hook eyes, stitched closed below back seam. Most had attached panties. The first outfits had a white tag printed Vogue Dolls, Inc./Medford Mass. in blue, and later tags after the mid '40s were printed "Vogue Dolls, Inc." with blue

"ink spot" design A round gold label printed "Vogue" on front of costume was also used from the '30s through the '40s.

Wig Characteristics: Good quality mohair wigs sewn to a backing strip and glued to the head.

Values: $250.00 – 300.00; Military Group $350.00+; Uncle Sam $400.00+.

Toddles 8" composition dolls wore military uniforms c. 1943; this soldier with bent right arm is from the Military Group. Courtesy McMasters Auctions.

TYPE #2

Painted Eye Hard Plastic 8" c. 1948 – 1950

Marks on Doll: VOGUE on head; VOGUE DOLL on back.

Continued on page 223.

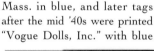

Vogue Toddles c. 1944 with mohair wig, two straight arms, in Tyrolean felt outfit.

Vogue Toddles white printed tag c. 1944-1946 sewn on outside of Tyrolean costume.

Vogue Toddles c. 1947 with mohair wig and straight arms, wearing costume listed as Debbie #8-1A, a flowered dress with organdy band at hem, matching bonnet.

A rare Toddles bunny in a pink flannel suit c. 1940s, with basket and papier-mache egg. Realized $750.00. Courtesy Frasher's Doll Auctions.

Rare Toddles Air Raid Warden c. 1943 wears a blue check suit and armband marked "C.D.1" for Civil Defense. Realized $575.00. Courtesy Frasher's Doll Auctions.

Type #1 Vogue 8" composition Toddles dolls c. 1930s and 1940s. Both dolls have painted side-glancing eyes and toddler bodies, but the doll on the left has a bent right arm, and doll on the right has two straight arms.

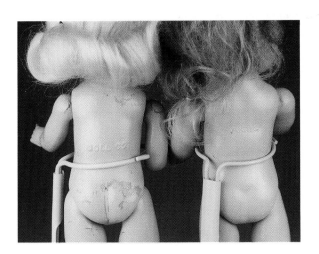

Vogue bought Toddles bodies marked on the back R&B or DOLL CO. as on left; their exclusive mold was marked "VOGUE" on back.

Vogue's painted eye hard plastic 8" doll c. 1948-49 with blonde mohair wig wears a pink flocked organdy dress trimmed with eyelet, with pink straw hat. Courtesy Peggy Millhouse.

The One Half Century Group is one of the most famous of Mrs. Carlson's Vogue designs in 1950 for both the 8" hard plastic painted eye and sleep eye dolls. Courtesy Vicki Johnson.

Vogue's painted eye hard plastic Crib Crowd doll with bent baby legs c. 1959.

Three Ginny closures: top left 1950–56 hook & eye; right c. '57 (on check shirt) octagonal snap; bottom left (on yellow skirt) gripper snap.

1951 Kindergarten Kiddies #29" "Tina" with sleep eyes, painted lashes and brows, bright cheek color, and blonde caracul wig, wearing a red chambray dress trimmed with woven heart braid. Original owner boxes with personal messages are a real treasure. Courtesy Sandy Johnson Barts.

Rare 1950-52 Miss Holly with original box with red felt jacket, bunny trimmed hat, and white felt skirt trimmed with felt holly appliquè and candy stripe ruffles. Courtesy Sandy Johnson Barts.

Some "transitional" strung sleep eye dolls c. '50-'52 had pale plastic, light hand-painted lashes and brows, and bright cheek color.

Inside Ginny dress: Unfinished waist seam, stitched closed below dress opening; back seam turned back and stitched to finish; deep hem; tagged ('54 tag shown or other).

Rare 1950 Crib Crowd Easter Bunny with pink poodle cloth suit and ears with pink felt trim, curly caracul wig, and bright cheek color. Crib Crowd dolls were the same as sleep eye dolls, with bent baby legs. Courtesy Shirley's Dollhouse.

(L) Ginny c. 1950 with bangs as part of wig and stitched to backing strip. (R) Ginny c. 1955 with bangs separate from stitched wig and glued underneath.

Boxes Marked: "Vogue Dolls, Inc." on box label. Boxes were solid light pink with lids. Dress tags had the Vogue "ink spot" logo; 1950 tags were white with "Vogue Dolls" printed in blue and two wavy lines on either side.

Doll Characteristics: The hard plastic strung 8" dolls were fully jointed with painted side-glancing eyes; two straight arms with metal loop arm hooks; straight legs with toe detail. The same doll with bent baby legs was called "Crib Crowd Baby."

Dress Characteristic: Same as Toddles, but many outfits had separate bloomers, holiday special styles, and regular line.

Wig Characteristics: Good quality mohair wigs sewn to a backing strip and glued to the head.

Value: $300.00+; with box $450.00+; One Half Century Group (each) $1,000.00+; Crib Crowd $1,500.00.

TYPE #3

Sleep Eye Hard Plastic 8" c. 1950 – 1953

Marks on Doll: VOGUE on head; VOGUE DOLL on back.

Boxes Marked: "Vogue Dolls, Inc." on box label. Boxes were solid light pink with lids until 1952 when bright fuchsia boxes with a "paper doll" design were phased in.

Doll Characteristics: The hard plastic, strung and fully jointed toddler dolls were like Vogue's painted eye doll, but now they had sleep eyes with painted lashes and brows; two straight arms with metal loop arm hooks; straight legs with toe detail. The doll was officially named "Ginny" in 1951. The same doll with bent baby legs was called "Crib Crowd Baby." Note: The doll's transitional years were 1950-52 when eyes had various multicolored rings and pupils, plastic tone varied from pale to pink, face coloring from light to bright blush. In '53 eye color was limited to blue and brown, and features were standardized and less pale; black Ginnys were sold in '53 and '54 and are rare today.

Dress Characteristic: Same as Toddles, but with gathered bloomers and new styles. Dresses were stitched closed below

Continued on page 227.

Transitional 8" hard plastic sleep eye doll with pale coloring, mohair wig in a rare pink #822 "Fitted Chest" with lid and built-in drawer c.'52. Realized $2,500. Courtesy Frasher's Doll Auctions.

1952 Sports Series "Beach," sleep eye Ginny with painted lashes in red sunsuit, rare round frame plastic glasses, and straw fan. Courtesy Sandy Johnson Barts.

1952 Sports Series "Roller Skater" with sleep eyes wears a yellow quilted costume with matching felt skirt trim and headband. Courtesy Shirley's Dollhouse.

1952 Debutante Becky #62 wears a rare ribbon hat with white organdy dress embroidered with blue and pink flowers. Courtesy Sandy Johnson Barts.

1952 Debutante Becky #62 from the back. Courtesy Sandy Johnson Barts.

Rare 1952 Frolicking Fables "Ballet" wears a lace ballet costume edged with gold braid and fabric rose, with gold flower headband and slippers. Courtesy Sandy Johnson Barts.

Ginny in her 1953 Talon Zipper A.M. #70 blue denim costume with separately boxed outfit #70 Talon Zipper Debut Series outfit.

1952 strung Ginny Type #3 with sleep eyes, Lucy #39, Tiny Miss Series, a green and white cotton dress with white organdy apron with a straw hat with green ribbon. Original pink Vogue box. Blonde braid wig with original green ties. Courtesy McMasters Auctions.

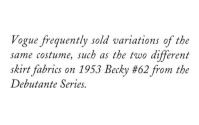

Vogue frequently sold variations of the same costume, such as the two different skirt fabrics on 1953 Becky #62 from the Debutante Series.

1953 Ginny "Ballet" with "Moving Eyes" marked on the box, in a delicate ribbon tutu fabric, tulle ruffles, and flower trim and headband. Note original "Ballet" wrist tag. Courtesy Sandy Johnson Barts.

1954 walking Ginny Type #4 with painted lashes, wearing a '55 Away We Go outfit #53, a two-piece TV lounging set with green pants, flowered top, plastic beads and glasses.

Rare 1954 Black Ginny in box printed "No.80/Hawaiian," in grass skirt, halter top, paper lei, flower trim in hair. Courtesy Laura Fluhr.

1954 black walking Ginny with painted lashes wears Candy Dandy #52, a yellow organdy lace-trimmed dress with green and yellow printed hem trim and straw hat with velvet flower trim. Courtesy Joyce Sziebert.

1955 walking Ginny Type #5 with molded lashes, wearing a '55 Tiny Miss #43, white organdy outfit trimmed with lace. Courtesy McMasters Auctions.

The 1955 Ginny Bon Bon Series dolls were molded lash walkers with full nylon dresses with parasols, straw hats, and satin slippers; #80 aqua dotted dress with pink hat (MIB $600.00); #81 white rosebud print dress with lavender waist band and hat ($550.00); #82 pink flocked dress, floral waist band, pink hat (MIB $525.00); #83 yellow dress with flocked white hearts, yellow hat (MIB $775.00); #84 blue dress with pink floral design, black velvet tie, straw hat with pink flowers, in box ($800.00); #85 red flocked nylon dress, red velvet bodice, red hat, no parasol ($275). Prices realized courtesy Frasher's Doll Auctions.

1955 Bon Bon #582 pink flocked nylon dress with petticoat, slippers, hat, purse, and umbrella. Courtesy Chree Kysar.

225

1961 bent knee walking Ginnys with green eyes and freckles and regular wig colors.

1956 molded lash, straight leg walking Ginny wearing "Camp Outfit #6032 from Gym Kids" series with rare original box. Vogue apparently was not licensed to use the "Brownie" insignia and name.

1957 bent knee walking Ginny Type #6 in outfit #7052 yellow organdy dress with white lace trim. Courtesy Barbara Van Orman.

Label for rare "Camp Outfit #6032" box.

1963-65 8" Ginny Type #7 had a vinyl head with rooted hair and a hard plastic bent knee body; shown with her original box.

1960 Wee Imp Ginny with carrot red hair, green eyes, and freckles, in rare outfits: (L) red and white stripes matches Brikette's outfit; (R) overall outfit matching Li'l Imp's outfit #4210. Courtesy Barbara Van Orman.

dress opening in the back and closed with hooks and eyes, but in '53, a Talon Zipper series was introduced.

Wig Characteristics: Early dolls had good quality mohair wigs, using up old stock, then synthetics of Nutex, Dynel, or Saran were phased in, sewn to a backing strip, and glued to the head. Transitional wigs varied in styles from shorter to long, and in many colors and shades. In '53 wig colors were limited to blonde, brunette, and auburn, and styles were limited to bangs or side-part bob, or braids.

Value: $375.00 – 450.00, add $100.00 with box; Black Ginny $2,000.00; Crib Crowd $1,500.00; Poodle cut $600.00.

TYPE #4 (photos, pg. 225)

Painted Lash Walker 8" c. 1954

Marks on Doll: VOGUE on head; GINNY/VOGUE DOLLS/INC./PAT.PEND./MADE IN U.S.A. on back.

Boxes Marked: Vogue Dolls Inc., bright fuchsia boxes with a "paper doll" design.

Doll Characteristics: Same 8" hard plastic dolls as 1953 (sleep eyes with painted lashes) but now with a head-turning, straight leg walking mechanism added.

Dress Characteristics: Same as '50-'53, still with hooks and eyes or a few with zippers. Vinyl side-snap shoes are introduced to facilitate the walking mechanism.

Wig Characteristics: Advertised as Nutex and limited to bangs or side-part; bobs or braids.

Value: $350.00; $450.00 with box.

TYPE #5 (photos, pg. 225)

Molded Lash Walker 8" c. 1955 – 1956

Marks on Doll: VOGUE on head; GINNY/VOGUE DOLLS/INC./ PAT NO. 2687594/MADE IN U.S.A. on back.

Boxes Marked: Vogue Dolls Inc.; bright fuchsia boxes with a "paper doll" design.

Doll Characteristics: Same 8" hard plastic doll as 1954 (sleep eyes, head-turning, straight leg walking mechanism) but now with molded lashes instead of painted lashes.

Dress Characteristics: Same as '54 still with hooks and eyes or a few with zippers. Shoes still a side-snap vinyl style.

Wig Characteristics: Advertised as Dynel or Saran in bangs or side-part; bobs or braids.

Value: Doll $225.00 – 350.00; $250.00+ in box; in Debutante or Bon Bon costumes $450.00.

TYPE #6

Bent Knee Walkers 8" c. 1957 – 1962

Marks on Doll: VOGUE on head; GINNY/VOGUE DOLLS/INC./ PAT NO. 2687594/MADE IN U.S.A. on back.

Boxes Marked: Vogue Dolls Inc.; bright fuchsia boxes with a "paper doll" design made a little narrower.

Doll Characteristics: Same 8" hard plastic doll as 1955-56 with sleep eyes, molded lashes, head-turning walking mechanism, but now with bending knees added. Green eyes and freckles were sold in '60 and '61.

Dress Characteristics: Same as '55-'57, still with hooks and eyes or a few with zippers. Shoes still a side-snap vinyl style.

Wig Characteristics: Advertised as Saran with bangs or side-part; bobs or braids. 1960 a "Wee Imp" Ginny with straight carrot red hair one year only.

Value: $175.00 – 225.00; $225.00+ in box.

TYPE # 7

Vinyl Head Walkers 8" c. 1963 – 1965

Marks on Doll: VOGUE on head; GINNY/VOGUE DOLLS/INC./PAT NO. 2687594/MADE IN U.S.A. on back.

Boxes marked: Vogue Dolls Inc.; tan folded boxes with teardrop-shaped acetate window on cover.

Doll Characteristics: 8" hard plastic body and vinyl head doll with sleep eyes, molded lashes; bent knees but without a head-turning walking mechanism; rooted hair.

Dress Characteristics: Same as previous years but with round metal gripper snaps with fluted edges. Fewer "fancy" styles and nylon knit panties; side-snap vinyl shoes.

Wig Characteristics: Advertised as rooted hair in "pixie" styles.

Value: $150.00; $175.00 in box.

Comparison of vinyl head of USA Ginny #7 on right and all vinyl Ginny #8 on left.

1965-72 8" USA Ginny Type #8 all vinyl doll with rooted hair.

TYPE # 8 (photos, pg. 227)
USA Vinyl Dolls 8" c. 1965 – 1972
Marks on Doll: GINNY on head; VOGUE DOLLS INC. on back.
Boxes Marked: Vogue Dolls Inc. marked on tan folded boxes with teardrop-shaped acetate window on cover.
Doll Characteristics: All vinyl 8" doll with jointed arms and straight legs, non-walker, sleep eyes with molded lashes.
Dress Characteristics: Simply made clothes with round metal gripper snaps with fluted edges. Shoes still a side-snap vinyl style.
Value: $100.00 in dress; $125.00 – 150.00 in box; $75.00 in Far-Away or Fairyland costume in box.

Vogue Doll Company 8" c. 1995 to date

Vogue sold the rights to Ginny in 1972, and her ownership changed over the years in order: Tonka, Lesney, Meritus, Dakin. Then in 1995 Ginny found a home with the team at the Vogue Doll Company. Happily, the company created wonderful outfits based on Mrs. Graves's original designs as well as exciting new designs. Ginny remains very collectible today.

Comparisons of Toddler Types #1 – #8

While Vogue's 8" toddler changed over the years, she maintained that cute little girl look. Also, her outfits were beautifully designed in the true spirit of Mrs. Graves's original costumes.

Ginny is pretty as a picture in her black dotted and yellow costume from the Hat Shoppe 2001 collection.

Today's Ginny as Little Red Riding Hood, from Fairy Tales Collection, 2001 collection.

Hard plastic 8" comparisons: (L to R) Type #2-strung doll with painted eyes; Type #3-strung doll with sleep eyes and painted lashes; Type #4-strung doll with sleep eyes, painted lashes, and walking legs.

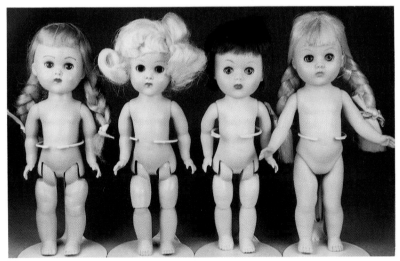

1950s Ginny on left compared to 1940s Toddles on the right, both in the same outfit. Vogue used knit costumes for brother and sister '40s composition Toddles and painted eye hard plastic dolls, and for sleep eye dolls in the '50s. Courtesy Shirley's Dollhouse.

Vogue's sleep eye 8" dolls with molded lashes comparisons (L to R): Type #5-walker with straight legs, glued on wig; Type #6-walker with bent knees, glued on wig; Type #7-vinyl head, with bent knees (non walker) and rooted hair; Type #8-all vinyl with rooted hair, straight legs.

Vogue's Alice in Wonderland L to R: Composition Toddles c. 1940s, hard plastic; painted eye c. 1948; hard plastic, sleep eye with mohair wig c. 1950; hard plastic, sleep eye with synthetic wig c. 1952.

Vogue's Dutch Girls L to R: Hard plastic, painted eye Dutch boy and girl c. 1948; hard plastic, sleep eye with mohair wig c. 1950; hard plastic, sleep eye walker with synthetic wig c. 1954; molded lash walker c. 1955.

Ginny in red checked shirt in the center compared to her many competitors in their 1950s gardening outfits. Upper left: Fortune's Ninette; upper right: Elite's Vicki; lower left: A&H's Gigi; lower right: Cosmopolitan's Ginger #2.

Painted eye 8" vinyl Ginnette c. 1956 in aqua and white dotted beach outfit #6507 matching Ginny. Courtesy Barbara Rosplock–Van Orman.

Sleep eye Ginnette c. 1957 in swimsuit #7625 matching big sister Ginny and Vogue's teen boy Jeff. Courtesy Barbara Rosplock-Van Orman.

Vogue 8" vinyl sleep eye Ginnette basic doll #2010 with original box, wearing 1958 batiste gown #2303; original glass bottle tied to her wrist. Courtesy Shirley's Dollhouse.

Babies

Ginnette 8" c. 1955 – 1969

Marks on Doll: 1955-63: VOGUE DOLLS/INC. on back. 1964-65: 6, 13, or 19 on head; VOGUE DOLLS/INC. on back. 1967: VOGUE DOLLS on head, VOGUE DOLLS INC. 1969: VOGUE DOLLS INC (c) 1967 ON HEAD; same as '67 on back.
Boxes Marked: Vogue Dolls Inc.
Doll Characteristics: An 8" all vinyl, fully jointed drink and wet doll. Eyes varied: 1955-56 dolls with painted eyes and lashes; 1956-69 sleep eyes, molded lashes and eyebrows; a drink and wet doll until 1962 and then again in 1964.
Dress Characteristics: Simply made clothes with round metal gripper snaps with fluted edges. Side-snap vinyl shoes.
Wig Characteristics: Molded hair until 1962 when rooted hair was introduced.
Value: Painted eye c. 1956-57 $100.00+ in box; sleep eye c. 1957 on, Doll only $60.00; $75.00 – 150.00+ in box.

Rooted hair 8" Ginnette on the left c. 1964 (wearing '68 outfit) is basically the same doll as Vogue's 8" rooted hair Ginny Baby on the right. Courtesy Marge Meisinger.

Jimmy 8" c. 1958

Marks on Doll: Back: VOGUE DOLLS/ INC.
Boxes Marked: Vogue Dolls, Inc.; boxes were blue, white, and pink using the Ginny paper doll logo.
Doll Characteristics: 8" painted eye Ginnette mold to introduced as Jimmy in 1958. He had painted lashes in the brochure, but some have no lashes; Made for one year only.
Dress Characteristics: Same as Ginnette.
Wig Characteristics: Molded hair.
Value: Painted eye c. 1956-57, $100.00+ in box. Sleep eye c. 1957 on: Doll only $60.00; $75.00 – 150.00+ in box.

Separately boxed Vogue outfits for Jimmy c. 1958. Courtesy Barbara Rosplock-Van Orman.

Vogue 8" vinyl sleep eye Ginnette in original box with flannel diaper.

Close-up of Vogue's sleep eye Ginnette with nursing mouth.

Vogue 8" vinyl painted eye Jimmy c. 1958 in original Ivy League plaid outfit #4150 with white jersey shirt and red vest. Courtesy Barbara Rosplock-Van Orman.

🍇 Wipco, Inc. 🍇

Lisa 8" c. 1950

Lisa was a "Dress-It-Yourself" doll, like many of the other inexpensive dress-me dolls sold on the '50s doll market. They were found everywhere from hardware stores to dime stores. Like many others, Lisa uses Cosmopolitan's Ginger doll body.

Marks on Doll: None.

Boxes Marked: Sold in plastic bags stapled to cardboard tags printed Lisa/Dress-It-Yourself/ Doll/Wipco Inc.; Wipco, Inc., 200 Fifth Ave. New York, N.Y.

Doll Characteristics: Hard plastic 8" doll non-walker c. 1950s with sleep eyes and molded lashes, good cheek color, mold line through center of the ear; arms with C-shaped hooks and separate fingers; straight legs with toe detail. Note: Lisa was a large eye Ginger (see Cosmopolitan section) with the walking mechanism removed, and the head is strung through the walking rod holes. Others like the Py-O-My Advertising doll used this doll (see Comparisons section).

Dress Characteristics: Sold undressed in bag with no panties.

Wig Characteristics: Wavy mohair with no backing glued to the head.

Value: $45.00 – 55.00 in original bag.

Wipco's 8" strung hard plastic Lisa c. 1950s was sold undressed in bag; she is a large eye Ginger with mohair wig and with walking mechanism removed. She was an inexpensive "dress me" type doll.

🍇 Woolworth's Exclusive Dolls 🍇

Woolworth's, often referred to as a "dime" store or as a "5 &10 cent store," is a vanishing breed of stores today. They offered affordable alternatives for a wide variety of products in almost every hometown across the country. Woolworth's was a wonderful source of inexpensive toys, and their small dolls were among their biggest sellers. For example, in 1956 Woolworth's advertised an 8" Pam toddler in their Christmas catalog (see Fortune section) to compete with the Ginny look-alike market.

Woolworth frequently offered name brands, but they also contracted others to label dolls under an exclusive Woolworth's label. The company adopted the name "Marie" for a series of small dolls and officially filed patents in 1961 for "Miss Marie" a 10½" fashion doll, "Little Miss Marie" an 8" fashion doll, "Baby Marie" a Ginnette look-alike, and "Little Baby Marie."

Woolworth's advertised that the Marie series dolls were "sold only at Woolworth's." While we can speculate about the doll's manufacturers, they are not documented, so we will categorize them as "Woolworth's dolls" for these descriptions.

Note: Woolworth's also filed patents for Tina Marie and Donna Marie in '61, but no information has been located on those dolls. Also, an 8" baby vinyl doll "Little Baby Marie" was sold in plastic bags and marked "Japan" on the neck. However, no Woolworth's identification was printed on the label.

Toddler

Pam 8" c. 1956

See page 87, Fortune section, for Ginger Type #2 dolls sold as "Pam" by Woolworth's, in boxes marked Fortune, with values.

Pam 9½", c. 1950s

See pgs. 96 and 97, Fortune section, for description and values of this size "Pam" presumably sold by Woolworth's. The boxes were marked Fortune.

Teen

Little Miss Marie 8" Late 1950s and 1960s

Marks on Doll: Unmarked.

Boxes Marked: Little Miss/Marie/ Sold Only At/Woolworth's.

Doll Characteristics: An 8" fully jointed all vinyl doll, with rooted hair, blue sleep eyes with molded lashes, dark brown brows, and three lashes painted at the corners; high-heel feet; painted toenails and fingernails.

Clothes Characteristics: Well-made casual and dressy styles for the low to mid-market, close with circular donut-shaped snap in the back.

Wig Characteristics: Rooted Saran type hair in bubble cuts with bangs.

Value: $45.00; in box $55.00+. Hard to find in box.

Baby

Baby Marie 8" Late 1950s and 1960s

Marks on Doll: Unmarked.

Boxes Marked: "Baby Marie/Drinks and Wets/ Sold only at Woolworth's" on an acetate case with blue cardboard base and top with cord carrying handle.

Doll Characteristics: 8" sleep eye drink and wet doll with a soft vinyl Ginnette-like mold with molded hair, open mouth, and sleep eyes with molded lashes. Her baby legs are slightly bent with separate toes and a wetting hole in lower back. Identification can be confusing because her vinyl head and body and her curled fingers on the right hand look so much like Vogue's Ginnette baby doll. However, Ginnette is marked Vogue, and Baby Marie is not marked at all.

Dress Characteristics: Baby Marie wore cotton dresses closed with a smooth round metal snap, a flannel diaper, and socks, and she had a plastic bottle packaged with her.

Wig Characteristics: Molded hair painted brown, single curl front center like Ginnette.

Value: $35.00 – 45.00 doll only; in case $75.00+, hard to find in case.

Woolworth's label for 8" Little Miss Marie in original folding window; outfit name is printed "Sunday Best." Courtesy Suzanne Vlach.

Little Miss Marie 8" all vinyl Woolworth's doll has sleep eyes with molded lashes and three lashes painted at the corners, high-heel feet, and painted finger and toe nails. Her red and white "Sunday Best" dress is trimmed with lace at the collar and sleeves. Courtesy Suzanne Vlach.

Close-up of Woolworth's 8" Little Miss Marie face shows lash and brow features painted in dark brown and small-pursed mouth. Courtesy Suzanne Vlach.

Back of Woolworth's 8" Little Miss Marie dress closing with a circular donut snap. Courtesy Suzanne Vlach.

Woolworth's unmarked 8" Baby Marie, an all vinyl, fully jointed, drink n' wet baby doll. She was sold in acetate cases in dresses or undressed. Courtesy Marge Meisinger.

Woolworth's 8" Baby Marie all vinyl drink n' wet baby wears a cotton flowered romper and bonnet closed with a round smooth circular snap. Courtesy Marge Meisinger.

British Dolls

Dolls from the U.S. and from England frequently mirror each other. This seems to have especially been true for post-World War II dolls as both countries eagerly incorporated hard plastics into doll making. The new hard plastic material was relatively indestructible and was far more practical for doll making than composition or bisque material. Also, hard plastic dolls could be washed without harm, so the hygienic issue was a big sales advantage in the '50s. No wonder that the small 8" toddler dolls quickly became popular in both countries.

By most accounts, the U.S. was slightly ahead of England in developing post-war hard plastic dolls. England did not recover quickly from the effects of the war; so doll making had low priority for using the new plastics. The first English dolls were primarily exported, so plastic dolls sales did not take off at home until around 1946. Once developed, the early UK plastic dolls were typically rather large and stocky walking and toddler dolls. In contrast, US post-war plastic dolls came to market slightly earlier, they were distributed for sale more widely at home, and the designs seemed more realistic by comparison. Despite these differences, it is interesting to note the many parallels as we study small dolls from the U.S. and the UK in the 1950s.

🍇 Rosebud Company 🍇

The trademark "Rosebud" was registered in England in 1947. At first, owners Eric Smith and his wife Hazel made composition dolls, as was common in that day. However, in 1950 they filed a patent for their injection molding process to make plastic dolls. Rosebud's first plastic dolls were primarily "Ma Ma" talking dolls, but other dolls quickly followed as described below.

Miss Rosebud 8" c. early 1950s
Marks on Doll: Miss/ Rosebud/Made in England; A rose was reportedly added to the logo after 1960, but no rose logos have been found on the dolls to date.
Boxes Marked: Some boxes are pale pink with window lids marked, "Miss Rosebud/Britain's Daintiest Doll/Made in England;" some blue folding Miss Rosebud boxes with baby photo "I am Baby Rosebud;" international dressed Miss Rosebud dolls are mostly found in unmarked gray or brown boxes.
Doll Characteristics: The darling 8" toddler doll officially introduced by Rosebud in 1954 was called "Miss Rosebud." We know that the cute little doll was actually available as early as 1953 when *Woman's Weekly Magazine* featured Miss Rosebud twins in knitting and sewing segments. However, it is not clear how much earlier they were on the market. The adorable strung Miss Rosebud doll was made of "strong lightweight plastic," was jointed at the head, arms, and legs, and had a cute face mold. Her sleep eyes had hand-painted lashes above the eyes, and she had bright cheek color; arm hooks were plastic C-shaped hooks, and the 2nd and 3rd fingers on the right hand are molded together and fingers on the left hand are separate at the tips; straight legs had good toe detail. The feet on some dolls were painted black, eliminating the need for shoes. Perhaps these dolls were targeted for the inexpensive souvenir market. But even these souvenir quality Miss Rosebud dolls were still appealing with bright cheeks and the Rosebud mark.
Wig Characteristics: The lovely wigs included pageboy and wavy styles out of mohair, curly astrakhan, and caracul. The

Continued on page 239.

All of these British dolls are dressed in bright yellow Leksand outfits from Sweden. Front: (L) Miss Rosebud (R) Amanda Jane Jinx; back: (L) Roddy (R) Pedigree one-piece body doll with jointed arms. The yellow fabric on Pedigree and Rosebud dolls is felt-like; prints vary. This is a wonderful example of all of the British dolls sent elsewhere for dressing. Courtesy Lee Ann Beaumont.

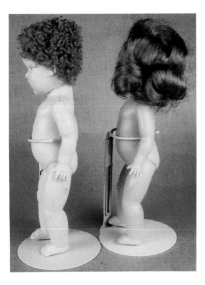

Comparison of English 8" Miss Rosebud hard plastic doll c. early 1950s on the left to Vogue's 8" hard plastic Ginny c. 1953 on the right. Miss Rosebud has a curly caracul wig and Ginny a synthetic wig. Note the strung dolls' similarities, but Miss Rosebud has more defined toes and smaller eyes. Later Miss Rosebud dolls had larger eyes, but still different from Ginny. Courtesy Marge Meisinger.

Side view comparison of Miss Rosebud on left and Vogue Ginny on the right, showing chubby toddler tummies and legs.

Back comparison of Miss Rosebud on left and Vogue Ginny on the right, showing y-shaped seat and similar leg and arm shapes.

Close-up of 8" Miss Rosebud c. early '50s with brunette mohair wig, small eyes with hand-painted lashes, blushed cheeks, and deep crease under nose, giving her a cute childlike look. Courtesy Marge Meisinger.

8" Miss Rosebud c. 1950s with beautiful mohair wig set in sausage curls. Her regal gown has a pink taffeta bodice and gathered flounce over a sparkle-dotted net skirt. This doll was shown in company flyer.

Miss Rosebud showing back of curled hairstyle and stitched-on gown that is not removeable.

8" Miss Rosebud doll section of a Rosebud brochure shows five of her costume styles: Sunsuit with floppy hat; Scotch Girl-Bonnie; Skier-Gwen; Marie Antoinette-style gown with elaborate wig; Fairy with net wings. Courtesy Lee Ann Beaumont.

Lovely 8" Miss Rosebud c. 1950s with painted lashes in the brochure's Fairy costume with net skirt and woven silver-tone top. Her blonde mohair wig is elaborately curled. She originally held a wand through a hole in her hand. Courtesy Lee Ann Beaumont.

The back of 8" Miss Rosebud Fairy showing silver-trimmed wings sewn to the costume top, cotton panties, and costume attached to the doll. Note the right hand holds a wand with star on top. Courtesy Lee Ann Beaumont.

Close-up of Miss Rosebud Fairy showing painted lashes and elaborately curled wig. Marge Meisinger.

Miss Rosebud with early narrower eyes and painted lashes wears an outfit of handsewn fabric over a gown similar to Miss Rosebud bride called June, perhaps lovingly dressed long ago by an owner as a bridesmaid. Courtesy Lee Ann Beaumont.

English 8" painted lash Miss Rosebud Coronation doll c. 1954 with a brown mohair wig in a pageboy set. She wears a white brocade gown, a stapled-on purple velvet robe with a white velvet trim and collar with black stitching, and a rhinestone tiara. This doll reportedly introduced the line at Toy Fair in UK. Courtesy Marge Meisinger.

English 8" strung Miss Rosebud c. 1950s with brown mohair wig, wears a white net bridal gown with embroidered floral pattern over taffeta bodice, a long net veil, and pink flower at waist. Courtesy Jo Barckley.

8" Miss Rosebud c. early 1950s with her original pink window box marked on the end, "Bonnie/Dressed as Scotch Girl." Her lovely mohair wig is set in a pageboy style with bangs, and her cheeks are brightly blushed. The kilt made from plaid taffeta ribbon with simple muslin panties underneath is not removable. Her black velvet jacket is trimmed with lace at the collar and cuffs and is stitched onto the doll, as is her matching tam. Her black leatherette shoes and black socks are removable.

8" Miss Rosebud Scotch Girl c. 1950s in red and gold variation of kilt colors, in gold and red taffeta. Courtesy Marge Meisinger.

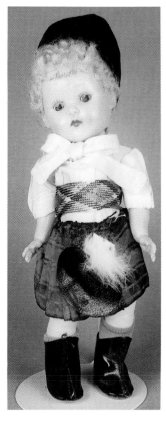

8" Miss Rosebud Scotch Boy c. 1950s with curly wig, black velvet cap, red plaid kilt, and white top. Courtesy Marge Meisinger.

English 8" strung Miss Rosebud brother and sister hard plastic dolls c. 1950s with painted lash sleep eyes in Swedish costume c. 1950s; marked Miss Rosebud. Authentic costumes call for red knit stockings. Courtesy Jo Barckley.

English 8" strung, painted lash Miss Rosebud c. 1950s with blonde mohair wig with pageboy bangs, wears a Polish costume with white organdy skirt trimmed with ribbon bands, red vest with gold trim, and red leatherette boots. Courtesy Jo Barckley.

Close-up of Dutch Miss Rosebud strung, painted lash dolls c. 1950; note the high cheek color.

Pair of 8" hard plastic, strung, painted lash Miss Rosebud Dutch dolls c. 1950. The original unmarked tan box is typical of dolls found in international costume; the Dutch boy was dressed in a black cotton suit with black felt hat and wooden shoes. Courtesy Lee Ann Beaumont.

English 8" strung, painted lash Miss Rosebud c. 1950s Dutch girl in sewn-on black costume with flower print trimmed apron; wooden shoes and lace Dutch cap. Courtesy Marge Meisinger.

English strung painted lash Miss Rosebud c. 1950s with blonde wavy mohair wig, in a gold dress with red and black woven apron, perhaps a Swedish costume. This same costume has been found on larger eye 8" Amanda Jane dolls marked "England," indicating costuming by a country buying various undressed 8" dolls from the UK. Courtesy Marge Meisinger.

8" Miss Rosebud doll c. early '50s with small eyes, painted lashes, and bright blush wears an inexpensive version of the Scotch costume, perhaps a souvenir doll. The black jacket is felt instead of velvet, the feet are painted black instead of shoes, and the wavy mohair wig is glued to the head instead of pageboy wig on a backing.

Skirt labels on two Danish dressed Miss Rosebud dolls, "Gudrun/Formby/Danish/Design/ Copenhagen Denmark" on left; "Mother /Denmark; GF/Handiwork" on right. Courtesy Marge Meisinger.

Back of Miss Rosebud removeable outfit showing red painted metal snap. Courtesy Marge Meisinger.

wavy mohair wigs are glued to the head with no backing. Other mohair wigs were in elaborate sausage curl styles. Later stitched wigs appear to be soft Saran types.

Value: Dressed and original $100.00+; $150.00+ in box and for rare costumes like the '53 Coronation Queen or '50s Fairy.

Miss Rosebud vs. Ginny (photos, pg. 235)

Even the seasoned Ginny collector, at first glance, can mistake the first Miss Rosebud dolls for their beloved Ginny, Vogue's best-selling 8" toddler doll in the early 1950s. While the dolls look incredibly similar, there are differences. Most noticeable, the earliest Miss Rosebud's eyes are slightly smaller, giving her painted lashes more prominence on the face.

A later Miss Rosebud doll with larger eyes without painted lashes and with removable costume. Her plastic body is a pinker plastic; original box is marked Magasin. Courtesy Marge Meisinger.

Also, Miss Rosebud has a deeper indentation above the lips, the toes are more clearly defined, and the fingers are wider. Another difference is that some Miss Rosebud dolls c. '53 had mohair wigs while Ginny introduced synthetic wigs in 1950. Miss Rosebud's painted lashes were eventually eliminated altogether, while Ginny switched to molded lashes beginning in 1955.

Clothing Characteristics: Other important differences between the 8" Miss Rosebud and Ginny lie in the costuming. While the early Miss Rosebud doll itself was of good quality, the outfit quality varied greatly. The first costumes were attached with glue and/or staples, such as Miss Rosebud's lovely brocade Coronation gown c. '53 was stapled onto the doll itself. Likewise, the Scottish Miss Rosebud costume had a glued-on ribbon bodice instead of a blouse, and the lovely Miss Rosebud fairy's tutu was not removable nor were the attached net wings. By contrast, Vogue's Ginny was promoted as "The Fashion Leader in Doll Society," and she was always dressed in beautifully coordinated outfits that were removeable and of the highest quality.

Later Miss Rosebuds

While dating is difficult, Miss Rosebud's plastic evolved into a less expensive-looking, pinker plastic over time, and her eyes became larger and her face color paled. Most of these dolls, while marked Miss Rosebud, have another country's tag on their dress and/or mark on the box. This leads to logical speculation that Rosebud sold the undressed dolls for costuming in other countries. Or, if Miss Rosebud's molds were sold off, the other companies likely changed mold characteristics for their own doll. These cases are undocumented, yet the Miss Rosebud dolls (and the other 8" British toddler dolls) found in foreign-tagged costumes make this likelihood hard to

Pair of marked Miss Rosebud dolls with painted lashes and brows. The girl has a silver tag marked, "Made in Denmark." The box is plain cardboard. The doll's bright matching costumes are not removable. Courtesy Lee Ann Beaumont.

Danish doll company used the Miss Rosebud mold with larger eyes and no painted lashes. This doll is in a colorful Dutch costume with baskets on wooden carrying bar on the shoulders. Courtesy Marge Meisinger.

Inexpensive 6½" Rosebud hard plastic play doll with one-piece head and body and strung arms, with wavy mohair glued to the head, sleep eyes, toe detail, marked "Rosebud/Made in England/ Patent Pending on back. Box printed, Rosebud Dolly/Britain's Finest Doll/Made in England." The price of 75 cents is marked in pencil. A picture of a baby on the outside is printed "I Am Baby Rosebud." This style box was reportedly sized for Miss Rosebud as well.

Miss Rosebud dress tag reads, "Danish Dolls, National Costume, AMAGER." Courtesy Lee Ann Beaumont.

Rosebud hard plastic '50s souvenir doll with mohair glued to the head, large sleep eyes, a one-piece head, body, and legs with strung arms and painted shoes and socks. This Scottish costumes appears to be the same as the inexpensive Miss Rosebud with painted feet. Courtesy Marge Meisinger.

Back of souvenir doll with Miss Rosebud mark. Courtesy Marge Meisinger.

Baby Rosebud, 6½" fully jointed black hard plastic baby with molded hair and glassene eyes. Courtesy Lee Ann Beaumont.

Baby Rosebud, a 6½" hard plastic baby c. mid '50s jointed at the head, arms, and hips with molded hair and early painted sleep eyes; marked "Rosebud" on the back. Courtesy Lee Ann Beaumont.

Baby Rosebud 6½" black baby above with "Rosebud" in script on back. Courtesy Lee Ann Beaumont.

Baby Rosebud 6½" black hard plastic baby with curly wig and "ROSEBUD/MADE/IN/ENGLAND" marked on the back in script. Courtesy Lee Ann Beaumont.

Baby Rosebud 6½" black hard plastic baby with curly astrakhan wig and glassene sleep eyes. Courtesy Lee Ann Beaumont.

discount. Collector and researcher Lee Beaumont's article notes this possibility in *Contemporary Doll Collector*, September 1999 issue.
Value: $100.00; $150.00+ in box. More for exceptional color or rare costumes.

Baby Rosebud 6½" mid 1950s

Rosebud produced darling 6½" Baby Rosebud hard plastic dolls in the mid 1950s. They had high cheek color, molded or curly astrakhan wigs, and they were jointed at the shoulders and hips; head is one piece with body; hands face the body, and the left hand has a thumbsucker formation. Both black and brown plastic babies with molded or curly wigs were part of the line. Researcher Lee Ann Beaumont shares that the first babies had "painted sleep eyes" and later babies had glassene sleep eyes. Also Ms. Beaumont found two types of markings: ROSEBUD/MADE/IN/ENGLAND (all caps); on black Baby Rosebud (in script) /MADE IN ENGLAND (caps). These "thumb sucking babies" were shown in *Woman's Weekly* magazines with instructions for knitted outfits. They are marked "Rosebud/Made/In/ England."
Value: Fluctuating values averaging $55.00; slightly more for black dolls with astrakhan wigs.

✿ Pedigree ✿

Pedigree originally produced a wide range of toys under the "Tri-ang" mark beginning in 1927, so they were well established as a quality toy maker by the time of the modern doll era. The Lines Brothers in England introduced the Pedigree trademark in 1942, and their first hard plastic doll was produced around 1946. They too manufactured and sold many walking and talking dolls, and even dolls with "flirty" eyes. While Pedigree dolls are difficult to find in the U.S. today, they had numerous factories around the world, including Canada, and many can be found in other countries as well as in England. The 14" Pin Up Doll, Saucy Walker, and Sindy are among their dolls. They also produced a number of small dolls for play as well as for souvenirs. The Delite was a popular undressed doll in the '50s. Also, according to Colette Mansell in *The Collector's Guide to British Dolls Since 1920s*, Pedigree made five different 7" boy and girl pipers dressed in Royal Stewart kilts. Also, the 1964 Pedigree catalog included a number of 7" character dolls in national costumes including Dutch, Welsh, and Swiss, as well as storybook characters such as Robin Hood, Red Riding Hood, and Bo Peep.

Authentic Tartan Dolls c. 1950s
Marks on Doll: "Made In England."
Boxes Marked: "Pedigree/Authentic Tartan/Dressed Doll."
Doll Characteristics: 7" plastic dolls with sleep eyes with or without molded lashes, one-piece bodies, and head with strung arms, painted shoes, and painted socks.
Costume Characteristics: Non-removable plaid cotton costumes and black or red felt lace-trimmed jackets.
Wig Characteristics: Boy has molded hair; girl has wavy mohair glued to the head.
Value: Fluctuates beginning at $30.00+; more with boxes.

Delite Doll
Marks on Doll: "Pedigree/Made in /England" over a triangle symbol on back; after 1959: "Made in England" on the back.
Boxes Marked: Pedigree/Delite/Doll/ 7in/ Made by International Model Aircraft Ltd. Merton, London S.W.19, England. Cardboard box measures 7" x 2½" x 2½". Wigged dolls are stamped "Wig" on end of box.
Doll Characteristics: *Prior to 1959:* 6½" hard plastic dolls had a one-piece body, head, and fixed legs, with strung arms; sleep eyes with no lashes and pink cheeks; strung arms have splayed fingers; feet had molded shoes painted white or black with no toe detail. *After 1959:* Ms. Beaumont advises of mold changes: "The Delite Doll's mold was changed c. 1959 and the doll's characteristics changed dramatically, no more splayed fingers and the doll has a closer look to Ginny a slimmer bodied doll." This doll was jointed only at the shoulders and has a painted-on body suit and molded shoes painted white. Ms. Beaumont also notes that Pedigree dressed these 6½" and 7" Delight dolls for their "Storybook and Character Dolls" series. For example, both sizes dressed in almost identical plaid-skirted costumes with white aprons were "Kathleen" from the Storybook and Character Series.
Clothing Characteristics: Early 6½" Delite Dolls were boxed wearing inexpensive thin nylon panties with lace trim; dresses for slimmer 7" dolls were braid trimmed and tagged Pedigree.
Wig Characteristics: The early box drawing shows a doll with molded hair, but some dolls have blonde or brunette wavy mohair glued to the head with bow glued to wig. The slimmer dolls also had glued-on wigs.
Value: Fluctuates around $35.00 for early doll; $40.00 for later slim doll.

Pedigree 7" hard plastic "Wee Lassie" c. 1959 dressed in Royal Stewart piper costume with strung straight arms, sleep eyes without molded lashes, mohair wig; original box. Courtesy Carol Rugg, photo by Patsy Moyer.

Close-up of sleep eye face without lashes of 7" Pedigree Wee Lassie with mohair wig. Courtesy Carol Rugg, photo by Patsy Moyer.

Pedigree's 7" hard plastic "Highlander" c. 1959 dressed in Royal Stewart piper costume with strung straight arms, sleep eyes, and mohair wig; original box. Courtesy Carol Rugg, photo by Patsy Moyer.

Close-up of sleep eye face of 7" Pedigree Highlander with molded wig. Courtesy Carol Rugg, photo by Patsy Moyer.

Pair of 7" Pedigree Tartan dolls with sleep eyes and molded lashes are jointed at arms (left arm bent), and have painted-on shoes. The girl's folded window box is marked, "Girl Highlander With Bagpipes (missing)/Royal Stewart/Triang Product/Made in Gt. Britain by Pedigree Dolls Ltd." Both dolls are marked "Made in England" on the back. Courtesy Lee Ann Beaumont.

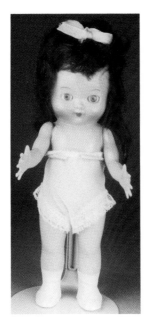

Close-up of 7" Tartan doll faces showing molded eyelashes, bent left arms, and mohair wig on girl. Courtesy Lee Ann Beaumont.

Pedigree 6½" hard plastic "Delite Doll" c. early 1950s with sleep eyes, brunette mohair wig, fixed head and legs, and jointed arms is typical of Pedigree's small plastic play dolls. Note the painted shoes and splayed fingers with palms facing the body.

Pedigree 6½" hard plastic "Delite Doll" c. 1950s with blonde mohair wig. Courtesy Lee Ann Beaumont.

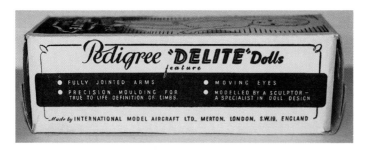

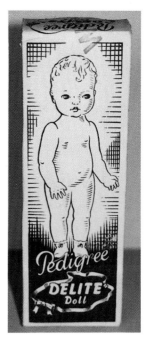

Delite Doll box for mohair wigged dolls, stamped "wig." Courtesy Lee Ann Beaumont.

Pedigree Delite Doll box with drawing of molded hair 6½" doll. Courtesy Lee Ann Beaumont.

Pedigree Delite Doll box advertising "true to life definition of limbs." Courtesy Lee Ann Beaumont.

Pedigree 6½" hard plastic "Delite Doll" c. early 1950s with sleep eyes, molded hair, and jointed arms, dressed in original Buffalo Bill outfit. He is marked "Pedigree (inside a triangle)/Made in England" on the back. Courtesy Lee Ann Beaumont.

Delite Doll c. 1959 with 7" slimmer body mold, one-piece head, body, legs, and head with sleep eyes in dress. Courtesy Lee Ann Beaumont.

Close-up of slim 7" Delite doll c. 1959 showing wide sleep eyes with molded lashes. Courtesy Lee Ann Beaumont.

Undressed slim 7" Delite doll c. 1959 with painted body suit, socks and shoes. Courtesy Lee Ann Beaumont.

Pedigree tag on 7" Delite doll's dress c. 1959.

🍇 Amanda Jane 🍇

"Jinx" 7¼" c. 1958

While incorporated in 1952, Amanda Jane did not make hard plastic dolls until c. 1958 when they introduced a 7¼" inch doll marked "England" on the back. Her name was "Jinx," and she looked remarkably like the American Ginny dolls and the English Miss Rosebud dolls. A few years later they changed the head for a vinyl mold with a less attractive "wide eyed" look. However, the early dolls would be very fine additions to the collector of Ginny-type dolls.

Marks on Doll: "England" on back.

Boxes Marked: Unknown but boxes were traditionally printed "Amanda Jane;" some were packaged in clear cellophane bag fastened to a cardboard top.

Doll Characteristics: 7¼"-7½" strung hard plastic dolls with sleep eyes; lashes painted above eyes and brows; arms with metal ring hooks like Ginny, and the 2nd and 3rd fingers on the right hand are molded together and fingers on the left hand are separate at the tips; straight legs with toe detail. Some dolls had painted feet for shoes and painted white socks; some had orange tone plastic, others had pink flesh tones.

Dress Characteristics: Jinx was advertised as "The miniature doll with the wonderful trousseau." Her removeable mid-market costumes were well designed: debutante, international, sleep wear, riding, party, sun, and school outfits. All dresses had hemmed skirts, and most were open-back with metal snap closure. Some dresses are found with "Amanda Jane" tags sewn in an inside seam. The company also sold boxed outfits. International costumes were bright cotton with ribbon trim. Undressed dolls may have been sold to companies in Denmark and elsewhere for dressing.

Wig Characteristics: Early dolls had mohair wigs, later dolls have been found with Saran wigs.

Value: $100.00; $150.00 in original bag.

Cover for Amanda Jane brochure 1960. Courtesy Lee Ann Beaumont.

Brochure page for "Jinx & Her Collection" showing boxed separate outfits and accessories. Courtesy Lee Ann Beaumont.

Brochure page for "Jinx #801" illustrated in the center, 8" doll with blonde or brunette wig, jointed legs and arms, and sleeping eyes. Courtesy Lee Ann Beaumont.

Typical brochure page advertising outfits for "#801 Jinx" and her beach, "Tomboy," school, riding, and knitwear "hand-knit" twin sets and accessories. Courtesy Lee Ann Beaumont.

Jinx lingerie, housecoat, and accessories from brochure. Courtesy Lee Ann Beaumont.

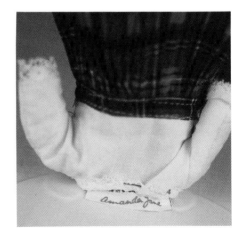

Jinx brochure features "Package sets," Girl Guide, and Nurse costumes. Courtesy Lee Ann Beaumont.

Separate Amanda Jane dress with tag sewn into neckline and metal snap closure. Courtesy Marge Meisinger.

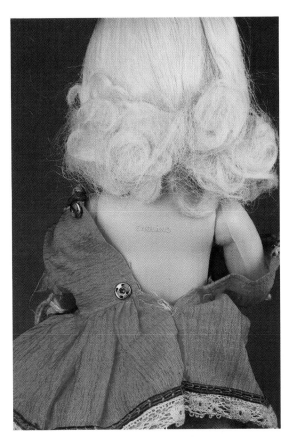

*Amanda Jane's Jinx 7¼"
undressed strung doll with
sleep eyes. The black
painted feet with painted
white socks were common
with international cos-
tumed dolls. Other Jinx
doll feet were unpainted.
Courtesy Lee Ann Beau-
mont.*

*Amanda Jane's Jinx 7¼" hard plastic strung
doll marked "England" c. 1956 with sleep eyes,
painted lashes and brows, and a mohair wig.
She wears an open-back pink dress with blue
trim with blue vinyl slip-on shoes.*

*Pink Amanda Jane Jinx dress closes with a metal snap; note
"England" mark on the doll's back.*

*Amanda Jane sleep eye dolls marked "Eng-
land," wearing dresses in bright international cotton costumes. Doll on left has a
dotted organdy apron; doll on right has a
woven apron and tall hat with painted feet
for shoes and socks. Courtesy Marge
Meisinger.*

*Amanda Jane Jinx sleep eye doll in
International Swedish Leksand cos-
tume in red tones. Courtesy Lee Ann
Beaumont.*

❦ Roddy ❦

This well-respected English company was established in 1934. In the late '40s they produced injection molded plastic dolls including popular walking and talking dolls such as a 16" Saucy Walker-type doll with a wig and open mouth. Roddy also made small display type dolls from 5½" to 8" in various fairy, little girl, and international costumes. Roddy's 8" doll was a darling Ginny-type toddler with sleep eyes described below.

Marks on Doll: "Roddy/Made in England" on back.

Boxes Marked: Unknown, but traditionally boxes were printed Roddy.

Doll Characteristics: 8" strung hard plastic (cellulose acetate) dolls with sleep eyes; molded lashes; arms with C-shaped plastic hooks and 2nd and 3rd fingers on the right hand are molded together and fingers on the left hand are separate at the tips; straight legs with toe detail. Some had plastic with an orange tone, others pink flesh tones. Undressed dolls may have been sold for dressing in other countries. Roddy reportedly also made a walking version of the 8" doll.

Costume Characteristics: The doll had an international wardrobe and other outfits which could be purchased separately. Outfits were well made for the mid-market with hemmed skirts.

Wig Characteristics: Some dolls have been found with Saran wigs with stitched parts.

Values: $75.00+; $100.00+ in box.

Roddy marked 8" hard plastic sleep eye doll with molded lashes. Her piper costume with woven plaid skirt, scarf, and matching cap, with white blouse is tagged "Faerie Glen Wear," a maker of separate doll clothes. The toy pipes are original to the doll.

Roddy marked 8" hard plastic sleep eye doll with molded lashes dressed in Dutch Girl outfit with heavy cotton striped skirt, woven apron, cotton top, and lace-trimmed cap. The doll's wig is synthetic with braids and bangs. Based on label, this doll was possibly sold for dressing abroad by another company or through an undocumented tie-in. Courtesy Marge Meisinger.

Close-up of 8" Roddy doll mark on back.

Close-up of 8" Roddy doll face.

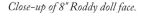

🍇 Sarold 🍇

Sarold sold many dolls, including an 8" toddler doll with a Saran wig in the 1950s. At a quick glance, she looks not only like Vogue's Ginny, but also like their English competitor's Miss Rosebud dolls.

Marks on Doll: The doll is marked "SAROLD/MADE IN ENGLAND" on the back.

Boxes Marked: Unknown.

Doll Characteristics: An 8" hard plastic strung doll with sleep eyes, with or without molded eye lashes, unusual eyebrows that are molded and raised on the face; straight arms with metal hooks; 2nd and 3rd fingers on the right hand are molded together and separate at the tips on right hand; straight legs with smooth feet and toes on some dolls. Others are found with painted black feet with toes. They have unusual body molds with narrow "pinched" torsos, the heads sit flat on the top of the neck, and they have small eyes and apple cheeks like early Miss Rosebud dolls. The doll is not as well made, and heavy glue seams are evident on the sides of the body and behind the ears.

Wig Characteristics: Saran wigs glued to head.

Clothing Characteristics: This doll was apparently also sold for dressing in other countries, as dolls marked Sarold are found in international costumes and in boxes marked, "Myfanwy/My Rare One/Welsh Dressed Doll."

Values: Fluctuate and can still be found for $25.00 – 30.00 but average closer to $50.00 – 75.00; $100.00+ in box.

Three 7½"- 7¾" strung hard plastic dolls "Sarold/Made In England" with sleep eyes, mohair braided wigs, and matching Scottish kilt costumes with tams. Courtesy Jo Barckley.

Marked Sarold 7½" hard plastic doll with mohair braids in a wool Welsh costume and felt hat. Note the unusual feet with toes painted black vs. most Sarold dolls with smooth feet.

Close-up of Sarold doll faces showing molded eyebrows on girl, not visible under hat on boy. Courtesy Lee Ann Beaumont.

Pair of Scottish attired 7½" hard plastic dolls c. 1950s marked, "Sarold/Made in England." Both have molded eyelashes, jointed at neck, shoulders, and hips, and smooth painted feet. Girl on the right has a wavy mohair wig. Courtesy Lee Ann Beaumont.

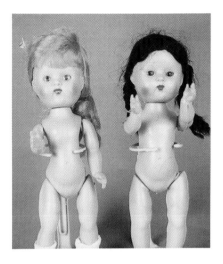

Marked Sarold 7½" hard plastic doll with mohair braids in a wool Welsh costume and felt hat. Note the unusual smooth feet. Original wrist tag and box are marked "I'm Myfanway (My Rare One). Courtesy Lee Ann Beaumont.

This 7½" Sarold doll in a clever fairy costume with painted feet, probably home-made, and possibly used as a cake topper or centerpiece. This doll is a good example of the popularity of fairy dolls in the '50s. Courtesy Lee Ann Beaumont.

Two 7½" hard plastic dolls marked "Sarold/Made In England" c. 1950 have unusual body molds with narrow "pinched" torsos and no toe detail; the heads sit flat on the top of the neck, and they have small eyes and apple cheeks like Miss Rosebud. Both are marked "SAROLD/MADE IN ENGLAND." The doll on the left has a synthetic wig and the doll on the right appears to have a mohair wig. Courtesy Marge Meisinger.

🍇 Faerie Glen 🍇

Faerie Glen sold a line of well-made clothing for dolls separately. Reportedly they purchased molds from Miss Rosebud and others to market as their own 8" dolls, Tonie and Sally twin dolls. Unfortunately the dolls are reportedly unmarked, and no photos are available, but they do bear a striking resemblance to Miss Rosebud dolls. The tagged piper costume shown on page 248 is on a Roddy doll. Since so few are known or have even been seen, no values are available.

Advertising Dolls

Fun From the '50s

Do you remember the little advertising dolls so popular in the '50s? Or maybe you spot them at garage sales and flea markets today. They represent a unique period in the post-WWII advertising era, and they are fun to collect. Re-energized households had more income to spend, and new products were hitting the market daily. The advertising industry was having a heyday, and many turned to cute little hard plastic dollies to entice product sales. Some dolls were included with the product itself, and many were sold at the store. However, most dolls were offered at low prices if ordered with product labels or box tops. This practice earned them the title "box top dolls" among collectors today.

Advertising Doll Background

Premiums weren't a brand new idea in the '50s. In fact, Campbell's Soup offered their Campbell Kid doll as a premium in 1910! However, '50s advertisers found a new life with hard plastic doll premiums for a number of reasons. First, hard plastic dolls were the "latest" and were big sellers on the '50s market. Second, they were small and could be easily mailed in brown cardboard boxes without breaking and without the padding or protection that drove up mailing costs.

Advertisers' third reason to favor plastic dolls for premiums is perhaps the most important for collectors to understand today. Incredibly, major '50s doll makers sold their undressed dolls to competitors and advertisers to re-dress and sell. So the advertiser or their representative could offer customers dolls that were "just like the big stores." In truth, the dolls that advertisers sold were usually of a lesser grade of plastic and often without features like eyelashes or walking mechanisms. Nonetheless, they looked like their first quality sisters on the '40s and '50s retail market, thus enhancing the premium offer.

Popular Premium Dolls

Companies such as Duchess Dolls, Plastic Molded Arts (PMA), A&H, and Virga showcased their retail market "display" dolls in large square boxes with display windows so that their lovely skirts could be flared out behind the doll. The costumes were stapled-on but could be elaborately trimmed with feathers, braid, or ruffles. Since advertisers could purchase these same dolls directly from the doll maker, they could easily provide a "no frills" version to customers. Maybe the feathers were left off, or the wig was of a lesser quality, but the doll was still cute.

Likewise, advertisers adopted toddler dolls as premiums in the '50s. Vogue's 8" Ginny doll led the toddler retail market, and her look-alike competitors soon flooded store shelves. They were playmate dolls, and most had removable clothing for additional play value. Not surprisingly, advertisers bought these same dolls for "no frills" toddler product incentives. Major makers like Vogue wouldn't sell to others, but Cosmopolitan, Ginger's maker, sold countless low quality toddlers to premium contractors in the 1950s. Thus, companies like Py-O-My could advertise a really cute toddler that looked like Ginger with a removable dress but without the retail doll's quality or extra features. Still, imaginative advertisers enjoyed the doll's selling power at the time, and it is a real treat to find these unique and curious little dolls today.

'50s Advertising Doll Review

Ad Dishwasher Detergent, Little Miss Addie, 10½" c. 1957

In 1957, Ad Dishwasher Detergent advertised the offer, "Little Miss Addie walks and moves her head. She moves her arms and closes her eyes. She has lovely blonde hair you will love to comb, and she is nonbreakable. A $6.95 value for only $3.00 and an AD Box Top. She wears a pin striped taffeta dress, a hat and a real fur mink." The doll was a 10½" hard plastic, straight leg walking doll with sleep eyes, molded lashes

Little Miss Addie, 10½" Ad Detergent doll with original box and brochure, wearing original pink striped dress and fur stole; on right 8" Ginger type doll in similar dress. Both dolls came in brown boxes marked "Little Miss Addie" with postage meter slug.

Little Miss Addie, 10½" Ad Detergent doll, with bridal gown and wearing two-piece sunsuit available separately. On the left is her original dress, and above are original brochures. Courtesy Linda Chervenka.

Blue Bonnet 7" Alaskan Eskimo doll.

with lashes painted under the eye, and a Saran wig. She is attributed to the Block Doll Co. and appears to be a first-quality doll. An 8" wide eye non-walking Ginger in matching dress is found today in a premium box postmarked Feb. 1958 with the same return address as the larger doll, perhaps as a later offer. While the advertisement does not document the 8" doll, "Miss Addie's sister" is handwritten on the 8" doll's box.
Value: $100.00 MIB.

Bab-O Cleanser, Little Miss Babbitt 10½" c. 1959

BAB-O Cleanser's maker, B.T. Babbitt Co., Inc. of New York City, offered "Little Miss Babbitt" for $1.00 plus a label from any of their products: Glim Liquid Detergent, Cameo

Copper Cleaner, Air-Gene, Hep Oven Cleaner Spray, and Vano Starch. The 10½" doll is an odd combination of parts, with Fortune's Pam head on a fixed leg body and strung arms, and a very wiry Saran wig. Seven different outfits were also offered.
Value: $35.00.

Blue Bonnet Margarine, 7½" c. 1960s

Packages of Blue Bonnet margarine spread offered various "Americana" dolls, 7½" hard plastic dolls with sleep eyes, painted lashes, strung head and arms, and fixed legs. They have sleep eyes with painted lashes. The Blue

Little Miss Babbitt advertisement on left, and 20" "Big Sister" on right.

Little Miss Babbitt, 10½" BAB-O Cleanser doll.

Campbell's Soup 9" Magic Skin doll.

Clicquot's Lotta Sparkle Doll, 9".

bows. An even easier way to identify the doll is by the Plastic Molded Arts or PMA mark on the back of some but not all of these premium dolls. Since the clothes are often stapled over the mark, the bows are a better clue for identification. Other distinguishing characteristic of the 6" and 7" PMA dolls are "pinched" noses, glued-on mohair or synthetic mohair looking wigs, arms with separate fingers, and C-shaped arm hooks.

Colgate Princess Doll c. 1951

This 5½" hard plastic doll had fixed legs and jointed arms with all fingers molded together with a separate thumb. She was probably a PMA doll, though this is not documented. Her sleep eyes had painted lashes and brows, and she wore a stapled-on dress advertised as "satin" with a wide red and white horizontal stripe. The Princess was advertised as a $1.29 value for 50 cents, and she was mailed in a two-piece brown box with an advertising flyer. The offer ended December 1951.
Value: $25.00.

Colgate Incline Walking Doll c. 1952

In 1952 Colgate Palmolive Peet Company advertised an unusual 6" plastic doll as "An Adorable Walking Doll" for only 50 cents and box top from Fab or Vel or two Palmolive wrappers. (Vel was a laundry product marketed for brightening nylon fabrics.) The ad stated, "This adorable walking doll not only walks down an incline but opens and closes her eyes." Most of the other premium dolls were either the pretty "display" type or Ginny toddler-type dolls, so this 6" chubby-type doll was unique at the time. She had a character doll look with oversized side-glancing eyes and oversized hands with widespread fingers. The doll was dressed in a "gay red polka dot pinafore" that was simply tied around the neck with a red ribbon. A flyer in the doll's box offered customers a form to order more dolls. This interesting doll "walks" via a unique gravity-powered

Bonnet Alaskan Eskimo had white boots, but Lestoil sold a similarly costumed doll c. 1959 with black boots.
Value: $25.00.

The Campbell Kid 9½" c. 1955

As early as 1910, Horsman sold their Campbell Kid doll on the retail market, a composition and cloth doll in four sizes that looked like the soup ad kids. Interestingly, it wasn't until the 1950s that Campbell offered premium dolls to customers, such as the 1956 "The Kid" doll for a label and $1.00. The first dolls were 9½" Magic Skin dolls by Ideal, later made in vinyl. The early Magic Skin dolls found today usually have deteriorated rubber bodies.
Value: $75.00.

Clicquot, Clicquot's Lotta Sparkle Doll 9" c. 1950s

This hard plastic doll is the same as Virga's 9" Playmate but without molded lashes. The wavy wig is glued to the head, and she has straight pin-hipped walking legs with toe detail. She wears a fur-trimmed taffeta dress and hood with matching panties, all stapled to the doll.
Value: $45.00.

Colgate Palmolive c. 1950s

Colgate Palmolive actively promoted products with premium dolls in the 1950s. They were primarily display type dolls from Plastic Molded Arts (PMA) dolls. This doll is easy to spot today for its molded "shoes" are painted and incised with three vertical lines to simulate

Colgate's Princess Doll, 5½".

Colgate's Walking Doll, 6".

Advertisement for Colgate walking doll c. 1951.

Curity advertisement c. 1952 with Miss Curity doll, 7".

Fab Miss America doll, 7½".

leg design. PMA is marked on the bottom of each doll's foot, perhaps indicating Plastic Molded Arts as the manufacturer.
Value: $30.00.

Curity, Miss Curity 7" c. 1952 – 1953

Curity, the well-known maker of first aid products, offered a Curity nurse doll on the 1950s retail market. Large nurse dolls were popular, such as Ideal's 14" hard plastic Curity Nurse doll, and the 7" nurse premium was one of the smallest. She was advertised c.1952 with strung head and arms, sleep eyes with painted lashes, fixed legs, and a plastic nurse's uniform. Her maker is unknown, but she is a display doll type.
Value: $40.00.

Fab Miss America 7½" c. 1950s

Colgate Palmolive's Fab Detergent "Miss America" premium doll was offered for $1.00 with no coupons needed. She was 7½" tall with strung arms and head with sleep eyes and painted lashes. Her fixed legs had feet painted white with a roll around the top with three lines incised for a bow. Her gown had a horizontal red and white pin striped taffeta skirt, blue ribbon waistband, and bodice made from a white ribbon criss-crossed around the neck and tucked into the waistband. The shoulders were trimmed with red fringe. Typically, this outfit was stapled in the back and was not removable. The one-piece brown box folded with a top opening.
Value: $25.00.

Fab Americana Doll and Album 7" c. 1954

Colgate Palmolive's Fab Detergent Americana doll was part of a series of eight 7" dolls costumed as historical women that sold for $1.00 each with a mail-in coupon. The doll had fixed legs, sleep eyes, glued-on mohair wig, and the characteristic PMA incised bow marks on the feet. The doll's gown had a red and white horizontal medium-striped long taffeta or rayon skirt and a blue felt bodice. Interestingly, a '50s gas station company reportedly also offered the doll dressed in this same outfit as a premium.
Value: $25.00.

Fab Americana doll, 7".

Fab Doll 9" c. 1955 – 1958

Colgate Palmolive's "Fab Doll" advertised, "I walk, I flirt, I sit, I stand, I turn my head, You wash and comb my hair, Real Shoes.... I am a full 9" tall /Verified value $2.98." She was offered for $1.00 per doll with Fab box tops. The 9" pin-hipped walker had sleep eyes, a blonde wig, and came with or without molded lashes. She was "Manufactured exclusively for Colgate-Palmo-

Fab Picture Dolls (Pam type) with pink plastic and straw hat variations, 8".

Fab Doll, pin-hipped walking toddler in dotted skirt, 9".

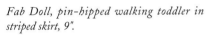

Fab Doll, pin-hipped walking toddler in striped skirt, 9".

showed the doll wearing a stapled-on taffeta dress with multicolor horizontal stripes. A second offer ended December 31, 1956, featuring the same 9" doll with a multicolor dotted taffeta dress. In 1958 the 9" Fab doll wore a pink cotton dress very similar if not identical to the Vel doll's dress described.
Value: $45.00; $55.00 in box.

Fab "Picture Doll" 8" c. 1957

Colgate Palmolive's Fab Picture Doll was a cute 8" toddler. Interestingly, two separate types of look-alike toddler bodies dressed in almost identical outfits were used for the offer.

TYPE #1: One of the "Fab Picture Dolls" offered was clearly documented in a 1957 Fab flyer offering the doll for "$1.00 each, plus 1 FAB box top...." The flyer pictures a sleep eye Ginger type doll with molded lashes, mold line through the middle of the ear, and straight walking legs. She was shown on the flyer wearing a pink taffeta dress trimmed with blue picot and closed with a simple metal snap, a pink straw hat and pink vinyl side-snap shoes with pink socks. The flyer pictured three additional outfits that could be ordered for an additional

live Co. by Plastic Molded Arts. Corp." One offer ending Jan. 1, 1956, charge plus a box top: Wedding Ensemble, $1.00; Daytime Costume (cotton dress and straw hat), 50 cents; 4-piece Sleepy-Time Lounge Set, 50 cents. Interestingly, this dress has the same distinctively decorated "p" pattern round metal snap as the Ginger doll. An undressed "Fab Picture Doll" is difficult to distinguish from Cosmopolitan's Ginger.
Value: $45.00; $90.00 MIB.

TYPE #2: A second type of "Fab Picture Doll" used Fortune's 8" Pam type doll with molded T-strap shoes. She was a sleep eye, walking doll with molded lashes, but her head mold line was behind the ear like a Virga doll. Both types of Fab dolls wore the same pink taffeta dress with blue picot trim and either a straw or vinyl hat with a molded-straw pattern.
Value: $55.00; $90.00 MIB.

Farberware, Nancy Farber 8"-9" c. 1958

Advertised as "Lovely blonde curls...eyes that close, head that moves as she walks, and charmingly dressed in a real chef's had and apron." No size was mentioned, and it is difficult to identify the photo for sure. Because of the $1.00 price, it is

Fab Picture doll, 8", box, and brochure.

Fab Picture dolls (Ginger type) as bride and in two dress outfits, 8".

assumed she is an 8"-9" Virga or Ginger type doll.

Value: No examples to price but estimate $55.00 based on rarity.

Frigidaire Princess 10" c. 1950s

This doll was an unusual premium because of her 10" height and the deluxe box presentation. While no documentation has been found, this doll was undoubtedly tied into a purchase c. 1950s rather than to a mail-in coupon offer. The bright purple-coated box lid was gold embossed "Princess Frigidaire (crown logo) / Frigidaire /Appliances." The bottom of the box is coated orchid stock, and the liner is pink. The hard plastic doll had bright cheek color, sleep eyes with molded lashes, mohair-like wig, and fixed legs with jointed head and arms. The silver threaded taffeta gown was stapled-on, and she was marked "Plastic Molded Arts" on the back. PMA also sold this type doll in different outfits on the retail market.

Value: $50.00.

Princess Frigidaire, 10".

Hawaiian Girl, 7½", display type.

Hawaiian Dolls, 7-8" c. 1950s

Hawaiian dolls were very popular as both souvenir and premium dolls in the '50s. Any product affiliations are unknown, but we list the dolls here because of their advertising nature. Some of the 7"-7½" display, 8" toddler, and 8" "chubby" hula dolls were boxed by Willadean of Hawaii, Honolulu; Mapela's at Waikiki; Lanaila Crafts, Honolulu; and others. They are very collectible.

HAWAIIAN GIRL 7½" c. 1950s

Display type doll, 7½" hard plastic pin-hipped walking doll with sleep eyes and painted lashes, jointed at the head and arms. Her walking legs have molded bows on the toes, and she wears a two-piece cotton halter and skirt glued onto the doll, with a grass skirt tied around the waist and paper lei around the neck.

Value: $35.00.

MAPELA'S AT WAIKIKI 8" c. 1950s

8" hard plastic unmarked doll c. 1950s with brown sleep eyes with molded lashes, black synthetic wig, straight walking legs with molded T-strap shoes, thought to be Pam by Fortune (see Fortune section for second example). She wears a

Miss Hawaii, 7½". Courtesy Mary Van Buren-Swasey.

Mapela's Hawaiian Girl, 8". Courtesy Peggy Millhouse.

Nancy Farber Walking Doll advertisement c. 1958. Courtesy Marge Meisinger.

Willadean of Hawaii, 8".

Face close-up of Willadean of Hawaii.

Hawaiian Boy, 7½".

Willadean cloth label.

Joy Walking Doll, 7½".

(L) Kellogg's vinyl head doll with molded T-strap shoes; (R) Kellogg's doll, smooth feet.

Kellogg's Bride Doll and trousseau, 8".

Kellogg's Bride Doll in blue dress, 8".

Close-up of Kellogg's Bride with molded shoes.

cotton sunsuit and crepe paper hula skirt and lei accessories. Her original box is marked Mapela's at Waikiki. Courtesy Peggy Millhouse.
Value: $100.00.

MISS HAWAII – Miss Hawaii 7½" strung hard plastic doll with sleep eyes, molded lashes with painted lashes under the eye, black glued-on wig, and feet with flat bows painted black. This is the same doll as Mary Lu by Doll Bodies, also boxed with Ginger dolls. Some dolls had a wrist tag reading, "Miss Hawaii with Dynel hair." Cotton sunsuit with tied-on grass skirt, and flower in hair. Her original box has this doll marked as "Hula Outfit" and also offers Muumuu and Holoku costumed dolls. Courtesy Mary Van Buren-Swasey.
Value: $75.00.

HAWAIIAN BOY – 7½" boy doll c. 1950s, a strung hard plastic doll with sleep eyes, molded lashes with painted lashes under the eye, molded hair with no wig, and feet with flat bows painted black. He wears a tie-on cotton swim bottom, a paper lei around his neck, and cotton hat with pom glued to his head. This is the same doll head and body as "Miss Hawaii" above and uses the Mary Lu by Doll Bodies.
Value: $45.00.

WILLADEAN of Hawaii, Honolulu – 8" girl doll c. 1950s with sleep eyes and no lashes, and head mold behind the ear. Her fingers on the left hand are separate, and on right hand has 2nd and 3rd fingers molded together with C-shaped arm hook. She is a head-turning walking doll with straight legs and flat feet with no toe or shoe detail, i.e., smooth-top feet. Her one-piece cotton suit is tagged "Willadean of Hawaii," and she has a paper lei around her neck, a grass skirt around her waist, and an orange pipe cleaner trimmed with a red flower around her head. This doll's body was also used for several Ginny look-alike dolls including A&H Gigi and Lisa, Dollyana Dorrie, and Riegel Miss 1962.
Value: $75.00.

Joy Walking Doll 7½" c. 1956 (photos, pg. 257)

One of the most collectible dolls was the "Joy Walking Doll" by Procter and Gamble c. 1956. This doll was unique because it was a walker while most companies offered a standard 6" to 7½" display type advertising doll with fixed legs. The height of this doll was almost 8", taller than most, probably due to the added walking mechanism. However, the rest of the doll had the same characteristics as other Plastic Molded Arts (PMA) hard plastic dolls: separate fingers, sleep eyes, and a "pinched" nose. The doll had molded shoes painted white with a round molded bow known to be used by PMA. The Joy doll's distinctive stapled-on outfit was a red and blue diamond print on white rayon taffeta. The doll was offered for "50 cents and the top from a Joy bottle carton-OR 50 cents and a piece of paper..." with the number from the can bottom. Full-page advertisements for the doll promotions were placed in major consumer magazines. If you have one of these, you have one of the few walking dolls of the display type.
Value: $35.00.

Kellogg's Bride 8" c. 1957

Cereal boxes provided prime advertising space for dolls and toys of all types. Kellogg's advertised one of the cutest doll premiums, a look-alike walking doll with a vinyl head and hard plastic body. Advertising states, "Her head moves as she walks, she stands by herself, her hair can be brushed, combed, waved, set, she's 8" tall!" and shows her sleep eyes with three lashes painted at the corners. One vinyl head Kellogg's Bride doll had molded T-strap feet. A second vinyl head doll was marked "U" on the neck and had smooth feet with no toe or molded shoe detail. This second smooth-feet type was the same as Uneeda's "Janie" doll (see Uneeda section.) The Kellogg's bride doll came with four trousseau outfits in return for $4.00 plus one Kellogg's Sugar Smacks or Rice Krispies box top. Four additional "Bride's wardrobe" costumes were also advertised as premiums.
Value: $95.00 MIB.

Kellogg's Mary Hartline c. 1954 (photos, pg. 261)

Television had a major influence on advertising, and some '50s premium dolls tied into TV shows and stars. "Super Circus" was a popular Saturday morning TV show launched in 1949. Mary Hartline, the show's pretty blonde bandleader, quickly became a major TV star, and advertisers scrambled to gain rights for promotions featuring Mary. The Mary Hartline dolls were box-top offers or in-store promotions. They were made by Ideal, and most measured 7¾" with brown eyes. They were marked "Ideal" in block letters and were probably subcontracted by Ideal to other manufacturers.

Kellogg's Mary Hartline, 7½", with original mailing box.

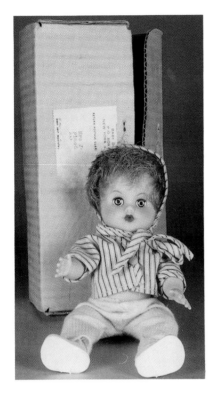

Lestoil doll, 7".

Little Miss Loft, 10 ½" c. 1950s.

Kellogg's Baby Ginger, 8".

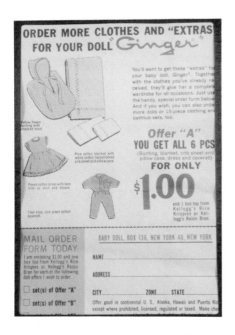

Kellogg's Baby Ginger premium offer.

Knorr Soup Doll set ad c. 1963-64. Courtesy Betty Strong.

Knorr Soup, English Knorr Dolls, 7½". Courtesy Betty Strong.

Kellogg's premium Mary Hartline dolls were almost identical to Ideal's 7½" Mary Hartline doll sold on the retail market. One way to distinguish between Ideal's premium and retail versions of Mary Hartline is the logo. The retail logo has "Ideal" in an oval, but the premium version may have "Ideal" in block letter. The doll's red cotton Mary Hartline costumes can have either a snap back or two buttons to close the costume. A different 7¼" doll was advertised in the 1954 Sears, Roebuck & Co. catalog and is attributed to Duchess Dolls, but she wears a felt costume and has a mohair wig, the only one known to have this type wig. These small hard plastic dolls are fun to collect because they are cute and are still rather reasonably priced on the secondary market.
Value: $80.00 MIB.

Kellogg's Baby Ginger 8" c. 1957 (photos, pg. 259)

Kellogg's premium Baby Ginger was an 8" vinyl drink n' wet doll with rooted Saran hair and sleep eyes dressed in "a 3-piece corduroy playsuit and white sandals...doll's outfit includes plastic baby bottle and diaper." She was offered for $1.00 plus one box top from Rice Krispies or Raisin Bran. Two additional clothing sets were also offered for $1.00 and one box top per set. Printed on the box, "Ginger is a Reg. T.M. of the Cosmopolitan Doll and Toy Corp." makes it clear that the premium and retail Gingers are the same; only the outfits differed, and the premium is unmarked.
Value: $30.00.

Knorr Soup, English Knorr Dolls 7½" c. 1963 – 1964

English Knorr Dolls were offered in pairs of 7½" hard plastic, jointed dolls with blue sleep eyes and full lips. Knorr boy and girl sets were dressed in eight different International costumes. Knorr is a Best Food product.(Photos, pg. 259.)
Value: $15.00 pr.

Lestoil 7½" c. 1954 (photos, pg. 259)

Lestoil offered a high-quality premium doll very close in quality to PMA's retail doll. The Lestoil 1954 offer featured dolls dressed in a choice of 15 "National Doll" costumes, and 11 different "Character Doll" storybook costumes. The 7½" hard plastic doll body and some costumes were identical to the PMA doll used by Colgate Palmolive. However, Colgate's gowns were ankle length, and Lestoil's gowns were 1½" longer in a thick, high-quality rayon/satin spread out attractively on display with elaborate stapled-on headpieces. They were advertised for "$1.00 and the label from a bottle of Lestoil for each doll you order." They were mailed in a good quality two-piece rectangular box.
Value: $45.00.

Loft Candies, Little Miss Loft 10½" c. 1950s – 1960s (photos, pg. 259)

No documentation is available, but it is assumed this doll was a premium or in-store offer in the '50s or '60s. She was a hard plastic doll with sleep eyes, molded lashes, good cheek color, and a wavy synthetic wig glued

to the head. Her body was jointed at the head, arms, and legs, with straight walking legs and high-heel feet. Her pink taffeta dress had taffeta pants sewn to the waist and closed with a metal circular snap; a felt hat was stapled to her head; vinyl heels.
Value: $45.00.

Lustre-Creme Starlet 8" c. 1953 – 1954

"Starlet" was promoted by Inez Holland House for Lustre-Creme Shampoo mid-1950s. The 8" doll had the characteristics of Fortune's retail 8" Pam doll, a Ginny look-alike. Starlet was a strung and fully jointed hard plastic doll with excellent face color, sleep eyes with molded lashes, a bright orange/blonde Saran wig, and molded T-strap shoes painted white. Her taffeta flower print tie-on gown had matching panties. The booklet in her box advertised, "Starlet is the

only doll in all the world with a complete wardrobe of 'forever fresh' textured, classic dressmaking clothes. Amazingly stain resistant, they wipe clean with a damp cloth." Outfits included a school dress, Sunday best dress, sportswear, and bridal outfits. Her box included dress patterns for a hostess gown, as well as a booklet on how to shampoo the doll's wig. Since pattern material is dated 1953, it is assumed the offer was in effect around that time.
Value: $95.00 MIB.

Lustre-Creme "Starlet" doll, 8".

Lustre-Creme "Starlet" 8" doll and patterns c. 1953.

Close-up of 8" Starlet doll with painted and molded lashes.

Mary Hartline dolls (L to R): 7" premium marked Lingerie Lou; 7½" retail doll marked Ideal on oval; 7½" premium marked Ideal in block letters.

Lustre-Creme 8" Starlet doll with box and brochure.

Mary Hartline 7" advertisement in Sears 1954 Christmas catalog, thought to be Lingerie Lou doll. Courtesy Marge Meisinger.

Lustre-Creme 8" Starlet fold-out brochure showing additional outfits for Lustre-Creme; Inez Holland House promotion.

261

*From Alden's 1952 Christmas catalog for 7½"
doll with mohair wig, unusual costume with
metallic trim, and removeable boots; Mary
Hartline maker unknown, but Howdy Doody
made by Beehler Arts. Courtesy Marge
Meisinger.*

*Post Grape-Nuts, Nancy doll in original
outfit variation, 7½".*

*Post Grape-Nuts, Nancy & Sluggo premium dolls
(reproduction outfits), 7½".*

Lustre-Creme 9" c. 1955

Inez Holland House marketed a 9" head-turning, pin-hipped walking doll as a "Movie Star" doll for Lustre-Creme shampoo with a 10-piece accessory kit including shampoo, brush, and other items. Some of these dolls wore the same pink dress as the Vel doll, showing the interchanging of premium dolls.
Value: $40.00.

Mars Candy TV Doll 7¼" c. 1950s

Mars Candy was a major advertiser on the '50s "Super Circus" TV show, and their 7¼" hard plastic Mary Hartline doll was a mail-in offer featured on the show. The doll was marked on the back, "This is An Original Lingerie Lou," and she had sleep eyes, a pretty blonde nylon wig, and was jointed at the arms and head with fixed legs. Her bright red costume was decorated with a stenciled musical staff design on the skirt and a heart with "Mary" was on the bodice as licensed by Mary Hartline Enterprises. Her boots were painted-on. Interestingly, Ideal made a virtually identical 7½" doll as a Kellogg's premium (see Kellogg's). The doll was likely a mail in-premium offer, for cash plus wrappers.

Note: Ideal made both premium and retail 7¼" and 7½" Mary Hartline dolls also. Lingerie Lou also sold their doll retail through Sears and other stores.
Value: $50.00.

Nestlé, Nancy Nestlé 9" c. 1954

Nestlé offered a 9" Virga type doll for their Nancy Nestlé doll: "Adorable lifelike plastic doll, over 9" tall. She walks, she turns her head, and winks her eyes. She can be dressed and

undressed." Her taffeta dress tied in the back, but the white cotton panties were stapled-on, and she wore red vinyl slip-on shoes.
Value: $45.00.

Post Grape-Nuts Flakes Nancy & Sluggo 7½" c. 1950

In 1933 cartoonist Ernie Bushmiller created a spunky little girl character named Nancy, and by the end of the 1930s, Nancy had a boyfriend, Sluggo. The two prompted very popular premium offers. Incredibly Nancy and Sluggo comics were still going strong in the

*Nestlé advertisement for Nancy Nestlé c. 1954.
Courtesy Marge Meisinger.*

*Nancy Nestlé-The Walking Doll,
9". Courtesy Marge Meisinger.*

late '40s and '50s when hard plastic dolls entered the doll market. Plastic Molded Arts 7½" hard plastic dolls were perfect for Nancy & Sluggo dolls, and it is believed that Post Grape-Nuts Flakes offered them as premium dolls. Just like in the cartoon, Nancy wore a felt vest and orange taffeta skirt with matching hair bow, and Sluggo had a red and white striped jersey, a black felt jacket, and gray flannel pants with a patch in the knee. Nancy had lamb's wool hair dyed black, but Sluggo's hair was painted black. See A&H section, page 17, for retail Sluggo and Girlfriend.

Value: $300.00+ each.

P&G Make Up Doll 11½" c. 1965

In 1965 Procter and Gamble offered a "Mary Makeup Doll" for free in return for product labels from various P&G products including Joy, Camay, and Downy. The unique aspect of the 11½" Mary doll was that color could be applied to her pale vinyl face and her light rooted blonde hair with a special coloring kit. The brochure in the doll's brown mailing box indicated that the customer was expected to purchase the make-up kit separately. The make-up kit was actually part of the "Tressy" line and was advertised: "She can change her make-up again and again. Included in Tressy's Cosmetic Kit are lipstick, eyeshadow, eyebrow pencil, nail polish, cosmetic sponges, instruction book." Horsman sold this same exact doll simultaneously on the retail market as Mary Makeup.

Value: $45.00.

Py-O-My, Patty 8" c. 1950s (photos, pg. 264)

Boxes of Py-O-My Blueberry Muffin mix offered 8" hard plastic sleep eye dolls with molded lashes for $1.00 plus a coupon from the outside of the carton. The head and arms are strung on, and the head does not turn. They are wide eye Ginger dolls with the walking mechanism removed. "I'm Patty your 8" walking Py-O-My doll." Six dolls were offered: Bride, Queen of Hearts, Patty Goes to Market, Patty's First Date, Apple for Teacher, and Mother's Helper. The dolls' feet were painted white with socks and slip-on vinyl shoes. Panties were made from nylon knit.

Value: $50.00.

Riegel Nightwear, "Miss Riegel 1962" 8" c. 1962

This 8" unmarked doll was sold sitting in a clear plastic bell with a label printed: "Miss Riegel/ 1962/ The Style Leader/ Year after Year/Nightwear Flannelettes/for all the family from/Riegel. Riegel/Fabrics that make fashion."

She was an 8" hard plastic, head-turning walker, fully jointed doll with sleep eyes and molded lashes. She has a Mindy Type #1 head with mouth paint downturned at edges and mold line behind the ear. Her straight legs had flat, smooth feet with no toe or molded shoe detail, and C-shaped arm hooks with 2nd and 3rd fingers on right hand molded together, separate fingers on left hand. Note: This is the same doll as A&H Dolls Gigi #1 and Lisa, and as Dollyanna's "Dorrie." Her good quality synthetic wig was stitched to a backing and glued to the head. One doll example was sold in a bell, wearing a thick flannel flowered nightgown with lace trim and a bow tie; white taffeta panties with picot trim; no shoes.

Value: $40.00; $55.00 in bell.

Tastee-Freez Dolls 7" c. 1950s

Tastee-Freez sold '50s "souvenir" dolls in their stores. They were 7" fixed leg dolls with painted-on white shoes and molded bows with tiny rounded edges typical of Duchess dolls. The doll's arms are jointed, and the 2nd and 3rd fingers are molded together. The Tastee-Freez doll had excellent cheek color, and sleep eyes with painted on eye-

P&G (Procter & Gamble) Mary Makeup Doll, 11½", 1965.

Post Grape-Nuts, Nancy doll face close-up, a PMA doll, boxed retail by A & H.

Post Grape-Nuts, Nancy doll, back.

Continued on page 266.

Riegel Nightwear doll in a bell c. 1962.

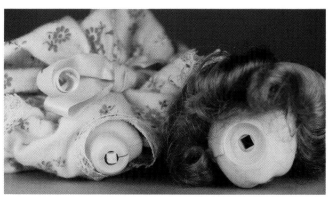

Riegel doll walking mechanism through neck.

Py-O-My Patty doll, original box and carton ad, 8".

Py-O-My Patty Queen of Hearts doll and original box, 8".

Py-O-My Patty box advertisement c. 1950s.

264

Miss Tastee-Freez, Ireland gown and yellow gown, 7".

Vel doll, 9", c. 1950s.

Miss Tastee-Freez, dotted gown, 7".

Waldorf doll tutu closes with gripper snap.

Vel doll face close-up of eyes without lashes, 9" doll.

Waldorf ballerina doll, 7".

brows and eyelashes. Many attractive costumes were offered, primarily stapled-on taffeta gowns, with a ribbon sash printed with the Tastee-Freez logo and the "America's Sweetheart" promotional slogan. The early '50s Tastee-Freez dolls had various nursery rhymes and designs printed on taffeta skirts and were marked "PMA" on the back. Mid-50s dolls were available in various gown styles, and it is known that at a much later date, cowboy and Indian dolls were also offered. These dolls were typically available in Tastee-Freez stores, and in 1956 she was offered for 99 cents after purchase of $2.00 of product.
Value: $25.00.

Vel Detergent 9" c. 1950s

Colgate Palmolive's 9" head-turning and walking "Vel" doll was a premium offer for both their Vel and Fab laundry products. The doll closely resembles Virga's 9" doll named Lucy and A & H's 9" Marcie doll with dimpled knees and toe detail. However, the advertising doll was apparently "no frills" version without molded lashes like the retail doll. The premium doll's medium quality synthetic wig was advertised, "You can wash, comb and set her beautiful long golden hair." Her pink cotton dress with white lace trim was tied in the back with a ribbon, and she wore white nylon socks and vinyl slip-on shoes but no hat. Box flyer: "Here is Vel, your new Vel Doll which you ordered in a Colgate offer. She is 9" tall and made of durable plastic...you can turn her head, walk, sit and stand." Also, "We hope that you have found....that it (Vel) is the best dishwashing detergent on the market, and provides the safest way of all to wash delicate fabrics, including sheerest nylon." "VEL" was printed on the doll's brown mailing box.
Value: $45.00.

Waldorf Doll 8" c. 1950s

Waldorf Doll was a slim, hard plastic walking doll with sleep eyes, straight legs with pin-hips, jointed knees, and high-heel feet. Her pink knit tutu with silver thread is removable and closes with a star gripper snap like Vogue Dolls, Inc. used beginning in '57. No advertising has been located to document or date the doll exactly.
Value: $25.00.

Unknown Premium Dolls

Bride Doll

This 7" hard plastic bride doll has jointed head with sleep eyes, strung arms with 2nd and 3rd finger molded together on the left hand, separate at tips on right; and fixed legs

with flat feet painted white with molded sharp-corner bows like Duchess and wears a white taffeta gown.
Value: $25.00.

Mardi Gras Doll

This 7" plastic doll is in a Mardi Gras costume similar to the Lestoil doll c. 1959 with jointed arms and head with sleep eyes, fixed legs, taffeta gown, pom-fringed felt hat, and mask, but she has high-heel feet.
Value: $25.00.

Whatever your collecting pleasure may be, advertising dolls can be very interesting to add to your list. Both doll collectors and advertising collectors often vie for "prize" specimens, creating a cross-over market and increasing demand for the advertising dolls. If the collector is lucky, they will find a doll in its original box with its product advertising. Without boxes, it may be a challenge to identify the dolls since, as we have outlined above, many were "adopted" by more than one advertiser. If doll boxes are not available, perhaps the collector will find the original advertisement for the doll to identify the outfit, doll type, etc. Whatever the method, advertising dolls are truly finding their place in today's collecting market.

Unknown 7" Mardi Gras doll.　　　*Unknown 7" bride doll.*

Premium dolls not shown: Roman Meal c. 1955, sold for $1 by Roman Meal; 8" Virga dolls in Virga type outfits with "p" pattern snaps, and tie-on hats. Shipped in brown mailing boxes.

Sewing Sets

Dress Me Dolls of the '50s

Collectors fondly recall little "Dress Me" dolls from the 1950s. Little "Moms" became mini fashion designers for the little undressed dollies and had lots of fun in the "stitch n' sew" craze. Today it is fun to find these lost '50s dollies and treasures from our sewing culture.

Sewing Kit Roots in the 1940s

Industrious pattern manufacturers in the 1940s likely spawned the 1950s sewing craze. The '40s pattern makers cashed in on increased domestic sewing during World War II, and they saw even more potential in pleasure sewing after the war. However, the sewing industry recognized that much of their task to build the home sewing market was educational.

If housewives were lucky, their own mom had passed along sewing skills. But if they had to learn on their own, the budding sewer had a problem. Pattern makers were eager to solve their sewing-skills dilemma and to sell a few products in the process. In the 1940s pattern companies put together sewing kits with mannequin dolls, patterns, and instructions for both moms and "young miss" sewers. More moms were now sewing away, and America's sewing spirit was rekindled.

The '40s home sewing activity had a trickle-down effect and soon inspired sewing kits for younger kids. At first these kid's sets were quite formal presentations with adult-looking mannequin dolls. These eventually gave way to colorful sewing sets for younger audiences. For example, in the '40s Pressman & Co. boxed a child's sewing set with a 6" child model doll, kid-size scissors, pre-cut fabric, and embroidery materials, etc. These cheerful sewing kits inspired even more child-friendly sets going into the '50s.

Pressman & Co. '40s sewing kit box lid had bright illustrations printed "Every Little Girl Loves to Sew" on the side. Courtesy Jo Barckley.

A late '40s Pressman & Co. "Sewing for Every Girl" kit featured a 6" composition doll with fabric, patterns, and thread. Courtesy Jo Barckley. MIB $40.00 – 45.00+.

This "Miniature Fashions for Young Fashion Designers" sewing set in wooden inlaid box includes gray instruction book c. 1943 "for older/more advanced students", 15" Fashiondol composition mannequin, patterns, and sewing aids. The doll has removable arms for fitting and pegs to hold feet in blue stand at right. The smaller doll and green Simplicity instruction booklet c. 1944 were purchased separately. The 1954 Marshall Field's Christmas catalog featured Simplicity's kits with hard rubber 15" Fashiondol and sewing kits for "ages 10 and up." Courtesy Jo Barckley. Box with patterns and mannequin $250.00 – 350.00; 12" mannequin with dress form/pattern, MIB $75.00 – 100.00; mannequin only $50.00 – 75.00.

Hassenfeld Bros. (Hasbro) offered c. 1957-'59 Jr. Miss Sewing Kit in a plaid hat box, including 7½" hard plastic doll with sleep eyes, strung arms, and mohair wig. Kit contained pre-cut fabric for dresses, scissors, and sewing accessories. Courtesy Jo Barckley. $75.00+.

Hassenfeld Bros. (Hasbro) offered c. 1960s Polka Dot and Plaid Sewing Set For The Junior Miss offering "Pretty Pre-Cut Costumes Ready To Sew" along with sewing accessories. Courtesy Jo Barckley. $40.00.

Necchi's Little Miss Seamstress Set includes an inexpensive 11" plastic doll with moving arms, needles, thread, material, and material to make housedresses. MIB $40.00 – 50.00.

1950 Fun Doll Sewing Kits

American and European designers inspired a rush of sewing creativity with their "hot" new '50s fashions. Now that households were sewing-savvy, women once again turned to their sewing machines to stitch the latest looks, and once again marketers tapped into the sewing sales. At first, they simply spiffed up the '40s sewing mannequin sets. For example in 1953, Butterick teamed up with Ideal Toy Corporation to promote a more streamlined "Butterick Sew-Easy Designing Set" which now contained patterns and Ideal's 14" adult hard vinyl mannequin. And Simplicity, who used to target "the modern miss," now appealed to "the little girl who likes to sew" in Chicago Marshall Field's '50s Christmas catalog. The updated set was basically the same as the 1940s set, but with a rubber 15" Simplicity/Fashiondol.

However, the recycled '40s mannequin dolls didn't last long in the '50s kid's sewing market. Instead, retailers began to incorporate the 7"- 8" hard plastic

display and toddler type dolls into clever sewing sets. The pattern companies lost sales to savvy toy makers as "Dress Me" dolls arrived in the "fabulous fifties." Kid-friendly sets for less serious sewing gained popularity, along with the paint-by-numbers and other sorts of hobby sets in the post-war economy. Madison Avenue advertisers recognized the sales potential of kids and made every effort to capture their attention. Bright graphics on sewing kit lids, pre-cut fabrics, and dolls that more closely

Little Miss Seamstress Set featuring Necchi Sewing Machine was a favorite of young sewers. The colorful lid featured the molded plastic machine in white. Played-with, $25.00 – 40.00; mint $50.00+.

Hassenfeld Bros. (Hasbro) 1955 boxed Junior Miss Sewing Kit with small plastic doll, pre-cut fabric, thread, embroidery pattern, and sewing accessories. Played-with, $20.00+; mint $35.00 – 40.00.

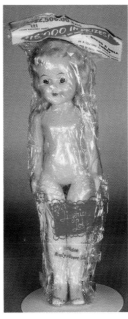

1957 advertisement for a Lingerie Lou "Dress-A-Doll Contest." The ad says that the dolls could be bought at F.W. Woolworth Stores in 7½" to 11½" sizes. The doll in the ad is the 7½" size.

Lingerie Lou 11½" doll in acetate bag for "Dress A Doll Today" contest for cash prizes advertised on the bag label. MIP $20.00 – 35.00.

These 7½" Lingerie Lou dolls in homemade costumes could been contest entries or just fun home projects. The contest ad states, "All dolls are donated to The March of Dimes at end of contest." Doll $45.00 – 55.00; MIB complete $125.00+.

Colgate Palmolive included "miniature replicas of Vogue Patterns" to sew a dress, coat, and nightgown with their strung 8" hard plastic Lustre-Creme Starlet premium doll c. 1953.

Lingerie Lou boxed set of two dolls and a pattern in "Make Your Own Dresses" set.

Vogue's Ginny doll c. 1950s had Vogue patterns to make matching little girl's dress. Shown with pattern book page is Ginny in her '58 red jacket outfit #1241 which had child's look-alike pattern #2741; Ginny's '58 pink organdy and velvet outfit #1335 had matching Vogue child pattern #2786. $175.00 – 225.00; in box $225.00+.

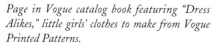

Talented sewers like Toni Ferry recreate '50s patterns today, like this Nancy & Sluggo set from original premium dolls (see Advertising Dolls chapter).

Page in Vogue catalog book featuring "Dress Alikes," little girls' clothes to make from Vogue Printed Patterns.

McCall's patterns c. 1954 for the original Ginny. Mint $12.00 – 15.00.

resembled play dolls all appealed to little sewers. Judging from sewing kit remnants found in attics today, few stitched beautiful doll dresses, but they no doubt had fun trying!

One well-respected toy company that got into the '50s sewing kit game was Hassenfeld Bros., better known as Hasbro today. Their 1955 "Junior Miss Sewing Kit" had a bright plaid box lid and included pre-cut material and accessories for various sewing projects. The plastic sewing doll was inexpensive with painted eyes and was jointed only at the arms. Hassenfeld's "Junior Miss Sewing Kit" from 1957 – 59 was tucked inside a red plaid hatbox including pre-cut fabric, scissors, thread, pattern, and a thimble. The doll included in this kit was a high quality Duchess display doll jointed at the head and arms with sleep eyes.

1950s Dress Me Dolls

Toddler "Dress Me Dolls" were a huge marketing success in the 1950s doll world. These hard plastic dolls were typically dressed only in panties by manufacturers also selling lucrative boxed outfits to complete her wardrobe. Vogue Dolls Inc. led this trend. Their 8" hard plastic toddler Ginny doll was the mid-market "Fashion Leader In Doll Society" dressed in wonderfully coordinated Vogue outfits. But in 1952 they featured Ginny clad only in panties to stimulate sales of their separately boxed outfits. The campaign was a big success, as stores sold four separately boxed outfits on average for every doll they sold. However, not everyone raced out to purchase new store-bought outfits for the scantily clad dolls. Many little "mothers" spent countless hours at home making their own frocks for dolly, so the toy sewing industry definitely benefited from the craze.

But Vogue wasn't the only one with a dress me toddler in the '50s. Competitors jumped aboard the trend, and unclad look-alikes in all price ranges lined shop shelves. 1952 Lingerie Lous advertised their 7½" boxed dolls in Christmas and mail order catalogs wearing only "plastic lingerie." Some companies tossed completely undressed dolls into cellophane bags for low to mid-market sales. Grant Plastics sold a nice look-alike tod-

dler doll in cellophane bags labeled "Adorable Dress Me Dolls" for sale in unlikely places such as hardware stores. By the mid-1950s, makers of high end or mid-market toddlers, such as Wendy, Muffie, and Ginger, added a dress me doll to the line.

In 1956 the enterprising Doll Bodies conducted a contest for outfitting their undressed dolls. They sold their 8" and 10Z\x" fully jointed Lingerie Lou dolls in cellophane bags with the tag reading: "Dress A Doll Today/In A Costume Of Your Choice/Grand Prize $2,500." Designs for costumes to outfit the doll that were submitted to the company by deadline qualified to win one of 122 cash prizes.

Home Sewing Crazy - Then and Now

Kids turned to the sewing machines in the '50s, and pattern companies were once again eager to help them (with a little help from their Mom) sew for their dolls. Companies such as Simplicity and McCall's provided patterns for doll wardrobes for sale in sewing stores. Doll promoters and premium makers also got into the act. In 1953 Colgate Palmolive promoted their "Lustre-Creme Starlet" premium doll and pattern to make her a nightgown and outfit. But Vogue Dolls, Inc., maker of the market reader Ginny went a bit farther in 1958. They teamed up with the Vogue Pattern Company to sell home sewing patterns matching little Ginny's darling dresses.

Years later, pattern companies were still providing wonderful patterns for dolls, such as Simplicity's Ginny Doll patterns c. 1992. With vintage outfits becoming increasingly difficult to find and prices escalating, many enjoy sewing for their dolls even more. Talented sewers provide professional assistance, such as Toni Ferry who has the knack for turning back the clock to create costumes from any era, such as Nancy & Sluggo, impossible to find premium dolls from the 1940s-50s. As the world becomes increasingly high tech, many find great satisfaction and comfort in sewing for their dolls. Yesterday's sewing kits become comfort food in our hectic lives today and reminders of simpler times.

J&P Coats & Clark's provided a lovely printed pattern for The California Doll crochet Bridesmaid projects c. 1950s. Dolls like the brunette 7½" doll could be purchased separately with Chadwick's Red Heart Yarn. Doll/flyer $20.00 – 35.00.

Doodle Dolls' crochet patterns were frequently made in colors to match wedding party bridesmaids, such as this lovely teal and pink gown. The 7½" doll has incised lines on her feet, simulating PMA-type bows. $25.00 – 35.00.

Twinkle Belle crochet doll kit by Bucilla included the 7½" jointed hard plastic doll along with thread and pattern for the project shown on the label c. 1950s. $25.00 – 45.00.

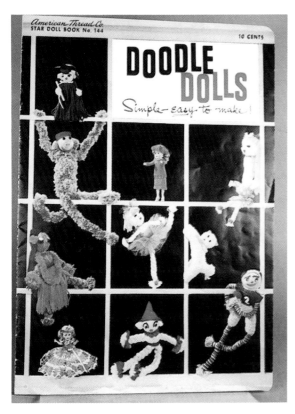

Baby Dolls were perfect for '50s sewing projects, such as American Thread's "Ruffle Bustle" 8" baby doll dress from their 1950 "Fair & Bazaar Suggestions" booklet. This 8" plastic '50s doll shown is similar to those made by Irwin Plastics.

Patterns for dress me and fashion dolls in crochet books like Doodle Dolls.

International Doll Company, Mollye, 7" undressed plastic doll with painted eyes; strung arms, fixed head and legs, no bows like Virga dolls. $15.00 – 20.00; MIB $35.00 – 40.00.

Create lovely, colorful Dolls
with *Dress-a-Doll-Disks*

Whether you're a beginner or have sewed for years, you'll find it fun and easy to make a beautiful doll like this in just a few hours with **DRESS-A-DOLL DISKS**. Easy-to-follow instructions are given for many colorful dolls—add your own touches for an original you'll be proud to say you made! Wonderful for gifts, party decorations, bazaars, club money raising projects!

Buy **DRESS-A-DOLL DISKS** in heavenly blue, candy pink, misty green, creamy yellow, orchid, and white at your favorite variety store. If they are not yet available locally, write Johnson & Johnson, 4949 W. 65th Street, Chicago 38, Illinois, for the name of the dealer nearest you. **DRESS-A-DOLL DISKS** are made only by Johnson & Johnson—your assurance of fine quality always.

Johnson & Johnson Filter Products Division,
4949 W. 65th Street, Chicago 38, Illinois
Copyright 1958, Johnson & Johnson, Chicago

Johnson & Johnson's 1954 advertisement for "Dress-A-Doll-Disks...fun, easy, profitable."

7½" plastic "Dress Me Doll" with sleep eyes and fixed legs is labeled for Allisons advertising, "Staple or pin clothes directly to the body." This doll was "Made in Hong Kong," possibly in the '60s or '70s. $10.00.

Duchess Dolls (see Duchess Dolls section) marketed this 7½" painted eye undressed doll in their late 1940s brochure for crochet doll projects. Note the sharp cornered bows on the feet typical of Duchess; undressed dolls were also sold with sleep eyes. $15.00 – 20.00; MIB $35.00 – 40.00.

Crochet Away!

In the hobby-friendly era of the 1950s, crochet doll kits were vigorously promoted in sewing departments and even displayed side by side with paint-by-numbers, wood burning, and all sorts of other fun craft kits. This was the era when the do-it-yourself spirit ruled, and one could never have too many how-to kits to keep themselves busy. For many collectors today, it is the crochet dolls that are among their fondest reminders of the 1950s hobbies when crochet enthusiasts never had a finer time.

Lots of cute little dolls dressed in elaborate crochet outfits have survived to present day because they were often put in display cases or saved as keepsakes passed through the generations. Those that recall crocheting away on the frilly little frocks enjoy collecting the original '50s dolls and pattern books they find today at antique malls, flea markets, and doll shows. They are lovely reminders of their cherished mementos. Yet others collect the dolls and patterns not because they are familiar, but because they are so colorful and pretty. However, the unfamiliar may wonder what inspired all that creative energy in the '50s, since the crochet doll hobby gave way long ago to Barbie and other fashion doll collecting. Crochet dolls still bring fond memories from '50s doll lovers.

Accessories

Many of the '50s doll makers boxed and sold separate doll accessories. However, there were scores of other companies that sold accessories only. Some specialized in certain accessories such as shoes or dresses, while others sold a wide variety of accessories. The following are a number of items on the '50s doll market.

Grand Wig Co., Inc. '50s advertisement for "Surprise Package for your Little Girl," including 8" walking doll with hats, three wig, dress, panties, shoes, socks, glasses, and a hanger. The doll looks like an unwigged Pam doll, and the straw hats are c. 1950s. Courtesy Marge Meisinger.

Doll & Craft World, Inc., "The Complete Doll Supply Source, 125 Eighth, St. Brooklyn, NY 11215 USA," c. 1960s. Silver center-snap leatherette silver doll shoes for 8" doll. Courtesy Marge Meisinger. MIP $45.00 – 75.00+.

Corona Hat Co., Inc., Lynbrook, NY "Miss Corona's hat and bag set of Genuine Imported Straw/ For all 10½" Slim Dolls." Hat also fits 8" Ginny look-alike dolls perfectly and is the same type used by Vogue with less expensive flower trim. MIB $40.00 – 45.00.

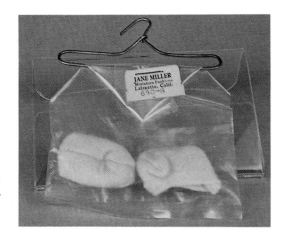

Jane Miller Miniature Fashions, Lafayette, Calif. Jane Miller made a wide assortment of dresses, shoes, outfits, and outfit sewing kits for various sized dolls in the '50s. These baby booties are for a doll approx. 8" tall, with "Jane Miller" cardboard tag. MIP $20.00 – 35.00.

Jane Miller tutu back with a round, smooth metal snap and typical company outfit tag.

A Jane Miller ballet tutu for 8" doll with satin bodice, attached panties, and tulle skirt very similar to Madame Alexander for 14" and larger dolls. $40.00 – 55.00.

Merry Mfg. Co. My Merry Wash-N-Wave Set. Includes "Merry Shampoo" and "Merry Wave Set," marked Merry Mfg. Co., also plastic curlers and terrycloth; back of box: Eugene L. Ach, 1109 Main St., Cincinnati 10, OH/Copyright 1950. $40.00 – 55.00.

M & S Shillman, Brooklyn, NY, tagged "Doll Accessory Package," "Every Little Girl's Delight," c. 1950s. Pair of 4½" wooden skis with attached vinyl slip-on shoes for 8" doll with poles with metal tips and leatherette straps, price tag 29 cents. MIP $30.00 – 50.00.

"Little Traveler" Steamer Trunk, maker unknown. Cardboard trunk for 8" -10" doll is printed with faux metal corners and travel stickers, very similar to Virga's "Bon Voyage" trunk c. 1957 (see Virga section). Mint $40.00 – 45.00.

Merry Toys advertises shaving, linen closet, and beauty shop kits, in December 1957 Good Housekeeping magazine.

274

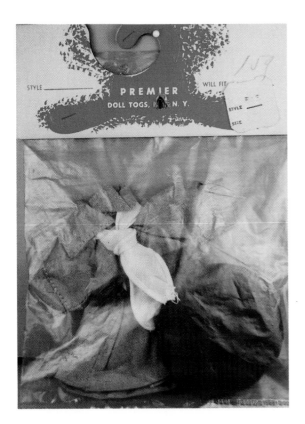

Premier Doll Togs, Inc. cardboard tag with perforated red dress hanger, green cotton Girl Scout uniform with three green painted smooth metal snaps, felt tam, yellow tie, green felt belt closes with green round metal snap; price in pencil $1.59. MIP $35.00 – 50.00.

S.B. Novelty Co., Inc. "Dolly's Tie Shoes," white tie leatherette shoes for 20" dolls. $25.00 – 30.00.

Premier Doll Accessories, Inc. (L) One pair white satin smooth bottom tie-on shoes with rib-edged white satin ribbon c.'50s. (R) Nylon hose and "fuzzy-bottom" cream satin tie-on shoes with less expensive flat-edged ribbon for 8" doll; package tagged Marshall Field & Company, 35 cents. MIP $20.00 – 35.00.

Premier Doll Togs, Inc., NY. Blue and white pin striped dress with puffed sleeves closes with square metal handsewn snap; white tie-on organdy apron trimmed with lace; price written on, 98 cents. MIP $25.00 – 45.00.

Premier Doll Togs, Inc., "Doll Fashions" two-piece romper outfit for 8" baby doll, closes with square handsewn metal snap. MIP $25.00 – 30.00.

Premier Doll Togs, Inc., Brooklyn 15, NY, "Doll Fashions." Three-piece cowgirl outfit for 8" toddler look-alike doll, check shirt with button, suedecloth vest and skirt trimmed with leatherette fringe. MIP $30.00 - 40.00.

Stashin Doll Mfg., Newark, N.J. "Baby Susie Doll Clothes, Designed to fit all 8 inch dolls!" advertisement c. 1950s. Penny and Andrea outfits are in Stashin section.

Premier Doll Accessories Co., Inc., "Toyland's Glamour Stylists for Dolls." Gold leather 8" doll tie-on shoes. Courtesy Marge Meisinger. MIB $30.00 – 45.00.

Not shown: Mae Marie, 8" unmarked, vinyl side-snap shoes, in box. Note: For additional separate doll outfits and accessories, see individual doll company sections including Cosmopolitan, Totsy, Virga, and Vogue.

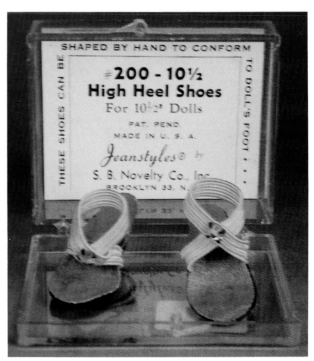

Premier Doll Accessories Co., Inc. One pair of good quality, unmarked pink vinyl side-snap shoes with blue socks for 8" dolls, unmarked bottom, c. 1950s. MIB $20.00 – 30.00.

S.B. Novelty Co., Inc. "High Heel Shoes for 10½" dolls/Pat. Pend, Made in U.S.A./ Jeanstyles (r) by S.B. Novelty Co., Inc., "These shoes can be shaped by hand to conform to doll's foot." $15.00 – 30.00.

BRUSHWARE ACCESSORIES

COMPARE
THESE UNUSUAL VALUES
PRICED FOR VOLUME SALES

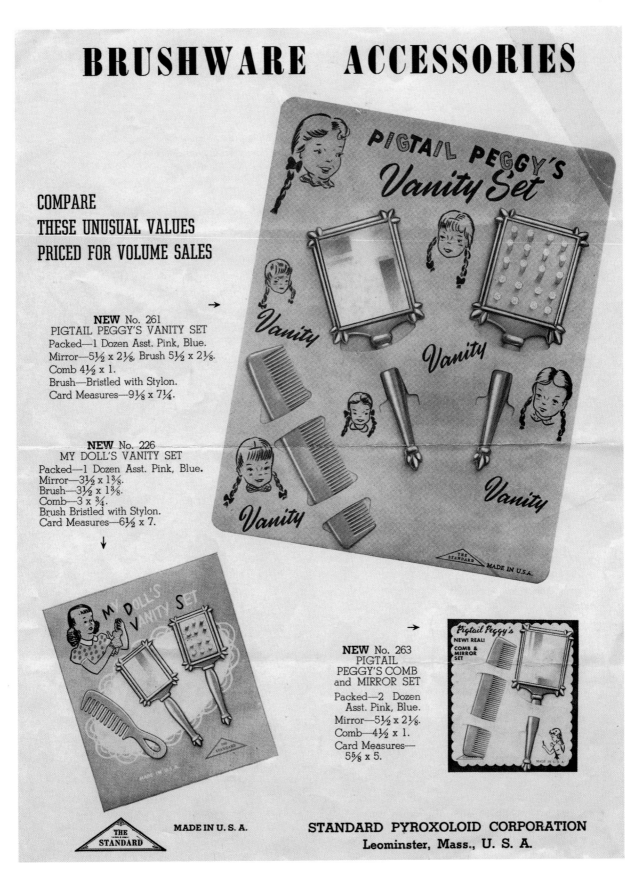

NEW No. 261
PIGTAIL PEGGY'S VANITY SET
Packed—1 Dozen Asst. Pink, Blue.
Mirror—5½ x 2⅛, Brush 5½ x 2⅛.
Comb 4½ x 1.
Brush—Bristled with Stylon.
Card Measures—9⅛ x 7¼.

NEW No. 226
MY DOLL'S VANITY SET
Packed—1 Dozen Asst. Pink, Blue.
Mirror—3½ x 1⅜.
Brush—3½ x 1⅜.
Comb—3 x ¾.
Brush Bristled with Stylon.
Card Measures—6½ x 7.

NEW No. 263
PIGTAIL
PEGGY'S COMB
and MIRROR SET
Packed—2 Dozen
Asst. Pink, Blue.
Mirror—5½ x 2⅛.
Comb—4½ x 1.
Card Measures—
5⅝ x 5.

MADE IN U. S. A.

STANDARD PYROXOLOID CORPORATION
Leominster, Mass., U. S. A.

Standard Pyroxoloid Corp. advertised child's vanity sets in the 1950s.

277

Doll Comparisons

It is often difficult to tell '50s toddler dolls apart, and unmarked dolls are a particular challenge. The previous chapters featured doll photos by individual makers. This chapter will compare dolls by different makers side by side. Space does not allow all of the possible combinations, so the most confusing comparisons have been selected, hopefully, to further aid identification.

Note: There may be other dolls in these categories that are not shown. Doll makers frequently substituted dolls and parts. It would be inaccurate to say that the following comparisons were always the case, but it can be said that they were most often the case.

Toddler Doll Comparisons

Unmarked Toddler Dolls

MINDY #3 VS. VIRGA #3 BENT KNEE WALKERS: The bent knee Mindy on the left and the bent knee Virga Playmate c. '57 on the right both use Ginger bodies. Mindy has the medium eye Ginger head and Virga has the larger eye Ginger head, but both have the Ginger center ear mold, and bent knee walker bodies with wide spread legs. (Virga did *not* use Ginger bodies on straight leg dolls.)

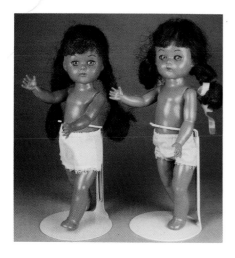

PAM VS. LUCY: At first look, Fortune's Pam on the left looks identical to Virga's Lucy (or Playmate) on the right. They both have the same head, body, and molded T-strap feet. One of the only ways to tell them apart is the arms: Pam on left has all separate fingers with peg-shaped arm hooks; Virga doll has 2nd and 3rd fingers molded together on both hands with C-shaped arm hooks.

PMA VS. HAPPI-TIME: (L) The PMA Type #3 straight leg walker on left and the Happi-Time bent knee walker on right are both Fortune Pam type dolls; both have the same head, separate fingers, peg-shaped arm hooks, and molded T-strap shoes. Eye sizes may differ.

PAM VS. LUCY: Pam type with pastel hair on left and Virga's Lolly-Pop doll with pastel hair on the right are essentially the same doll with almost identical heads and molded T-strap feet. However, differences are: (a) The arms are different with C-shaped hook for Virga and peg-shaped hook for Pam; (b) The Pam doll may or may not have slightly smaller eyes like this one.

LARGE-EYE GINGER MOLD DOLLS: (L) Midwestern's Mary Jean has had the walking mechanism removed and feet painted white. Not shown: Other non-walking large-eye Gingers; Admiration's Carol-Sue, Commonwealth Plastic's Carol. (R) Active's Judy head-turning walker without painted feet. Not shown: Many other competitors used the Ginger head-turning walker too including Gigi #3 and Julie.

Dolls With Lashes Painted Under Eyes

(L to R) *Norma* with painted white T-straps; Doll Bodies Roberta, and *Grant* Type #2 with painted molded bow feet; *Grant Plastics* with painted toes; *PMA:* Nancy (see Advertising Dolls) with painted black T-straps but can also be painted white. Dolls not shown with painted lashes under eyes: Dubell's Little Princess, PMA's Joanie Pigtails with molded T-straps; Stashin's Penny; Carlson's toddlers.

Vinyl Head Toddler Dolls

All of these, dolls have their maker's mark shown in italics on the neck. (L to R) Cosmopolitan's "GINGER" with toes; Fortune's "PAM" with toes and either flat feet or Cha Cha heels (same head); "Virga" with molded T-strap feet; "PMA" with molded T-strap feet.

British and International Dolls

(L to R) Early Miss Rosebud with painted lashes; Roddy with molded lashes; unidentified 8" Lapland doll with molded lashes.

(L to R) Early '50s Miss Rosebud strung with painted lashes; Vogue's '53 Ginny, strung with painted lashes.

Later '50s Miss Rosebud without painted lashes and pinker plastic.

Ear Molds – Toddler Dolls

Feet Comparisons – Toddler Dolls

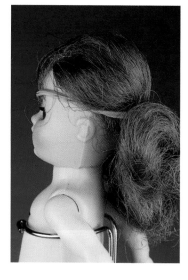

SMOOTH FEET DOLLS (L to R) These dolls have flat feet with smooth tops, i.e., no toe detail or no molded shoe detail. *Elite's Vicki Lee* with feet painted white; *A&H's Lisa* (brunette); *Dollyana's Dorrie*; *A&H's Gigi* Type #1. (Dolls with smooth feet not shown; Gigi in plastic bell; Riegel Miss 1962; Uneeda's Janie with vinyl head, Mego's Julie, Linda Doll Co.'s Linda.)

Ear seam behind ear (various shaped ears) on hard plastic toddlers without Ginger type heads including Ginny, Muffie, Wendy, Virga straight leg, Fortune's Pam, A&H's Gigi Types #1 & 2, Elite's Vicki.

(L to R) 1. *Molded T-strap shoes*: Virga's Lucy; Fortune's Pam; Norma (ptd. wht.); PMA (or ptd. wht. or blk.); PMA Joanie (or ptd. wht.); Norma (ptd. wht.); Virga Lucy; Virga Lolly-Pops; Nirsek Janie Pigtails. 2. *Cosmopolitan's Ginger* with dimples and toenails, and all dolls using Ginger bodies. 3. *Vogue's Ginny* with toenails, no dimples.

Ear seam through center of ear on Cosmopolitan's Ginger and on dolls using Ginger mold heads including Elite's Vicki Lee, Fortune's Jeanette and Ninette; Admiration's Carol Sue; Py-O-My advertising doll; Riegel Miss 1962; Terri Lee Girl Scout; Wipco's Lisa; A&H Julie; and others.

Advertising doll with flat smooth feet, "Willadean of Hawaii" (see Advertising chapter).

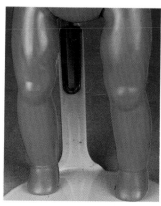

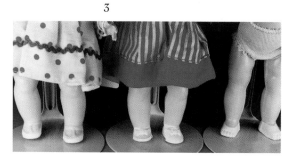

1   2   3

(L to R) Cosmopolitan's *Ginger* with dimples and toenails, and all dolls using Ginger bodies; Vogue's *Ginny* with toenails; Alexander's *Wendy* with toe nails; Nancy Ann's *Muffie* with dimples and toenails.

DOLLS WITH WHITE PAINTED FEET (L to R). *T-strap shoes*: Norma; dolls not shown with T-straps: Joanie Pigtails, Joanie Walker. *White painted flat bows*: Doll Bodies' Mary Lu. Not shown with painted. flat bows: Roberta toddler; Stashin's Penny; Grant Type #1. *White painted toes*: Grant Type #2; not shown with painted toes: Midwestern's Mary Jean; Admiration's Carol-Sue.

Arm Hook Comparisons – Toddler Dolls

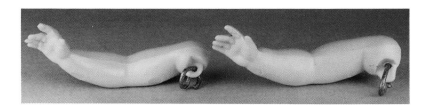

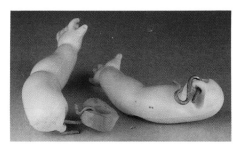

(L) Nancy Ann's Muffie metal ring in hole with square cut-out. (R) Vogue's Ginny, metal ring in hole with round cut-out; after mid '50s may have no cut-out.

Alexander's Alexander-kin (Wendy), S-shaped metal hook in a hole.

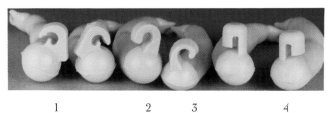

On left: Large thick C-shaped Virga's Lucy & Playmates; on right: Small thinner C-shaped hooks for Active's Mindy.

(L to R): 1. *Two C-shaped hooks* with flat right edge and small hook at bottom, Cosmopolitan's Ginger, and Ginger type dolls; 2. *single thick 3. C-shaped hook*, Virga's Lucy and Playmates; *single thin C-shaped hook*, Uneeda's vinyl head Janie; 4. *pair of peg-shaped hooks*, Fortune's Pam, Elite's Vicki, PMA Toddler.

Hand Comparisons – Toddler Dolls

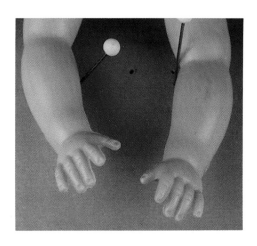

(L to R) Lisa, Dorrie, Linda. Smooth feet dolls with 2nd and 3rd fingers molded together on right (see pg. 282 for photo).

Second and third fingers molded together on both hands, used by Virga's Lucy and Playmates.

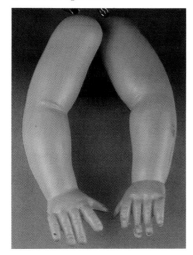

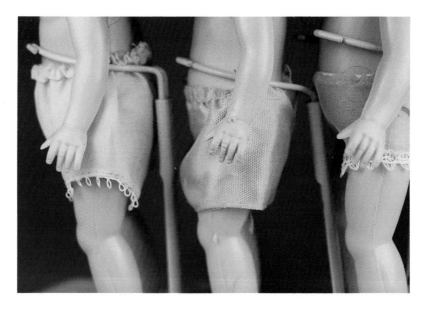

Second and 3rd fingers molded together on right hand with pointing index finger; fingers separate from knuckles on doll's left hand; with and without second creases at elbow; plastic colors and finger width may vary. Used by A&H's Type #1 Gigi; Active's Mindy; Unique's Jeanie; some smooth-feet dolls also used these arms.

Second and 3rd fingers molded together on the right; separate fingers from knuckles on left, however the 2nd and 3rd fingers may appear molded together completely, depending on the unmolding process. (L to R) Lisa, Dorrie, Linda. Not shown: Mego's Julie with T-strap shoes and others use these arms.

Display Doll Comparisons

Display Doll Feet (unpainted, white or black)

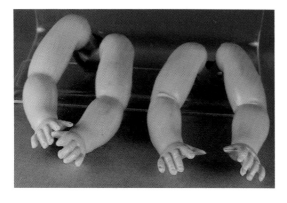

(L) Virga with 2nd and 3rd fingers molded together on both hands. (R) Mindy with 2nd and 3rd fingers on doll's right hand molded together, separate from knuckles on the left.

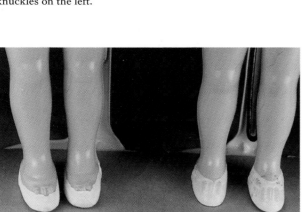

Rectangular bow, one horizontal crease, rounded corners: Joy walking doll (see Advertising dolls).

(L) Rectangular bows, one horizontal crease, rounded corners: Admiration; Chiquita. (R) Rectangular bows, two horizontal creases, rounded corners: Corrines, PMA.

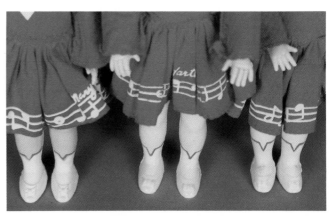

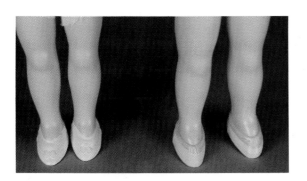

(L) Small butterfly bows mid foot: Lovelee; Dream Girl; Tastee-Freez (see Advertising Dolls). (R) Three incised marks for bows: Happi-Time; Marcie; PMA; Lady Hampshire; Fab 6" advertising dolls.

Mary Hartline doll feet (L to R): Sharp corner bows, marked Lingerie Lou; rectangular bows, one horizontal crease, rounded corners marked Ideal in oval; sharp corner bows, marked Ideal in block letters.

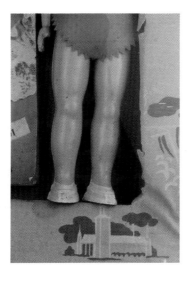

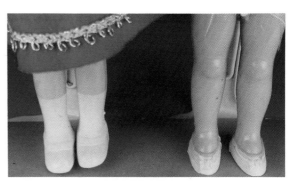

(L) No bows, one roll around top or bottom of foot: Midwestern; Virga; International Doll Co. Mollye. (R) Sharp corner bows: A&H; Duchess; House of Dolls, Chicago; Lingerie Lou.

Rectangular bow, one horizontal crease, rounded corners: Hawaiian walking doll (see Advertising Dolls).

Sharp corner bow: Lingerie Lou Dress-me Doll.

9" Hard Plastic Doll Comparisons

(L to R) *Fortune's 9½" Pam* with regular jointed legs; *Virga's 9" Lucy* with wavy mohair and synthetic wigs and pin-hip joints; *Virga's 9" Lucy* with stitched wig, and pin-hip joints. (Not shown using same doll as 9" Virga doll: Marcie Daily Dolly.)

Vinyl 8" Baby Doll Comparisons

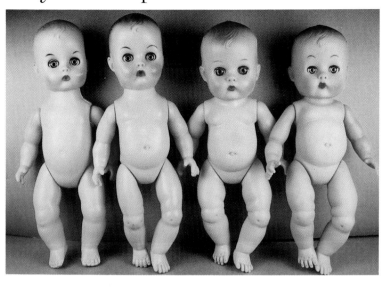

(L to R) *Marlon Creations*, all soft vinyl, unmarked but same as *Baby Susan* all soft vinyl, marked "Baby Susan."

(L to R) *Baby Susan look-alike*, all rigid vinyl with smaller head and less defined toes; manufacturer unknown. *Marked "Baby Susan,"* rigid vinyl with larger head. *Ginnette by Vogue*, all vinyl with bent right hand fingers, marked "VOGUE" on back. *Marked "AE,"* all vinyl with bent right hand fingers (possibly PMA).

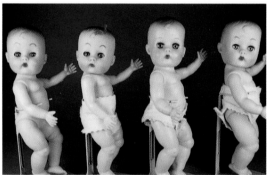

(L to R) *Marlon* Creations, all vinyl, unmarked, with molded eyelashes and lashes painted under eyes. *Baby Susan*, all vinyl, marked "Baby Susan," with eyelashes painted under the eyes. Both came in Marlon boxes.

Side view of four 8" babies above. The two on left are vinyl with hard plastic arms and straight fingers, and two on right are all vinyl with bent right hand fingers.

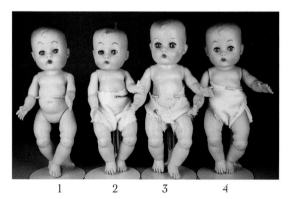

(L to R) *Marked "Baby Susan,"* all rigid vinyl. *Baby Susan look-alike*, all hard plastic with smaller head. *Vogue Ginnette*, all vinyl, marked "Vogue" or "Vogue Dolls, Inc." on back.

VINYL & HARD PLASTIC, SLEEP EYES 8" (L to R) 1. *Unmarked* vinyl 8" baby with r.v. arms. 2. *Unmarked* vinyl with r.v. arms; rooted forehead lock (one row), unknown maker. 3. *Ginnette* 8" "VOGUE" mark on back; all vinyl with bent right hand fingers. 4. *Marked "A-E"* all vinyl with bent right hand fingers (possibly PMA).

Composition, Painted Eyes,
8" Baby Doll Comparisons

(L to R) *Madame Alexander* "Dionne Quint" (also came with bent baby legs); *Vogue* "Sunshine Baby" with bent right arm; *unmarked* generic baby; *R&B* "My Dream Baby" with center forehead curl.

Close-up of babies above.

(L) *Unmarked* baby; (R) *Vogue* "Sunshine Baby" with bent right arm.

❧ Bibliography and Resources ❧

Museums

Bethnal Green Museum of Childhood
Cambridge Heath Road, London E2 9PA
(close to Bethnal Green Underground Station)
Tel: (recorded information) 0181-980-2415

Wenham Museum, A Museum of Social History
132 Main St.
Wenham, MA 10984
Tel: (978) 468-2377
Website: www.wenhammuseum.org

Primary Research Material

Dollmaker brochures 1950s & 1960s
Playthings magazines (1922-1960s)
Retail catalogs: FAO Schwarz, Marshall Field, Sears, Aldens, Wards.
Interviews with doll collectors and experts: see Acknowledgement section.

Books

Anderton, Joanne. *Twentieth Century Dolls*. Trojan Press, N. Kansas City, MO, 1971. *More Twentieth Century Dolls*. Wallace-Homestead, Des Moines, IA, 1983.

Baird, Frances. *British Hard Plastic Dolls of the 1940s & 1950s*. New Cavendish Books, London, 1998.

Finnegan, Stephanie. *Madame Alexander Dolls: An American Legend*. Portfolio Press, 1999.

Foulke, Jan. *Blue Book, Dolls & Values*. Hobby House Press. (annual).

Hart, Luella. *Directory of United States Doll Trademarks*, 1888-1968, Self published 1968.

Izen, Judith and Carol Stover. *Collector's Encyclopedia of Vogue Dolls*. Collector Books, Paducah, KY, 1998.

Izen, Judith. *Collector's Guide to Ideal Dolls*. Collector Books, Paducah, KY, 1994 & 1999.

Judd, Pam & Polly. *Composition Dolls 1928-1955*; Hobby House Press, 1991; *Hard Plastic Dolls I & II*. 1990 & 1993.

Mandeville, Glenn. *Ginny...An American Toddler Doll*. Hobby House Press, 1994.

Ginny-America's Sweetheart. Hobby House Press, 1998; *Madame Alexander Dolls*. Hobby House Press, 2000.

Mansell, Colette. *Collector's Guide to British Dolls Since 1920*. Robert Hale, London, 1983.

Miller, Marjorie. *Nancy Ann Storybook Dolls*. Hobby House, 1980.

Millhouse, Peggy. *Doll Clothes Restoration*; *Doll Wig Restoration*. Booklets. Published by author: 510 Green Hill Rd., Conestoga, PA 17518.

Moyer, Patsy. *Modern Collectible Dolls I-IV*. Collector Books, 1996-2000; *Doll Values*, Collector Books, 1997-2000

Niswonger, Jeanne. *Ginny & Vogue Dolls, 1998*; *The Ginny Doll Family*. Self-published, 1996; *That Doll Ginny*, 1978. Self-published: 305 W. Beacon Rd., Lakeland, FL 33815.

Roberts, Sue Nettlingham and Dorothy Bunker. *The Ginny Doll Encyclopedia*. Hobby House Press, 1994.

Robison, Joleen Ashman & Kay Sellers. *Advertising Dolls*. Collector Books, 1980 & 1994.

Roth, Lillian and Heather Browning Maciak. *The Muffie Puzzle*, 1996; *The Muffie Puzzle-New Pieces*, 2001. Self published: 403 Euclid St., Santa Monica, CA 90402-2127.

Smith, Patricia. *Modern Collectors Dolls I-VII*; *Doll Values*, *Twelfth Edition*, Collector Books, 1996; *Vogue Ginny Dolls*. Collector Books, 1985; *The World of Alexander-Kins*. Collector Books, 1985.

Strahlenforf, Evelyn Robson. *The Charlson Standard Catalogue of Canadian Dolls*. Toronto Press, Toronto; *Dolls of Canada*. Toronto Press, Toronto, 1986 & 1990.

Sydney Ann Sutton in "Scouting Dolls Through the Years." Self Published.

Zillner, Dian. *Dolls and Accessories of the 1950s*, 1998. Schiffer; *Collectible Television Memorabilia*. Schiffer, 1996.

Magazine Articles

"Schiaparelli Chic" by Billy Boy; *Dolls* magazine, October 1992, p. 78-83.

"Miss Rosebud, An English Beauty" by Lee Ann Beaumont, *Contemporary Doll Collector*, September 1999, pgs. 40-45.

Magazines

Antique Trader, Collector News, Doll Reader, Contemporary Doll Collector, Dolls magazine, *Doll* magazine (UK), *Doll World, Antiques & Collecting* magazine, *Toy Shop, UFDC Doll News, Warman's Today's Collector.*

🍇 Index 🍇